ST. VINCENT DE PAUL OF BALTIMORE

THE STORY
OF A PEOPLE
AND THEIR HOME

ST. VINCENT
DE PAUL
✤ OF ✤
BALTIMORE

THOMAS W. SPALDING AND
KATHRYN M. KURANDA

MARYLAND HISTORICAL SOCIETY
BALTIMORE

The Maryland Historical Society
201 West Monument Street
Baltimore, MD 21201

Founded 1844

First Edition

Designed by Martha Farlow
Manufactured in the United States of America

LIBRARY OF CONGRESS CATALOGING-IN-PUBLICATION DATA
Spalding, Thomas W.
St. Vincent de Paul of Baltimore : the story of a people and their home /
Thomas W. Spalding and Kathryn M. Kuranda.
p.   cm.
Includes bibliographical references and index.
ISBN 0-938420-49-6
1. St. Vincent de Paul Church (Baltimore, Md.)—History.
2. Baltimore (Md.)—Church history.   I. Kuranda, Kathryn M., 1955–
II. Title.   III. Title: Saint Vincent de Paul of Baltimore.
BX4603.B3S78   1995
282'.7526—dc 20   94-47237 CIP

CONTENTS

PREFACE AND
ACKNOWLEDGMENTS

"A key to understanding the history of American Catholicism is the parish," Jay P. Dolan has written.[1] He might have said "the key." It is the level at which faith is lived out in the concrete. Parish "histories" abound, but most are memorial volumes devoid of historical merit. Today the parish serves increasingly as a laboratory for the analysis of social, devotional, and other patterns in American Catholicism, but there have been few examinations of the parish as parish.[2] In 1987 a group of historians at the University of Notre Dame completed a comprehensive historical analysis of American Catholic parishes from 1850 to the present.[3] But it inspired few professional historians to dissect the individual parish with its myriad ministries and activities that touched the life of the ordinary Catholic at the lowest but most intimate level.[4] An invitation to do the history of a particular parish in Baltimore provided the present writer the opportunity to do just that.

Since the parish of St. Vincent de Paul in Baltimore was established in 1840–41, renovation projects reflecting an evolving parish have been undertaken approximately every fifty years. To coincide with its 150th anniversary, the parish undertook in the summer of 1990 its fourth major rehabilitation under its thirteenth pastor, Rev. Richard T. Lawrence. In anticipation of this event, the parish commissioned a history of the parish and an architectural study of the church building itself. I agreed to do the history, part 1, the story of the people. R. Christopher Goodwin & Associates, Inc., of Frederick, Maryland, were engaged to do the architectural study, part 2, the story of their home.

Although Kathryn M. Kuranda, who has a master's degree in architectural history, served as organizing historian for part 2, it is the result of a collaborative effort. Her associates were Michelle T. Moran, archivist; Martha R. Williams, historic site specialist; and Augustine J. Fahey, graphics coordinator. All brought their particular expertise to the historical research and architectural drawings involved in the preparation of the second part of the book.

As author of part 1, I wish to express my gratitude to Fr. Richard Lawrence, pastor of St. Vincent's, not only for the invitation to write this history but also for the freedom he allowed me to write it as I saw it. At the same time he was ready to contribute from the store of information he commands on the last quarter century of the parish's life and, when pressed, to share his insights into many aspects of its development.

I would like to thank in a special way Rev. Paul K. Thomas, archivist of the archdiocese of Baltimore, for his generous and thorough assistance in providing documents and checking facts, as also Rev. John Bowen, SS, archivist of the Sulpician Archives. I wish to thank Father Bowen, Dr. Christopher Kauffman, and Rev. Michael Roach for their careful reading of the manuscript and constructive suggestions. I must also express my appreciation for the friendly assistance of the staffs at the Enoch Pratt Free Library, the Baltimore Life Museum, and the Peale Museum. Of the many who have responded generously to my request for interviews I would like to mention Fathers Edmund Stroup and Joseph Wenderoth, Albert Puliafico, Anne Freebruger, Albert Reichelt, Ruth Martin, and Sr. Annella Martin, RSM.

With gratitude I acknowledge the support and assistance of colleagues and staff of Spalding University of Louisville, Kentucky; I thank Br. James Kendrick, CFX, for proofreading; Andrew Tomlinson for his graph, Louis Mercorella for stylistic advice, and Therese Boyd for editing. And I am grateful to Robert J. Brugger and Martha Farlow of the Maryland Historical Society and the Johns Hopkins University Press for their assistance and encouragement.

R. Christopher Goodwin & Associates wishes also to acknowledge the assistance rendered by Father Lawrence and me, as well as the staff of the Maryland Historical Society.

Thomas W. Spalding, CFX
Spalding University

ST. VINCENT DE PAUL OF BALTIMORE

INTRODUCTION

Few parishes, perhaps, better demonstrate the evolving nature of the Catholic parish in the United States than does St. Vincent de Paul of Baltimore. In its 150 years it has taken almost as many shapes as had the entity defined as parish by the Council of Trent some 300 years before St. Vincent's was founded. A term older than *diocese* itself, *parish,* by decree in the mid-1500s, became the territorial parish, a clearly delimited subdivision of the diocese under a pastor charged with "the care of souls" (*cura animarum*).[1] In post-Reformation Britain and its colonies, however, there were no Roman Catholic parishes, only missions, and it was from these that parishes evolved in the United States.

It fell to Bishop John Carroll of Baltimore, the first Catholic bishop in the United States, to determine the character of the American substitute for the territorial parish. As his model Carroll chose the Episcopal parish with its elected vestry charged with temporal affairs. The quasi-parishes of the Carroll church were, therefore, largely the creations of elites: the country gentry or urban merchants.[2] St. Vincent de Paul of Baltimore would be the last of such Carroll churches in the premier see, the last to be incorporated, in 1841, by a board of trustees from fairly affluent mercantile families.

Their home, the church building itself, would afford one of the best examples of how a particular edifice was designed, and later redesigned, to meet and to mirror the attitudes and values of a particular population. The original Georgian structure, in its stateliness, simplicity, and order, reflected the architectural preferences of Baltimore's elite of the federal era. Pew doors, a first balcony for the less well-to-do, and a second for slaves and free blacks exemplified the social demarcation the elite demanded.

By the 1840s, however, when Catholic immigrants, unschooled in the management of church affairs, poured into the nation, trusteeism was already in retreat.[3] Hardly was the plaster dry on the Georgian edifice before its worshiping community was compelled to redirect its energies. Although it would retain a core of the old elite, who were largely responsible for its successes, St. Vincent's would, with its many organizations and activities, become a model immigrant parish, the leading Irish parish of Baltimore. Its church building would in the 1870s, the 1880s, and the 1890s be refashioned to reflect the immigrants' need to be immersed in rich and moving symbols of the sacred in a home that signaled their presence, their arrival, to the larger community.

In the 1880s the word *parish* displaced *church* in the listings of the *Catholic Directory,* even though the canonical parish as redefined in the code of canon law of 1918 would not find official acceptance in the United States until 1924.[4] By the latter date parish life in the immigrant church had reached its fullest expression. Two decades before, however, St. Vincent's was in decline, the victim of civic, mercantile, and industrial encroachments. It was, as early as the 1910s, the first Catholic parish of Baltimore to be threatened with extinction. But it was also the first to offer the Catholics of greater Baltimore a service that attracted enough worshipers to keep it afloat. Initially the attraction was a popular preacher, but soon it was the printers' mass that made it famous. With its late mass and lunch-break devotions St. Vincent's became the second parish for a growing number of Baltimoreans.

The revenue derived from its transient clientele enabled a talented pastor to mark the parish's hundredth anniversary by another renovation. This one, however, would not reflect the immigrant character of its small residential base, now mostly Italian, but that of the growing middle class of Catholic Baltimore who attended the printers' mass. With a style that was more Williamsburg American than European baroque, it bespoke assimilation. While the 1940–41 renovation sought a return to the simplicity of the original structure, it looked also to the future.

Demographic shifts initiated a transformation of parish life in greater Baltimore even before the reforms of Vatican Council II. The middle-class exodus to the suburbs brought a greater sophistication in parish organization as well as in architectural tastes. In the quarter century between the opening of Vatican II (1962) and the 200th anniversary of the archdiocese (1989) ten new parishes would be created in the suburbs and eight old ones closed in the inner city.[5] Those that survived were closest to the central business district. Each offered a special service or services to Catholics whose theological and liturgical needs were not well served in the circumferential parishes.[6]

Urban renewal and changes in church attendance that resulted from Vatican II again threatened St. Vincent's with extinction. But once more it became a magnet, offering the most vibrant liturgy in greater Baltimore and the best opportunities for service to the inner city and the church at large. In the process it became a metropolitan parish, attracting a stable body of communicants who regarded St. Vincent's as their only parish. In time this commuting community would undertake another renovation of its home informed by a new perception of itself as "church."

By the 1980s the Tridentine concept of territorial parish seemed to many, even in the Vatican, inadequate for the postconciliar church. On March 20, 1982, the cardinal prefect of the Sacred Congregation of the Clergy informed the archbishop of Baltimore, and other "pastors of the great cities of the world," that a plenary session of the congregation would be called to address a "study of the great problem of the parish today, with special reference to urban areas."[7]

In an accompanying paper the congregation declared that the roots of "the crisis of the parish as an institution" were to be found in the transition from an agrarian to an industrial world. The "anonymous" character of industrial society had impeded the development of the territorial parish as a community capable of filling the spiritual needs of its members. The doctrinal implications of the question, the paper insisted, were manifold. Was the parish a suitable institution for actualizing the mystery of the church? Could the dicta of Vatican Council II regarding the "particular church" (diocese) be applied also to the parish? Could the parish be a true community as opposed to a juridical institute? Did the notion of parish as "service station" produced by the consumer mentality adequately reflect the reality? Should the parish be viewed as object, in this sense, or as subject, in which the parishioners were not simply recipients but active agents in discharging the functions of a parish? Should the church recognize the "'charisms,' 'ministries,' and 'services'" of the parishioners under the "vigilant care" of an ordained pastor whose role it was to authenticate the charisms of others? What was the proper function of the parish council? How was the dictum "All are responsible for the Mission of the Church" to be interpreted? Only by addressing such questions could the Sacred Congregation arrive at a working definition of *parish*.[8]

Archbishop William D. Borders created a committee under the chairmanship of Rev. Richard T. Lawrence, pastor of St. Vincent de Paul, to formulate a response.[9] Reflecting on Baltimore's experience, the committee suggested a theology of parish based on the teachings of Vatican II regarding the particular church or diocese. All of the basic roles and ministries of the local church in the first centuries were operative in the parish today: that of oversight exercised then by the bishop but now by the pastor; that of collegial decisionmaking exercised then by the presbyterate but now by the parish council; and that of service exercised by the diaconate but now by the parish staff.

With regard to models suggested by the Congregation of the Clergy, the authors proposed as an alternative to the "elective" parish one in which parishioners from outside would adopt a territorial parish with a small residential base and accept responsibility for the parochial ministries within its geographic limits. "In effect, the parish is elective in regard to the subjects of ministry but territorial in regard to the objects of ministry." Baltimore parishes, the authors revealed, ranged from a 3 percent to 85 percent nonresidential membership, although most were less than 10 percent. St. Vincent de Paul claimed the 85 percent from without and was itself the best example of what the authors were proposing.

Father Dick Lawrence was not only chairperson for the committee of surrogate respondents but also the principal author of the concept that dominated the response: the parish as the particular church in its primitive form. Four years later he would, at the behest of the archdiocesan Division of Collegial Services, gather a group of parishioners to produce a videotape on "The Ministry of the Parish Council." In it they developed the concept in more detail. The parish, these parishioners insisted, was a church, in the sense of "the church at Ephesus" or "the church at Corinth," exercising the basic ministries of *kerygma* (proclaiming the word), *koinonia* (building community), and *diakonia* (rendering service). With regard to roles, the parish council, in its decisionmaking capacity, represented a latter-day *presbyteroi*. The tape sold well, some 750 by 1991.[10]

By then the pastor of St. Vincent's had refined the historical and theological underpinnings even more. "If we see the parish as a church," he would tell an academic conference in 1992, "then it follows at once that the mission of the parish is the mission of the church."

No part of the mission of the church may legitimately be neglected by a parish which desires to think of itself as a church. Such notions as branch office of the diocese, sacramental filling station, inbred support group, cozy insular family, and activist cell of the kingdom are at once revealed as inadequate.

No parish, he insisted, had the right to choose which of the models Fr. Avery Dulles had identified, namely, community, sacrament, herald, and servant.

> It must celebrate its liturgy well; it must be a community of welcome; it must provide for the initiation of new members and the religious education and spiritual development of all its members. It must reach out to the poor and oppressed both within and without its boundaries. It must announce the gospel by its life as well as by its word. Some parishes, just as some Christians, will be better at some of these ministries than others. But, unlike individual Christians, no parish that wants to claim the name of church can specialize in some ministries and leave the rest to others. To be a church is to accept the fullness of the church's mission.[11]

Under its latest pastor St. Vincent's would move beyond the "niche marketing" pursued by the metropolitan parishes of downtown Baltimore and accept the ministries and roles that characterized the primitive church.

Although a metropolitan parish in its membership, St. Vincent's would become, as the authors of the response to the Vatican inquiry described it, "elective in regard to the subjects of ministry but territorial in regard to the objects of ministry." St. Vincent's would never ignore its traditional boundaries nor those who lived within them. There would always be an interaction between parish and neighborhood, the parish changing with the neighborhood.

While St. Vincent's boundaries would be modified with the establishment of new parishes, it was identified with a part of Baltimore known as Old Town until the urban renewal of the 1960s and 1970s. Then it would return to the name of its origin: Jonestown. Chartered in 1732 as a separate entity, Jones Town was absorbed by the city founded three years earlier on the other side of the Jones Falls called Baltimore Town. As it edged southward along the Falls, however, it was given the name Old Town.[12] Until the 1970s the name Jones Town was forgotten.

Rarely did anyone attempt to define Old Town geographically. At the 1950 banquet of the Old Town Merchants and Manufacturers Association, a body founded in the 1880s by the businessmen concentrated on

Gay Street, the speeches made it evident "that the history of Old Town gets more confused as the years roll on." Although many at the banquet located the heart of Old Town just to the east of the old Gay Street Bridge, the mayor said he always thought of it as just across the Baltimore Street Bridge.[13] With the urban renewal of the 1970s, especially the Gay Street Mall north of Orleans Street, it moved northward again under the name Oldtown.

In 1974 the pastor of St. Vincent's, realizing that the parish environs had no neighborhood association to represent it, revived the name Jones Town, as Jonestown, by creating a corporation that called itself the Jonestown Planning Council. The name was accepted by the city of Baltimore and such bodies as the U.S. Department of Transportation in their endless hearings on the extension of Interstate 83, a well-traveled artery that came to an abrupt halt at the back of St. Vincent's. Even then there was confusion. In a final report (1983), Jonestown was defined on one page as lying between Fayette and Pratt streets and on another as bounded by the Fallsway, Hillen and Orleans streets, Central Avenue, and Pratt Street.[14]

The history that follows is one of definition, of a people and its home attempting to define or redefine itself as its environment changed. It will have, therefore, an ecological as well as ecclesial, socioeconomic, and even political dimension. St. Vincent de Paul was the product of many forces and factors that came together in 1840. To the extent this history is able, it will try to carry them all through the 150 years that followed.

PART ONE

THE PEOPLE

CONVERGENCE

1606–1840

The community on Front Street that called itself St. Vincent de Paul Parish was the product of a number of forces that came together toward the end of the 1830s. The oldest was economic. Until the late 1600s the land on which the parish would locate was known only to the Susquehannocks who encamped about a thousand feet above what was then the shoreline of the Northwest Branch of the Patapsco River on a tributary that would be called the Jones Falls.[1] As early as 1606, however, Capt. John Smith of Virginia, in search of new sources of wealth, sailed into the Patapsco. He called it the Bolus, Latin for bole, a reddish clay rich in iron ore. Among the partners who would establish a successful ironworks in the area 125 years later was Charles Carroll, Esquire, of Annapolis.[2]

A TOWN ON THE PATAPSCO

Gambling on the Patapsco as the logical site for a future port, Squire Carroll's father, Charles Carroll the Settler, had acquired for Charles and his brother Daniel some 500 acres on the Northwest Branch. Edward Fell took out a warrant for a part of it in 1726. The Carrolls successfully contested the claim. Three years later, when the owner of a tract on the Middle Branch refused to surrender it for a proposed town, Charles and Daniel petitioned the General Assembly of Maryland to plant the town on their land on the Northwest Branch. Baltimore Town was officially erected by an act of the Assembly dated August 8, 1729. The next year seven commissioners laid out sixty lots on sixty acres of the Carroll land west of the Jones Falls. The Carrolls would acquire and sell almost half of them.[3]

Charles and Daniel Carroll were Roman Catholics. So was John Digges, who in the early 1730s laid out a wagon road from his extensive holdings at Conewago in Pennsylvania to Baltimore (later Hanover Pike and Reisterstown Road) and in the town itself put up a warehouse on Lot 54.[4] Conewago would give two pastors to the future parish.

In 1726, the same year that he sought unsuccessfully to acquire the Carroll acreage, Edward Fell had a survey run on the land to the east of Jones Falls, named for David Jones. Jones was perhaps the first to take up land on this watercourse that would divide the future city diagonally from northwest to southeast. On the land surveyed for Fell he built a store, and others settled around it.[5] On August 8, 1732, the General Assembly erected Jones Town on ten acres east of Jones Falls, "whereon Edward Fell keeps store." The town was divided into twenty half-acre lots along two streets "or one street with three courses, corresponding with the meanders of the bank of the falls."[6] On one of these, Lot 10, the southernmost closest to the Falls, acquired by Daubney Buckler Partridge in 1737, would be built a church a little over a century later. On Lot 9 just above it, acquired by Capt. Robert North in 1740, would be built a brick residence that would become a rectory.[7]

The street closest to the Falls was named Jones Street, which, "by the sacrilegious interference of the ministers of the law," grumbled the historian J. Thomas Scharf, would be changed to Front Street. "Sacrilegious," Scharf explained, "because the ancient landmarks and names of towns, cities, &c., should be preserved and cherished reverentially as are family heir-looms."[8] In 1745 ministers of the law made Jones Town a part of Baltimore Town, but for its residents it would maintain a distinct identity that, with additions to the south, would come to be called Old Town.

Charles Carroll sold the twenty-eight acres of marshland between Old Town and Baltimore Town, and Gay and Frederick streets were run through it.[9] This portion of the city just to the west of Jones Falls was likewise destined to be a part of the future parish. Gay Street replaced the name Bridge Street east of the Falls, and another bridge carried what is now Baltimore Street east of the stream. The area between Gay and Baltimore would constitute the heart of Old Town. In 1763 streets were platted in this area on land acquired by two English merchants who made Baltimore their home, Jonathan Plowman and Brian Philpot, extending Old Town southward on a distinctive bias from the rest of a city oriented north and south.[10]

The eastern border of Old Town was Harford Run, now Central Av-

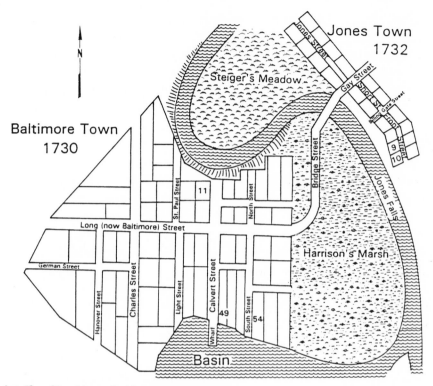

Lot #9: Site of future St. Vincent de Paul rectory.
Lot #10: Site of future St. Vincent de Paul church.
Lot #11: Property of Edward Fottrell of Baltimore Town.
Lot #49: Property Charles Carroll of Annapolis.
Lot #54: Property of John Digges of Conewago & Baltimore Town.

Baltimore Town and Jones Town, as originally laid out. Jones Town would extend south and west to become Old Town, the neighborhood of St. Vincent de Paul Parish. JAMES DILISIO

enue. This creek marked also the western border of Fells Point as it crept northward. Fells Point was named for Edward Fell, nephew of the Edward who kept store on Jones Falls. The town laid out by the nephew in 1763 had a better harbor than Baltimore Town and for a decade stoutly resisted absorption by the latter.[11]

THE FACTORS OF GROWTH

Baltimore, a town of millers and traders, had a very different character than had Annapolis some thirty miles south. The latter, a seventeenth-century creation of the southern counties and the Eastern Shore, was the gathering place politically and socially for aristocratic tobacco planters of the Established Church possessed of indentured servants, slaves, and debts that rendered them almost wholly dependent on British merchants. Baltimore, on the other hand, was the emporium of independent small farmers, nonconforming wheat growers, to its north and west. The depression of the tobacco market and great demand abroad for iron and wheat accounted for the rapid growth of Baltimore at the expense of Annapolis.[12] The center of gravity shifted in the early 1760s when the Ellicott brothers, staunch Quakers, moved from Pennsylvania to put up a flour mill on the Patapsco. The mill was in part responsible for the decision of Charles Carroll of Carrollton, son of Squire Carroll, to concentrate his energies at Doughoregan Manor nearby and convert from tobacco to wheat cultivation.[13] Although Carroll would inherit the Annapolis town house of his father, he would ride more often from the manor to nearby Baltimore, where in his old age he would winter in a mansion he had helped his son-in-law Richard Caton acquire in Old Town.

Demography was another force that shaped the Catholic community of Old Town. A constant influx of different national, racial, and religious groups would continually alter the character of the city as a whole. The old families that had moved in from the southern counties and the Eastern Shore, Germans and Scotch Irish from the hinterland, and merchants from England and Scotland, would be continually enriched by a succession of refugees—Acadians, French emigrés, Irish '98ers, and wealthy Creoles from Saint-Domingue (Haiti) and their slaves.

By 1790 Baltimore counted 13,500 souls, by 1800 31,500, and by 1830 80,600. By the mid-1790s it was already the third largest city in the nation after New York and Philadelphia, boasting in addition to its flour mills, cotton mills, and paper mills a collection of sugar refineries, rum distilleries, tobacco, rope, nail, and shoe factories, tanneries, lumber yards, and boat yards.[14] Baltimore's growth was stimulated by war—the French and Indian War, the American Revolution, the wars of the French Revolution and Napoleon Bonaparte, the War of 1812, and the wars of independence in Latin America. To the city of profiteers and privateers came a number of enterprising foreigners—Robert Oliver from Ireland, William Patterson from Scotland, Richard Caton from England, Lewis Pascault and Henry Didier from France, to name only a few. Some of them won social acceptance by marrying into the Carroll family. Such firms as D'Arcy and Didier took on experienced sea captains from New England, one of the most daring a John Daniel Danels from Maine, of whom we will hear more.

Health problems played a role in propelling large parts of the population northward, especially into Old Town. From 1793 to 1801 and again in 1819, the bustling Fells Point was beset by a series of epidemics of yellow fever that sent most of its middle-class residents scurrying to higher ground. Although many of the merchants had their wharves on the waterfront, they preferred to live uptown.

Many built or bought comfortable homes on Front Street, which by the 1830s would become the principal boulevard of one of the best parts of the city in which to live. The adjective applied most often to this part of Old Town was "fashionable."[15] "Even today," a future pastor, Rev. John Sinnott Martin, would write as late as 1941, "the observer can detect the remnants of by-gone glories in the varied widths and heights and architecture of the dwellings that still stand in Old Town. Pieces of iron railings, foot scrapers, hitching posts, carriage steps and grille work, still witness to a time when this was the Guilford of old Baltimore."[16]

Before it became a residential haven for the well-to-do, however, Old Town was one of the city's principal working-class districts.[17] Day laborers inhabited even its prominent streets. A number of manufacturing enterprises failed in the 1780s, like the first steam-powered grist mill of the city on Pratt Street, but a brewery was established in 1783 on Lombard at Front (now Brewer's Park) and acquired by Edward Johnson, a prominent Jeffersonian and friend of the workingman. Johnson in 1808 acquired a newly built home across the street, which, after passing through one or more hands, would in 1818 be acquired by Richard Caton. The brewery was acquired by the Clagett family, who would make it the best known of Baltimore's many breweries, producing some 10,000 barrels annually in its peak years.[18] In 1828 the Phoenix Shot Tower was raised at Front and Fayette for the manufacture of rifle shot. Some 240 feet high, it remains a neighborhood landmark. The next year what became the Front Street Theater was erected on Front at Low Street to accommodate some 3,000 spectators for some of Baltimore's most spectacular performances. Edwin Booth lived not far away on High Street.

Still, as late as 1798, 98 percent of Old Town was open space or roadways.[19] Between then and the War of 1812 it filled rapidly, especially the streets laid out by Plowman and Philpot. A few of the early homes still stand. One is the residence at Pratt and Albemarle built in 1793 where Mary Pickersgill stitched the flag for Fort McHenry that gave it the name

Commo. John Daniel Danels (1783–1855), one of St. Vincent's original incorporators, made a fortune as a privateer. His title and the sword he wears
were the gift of the Republic of Colombia, whose independence he helped
win. MARYLAND HISTORICAL SOCIETY

of Flag House. Another is the building found today at 9 N. Front Street,
constructed in 1805, the home of Thorogood Smith, the city's second
mayor, which as an outstanding example of the federalist style would es-
cape demolition. The home on Lombard and Front acquired by Richard
Caton with the help of his father-in-law, Charles Carroll, underwent the
last of several renovations and enlargements that made it the stately
home it is today. On Lombard Street nearby stand several other federal-
style townhouses that date from the late eighteenth or early nineteenth
century. One, completed in 1796, became the home of John Hutchinson,
whose career will soon be detailed.

FIVE FUTURE PARISHIONERS

Five individuals of different backgrounds settled in Old Town who in different ways illustrate the upward social mobility that a rapidly expanding city readily provided: Dr. Franklin J. Didier, John Ignatius Gross, Commodore John Daniel Danels, John Moore FitzPatrick, and John Hutchinson. Three would become parishioners of St. Vincent de Paul Parish, as would the widows of the other two.

Dr. Franklin J. Didier was the grandson of Henry Didier, who had come to Baltimore from France in his own ship in 1774 to build a fortune in trade. The latter's son, another Henry, helped organize the shipping firm of D'Arcy and Didier. In Henry Didier's employ—some say he had adopted him—was Henry Poe, brother of Edgar Allan Poe, undoubtedly a reason Eugene, son of Dr. Franklin Didier, would become one of the first authorities on the writer and poet.[20] Franklin, in any event, chose not the mercantile career of his father and Uncle Edmund but medicine. He took up residence at Lombard and Exeter streets with his wife, Julia Lemoine, with whom he had a daughter and three sons. The oldest, Edmund, would be the seventh pastor of St. Vincent de Paul Parish.

John Ignatius Gross (1798–1869) was the grandson of Anthony Gross, who had come from Alsace in 1765. John's father, Lewis, had formed a partnership with in-laws, Gross and White, a grocery firm. At least three of Lewis's six sons settled in Old Town. Lewis Jr. was a confectioner and manufacturer of soda water and James, or Jacob, a hardware salesman, but the most successful was John Ignatius, an auctioneer and commission merchant and later judge of the Orphans Court.[21] He would become one of the leading incorporators of St. Vincent de Paul Parish.

Another employee of D'Arcy and Didier was John Daniel Danels (1783–1855), a sea captain who had come from Maine to Baltimore at the time of the War of 1812 because of the opportunities it offered in trans-Atlantic trade. There he married Eugenie Caze, a member of one of the wealthy Creole families driven from Saint-Domingue, whose dowry was said to have been her weight in gold. After a number of daring escapades as a privateer during the war he went to South America ostensibly to further the cause of independence from Spain. In 1818–19 he roamed the coast as privateer or pirate, depending on legal niceties. In 1820–25 he added three ships to the modest navy of Simon Bolivar to blockade the coasts of Venezuela and Colombia. For this service he was awarded the title of commodore and a pension. After accumulating a considerable fortune and several suits at law in the process, he settled with his family on Albemarle Street.[22] He would be another of the leading incorporators of St. Vincent's.

Less exciting but more typical was the career of John Moore Fitz-Patrick (1794–1846). He had come to Baltimore about 1812 with his brothers from Ireland. They were natives of county Longford, horse country, and the Irish had a near monopoly on occupations connected with horses in Baltimore. FitzPatrick worked for a stage line until he accumulated enough capital to open his own livery stable at the Centre Market on Lombard. The first pastor of St. Vincent's would keep his horse and buggy there. John FitzPatrick married Elizabeth Kennedy, whose family lived on Fayette Street in Old Town. She had a brother Michael who was an actor at the Front Street Theater. When John Moore FitzPatrick died, the widow moved to a house on Front Street opposite St. Vincent de Paul Church.[23]

An even better example of upward social mobility was the career of John Hutchinson (1801–40). A destitute immigrant from Great Britain, he was apprenticed at age 18 to a Thomas Perkins, a wheelwright. In 1827 he opened his own shop, when Baltimore with a population of about 80,000 could accommodate twenty-three wheelwrights. In 1828 he married Mary Ann Jones at the Cathedral of the Assumption and acquired an apprentice of his own. Hutchinson entered into a partnership with a former fellow apprentice, and in 1834 they acquired the three-story house on Lombard at Albemarle down from the Caton mansion. The next year Hutchinson also opened a grocery. (Grocery stores at the time limited themselves mostly to the sale of coffee, tea, sugar, fruit, and liquor.) In 1836, however, the partners acquired the shop where they had worked as apprentices at Pratt and East Falls Avenue. In 1840 John Hutchinson died and was buried in the churchyard of St. James. He left his widow the considerable sum of $5,000, one-fifth of which she would invest in the building of St. Vincent de Paul Church.[24]

THE ROMAN CATHOLIC CHURCH OF BALTIMORE

The final and most important force at work in the creation of the Catholic community that found a home on Front Street was religion. In Baltimore there were a handful of Irish and perhaps a few German Catholics before the Acadians arrived in 1756. Largely for these dispossessed Canadians, victims of the French and Indian War, was mass said regularly by one or another Jesuit in a brick building on Charles Street built by Edward Fottrell before his return to Ireland.[25]

The removal of French rule from North America in 1763 brought a period of untroubled expansion for the Roman Catholics of Maryland. On June 4, 1764, Squire Carroll of Annapolis deeded to Fr. George Hunter Lot 157 on Northwest and Forest streets (later Saratoga and Little Sharp), but it was not until 1771 or 1772 that St. Peter's was built.[26] This modest brick edifice, with an extension of 1784, would become a cathedral when John Carroll, a former Jesuit, was named first bishop of Baltimore—first bishop of the United States—on November 6, 1789. By then there were ten other churches in Baltimore, four of them built by the Methodists, who had stolen a march on the other denominations.[27]

From 1790 to 1810 the Catholic population of Baltimore rose from 7 to 12 percent of the population, or well over 5,000 members. By then Roman Catholics constituted the largest denomination but counted the greatest number of unskilled laborers. The latter, however, would decline from 51 percent of the membership in 1800 to 39 percent in 1830 while middle-class Catholics would grow from 17 to 28 percent.[28] More important was the development of a Catholic upper class whose needs more than those of the middle and lower classes determined the character of the Catholic Church in Baltimore during the early national period. Catholics among the decisional elite of Baltimore, according to a study that may have underestimated the numbers, grew from 2 percent in the first decade of the century to 7 percent in the third.[29] This modest elite was an amalgam of old Anglo-American families, enterprising Irishmen, German merchants, and the French and Creole families already mentioned.[30] These were the pewholders, from whom were elected the trustees.

A second parish, St. Patrick's, was created for the largely Irish Catholics of Fells Point in 1792, and a church for the Germans on Saratoga Street, St. John's, was blessed by Carroll in 1802. Several lots were acquired for a new cathedral in 1796 in the lower part of Old Town on Philpot's Hill between now Granby and Stiles on Exeter Street. But the decision was later taken to build on land acquired from Col. John Eager Howard on Charles Street at Mulberry just over the city line. In 1806 the cornerstone was laid for an imposing cathedral that was not completed until 1821.[31]

In 1808 Baltimore became the seat of an archdiocese and John Carroll an archbishop. Until his death in 1815 Carroll continued to approve the trustee arrangement he had first encouraged for the founding and funding of parishes despite the fractious trustees of the port cities—New York, Philadelphia, Norfolk, Charleston, and even Baltimore, where the Germans at St. John's proved unruly. Carroll looked to the Episcopal Church as a model with its stable vestry charged with administrative affairs. His successor, Leonard Neale, had little use for trustees, and Neale's successor, Ambrose Marechal, induced the pope in 1822 to issue the papal brief *Non sine magno* designed to minimize their power. Parish property in the future, it decreed, should be held by the bishop. Under Archbishop James Whitfield, Marechal's successor, the Maryland Assembly in 1833 granted the power of corporation sole to the archbishop of Baltimore.[32]

Until 1833 the Catholics of Old Town had no church of their own. As early as 1773 the Baptists had erected the first church in Old Town where the Shot Tower now stands at Fayette and Front. A Quaker meetinghouse was raised at Fayette and Aisquith in 1781 and a German Reformed church at the Lombard Street bridge on Front Street in 1785, which not long after was sold to the Episcopalians for their second parish in Baltimore (Christ Church).[33] But Old Town's Catholics had to travel several blocks west to the cathedral or St. John's or south to St. Patrick's.

The first Catholic institution in Old Town was a nunnery. In 1830 Archbishop Whitfield persuaded the Carmelites of Port Tobacco in Charles County to move to Baltimore and open an academy. He had the perfect place, he told the mother superior. "The neighborhood is quiet and the situation sufficiently central so that it is believed you could easily obtain 50 or 60 scholars from Old Town, Fells Point, and the neighborhood of Central Market." Bel Air Market, he added, was also close by. Both markets had an abundance of fish. (By rule the Carmelites ate no fleshmeat.) The house could be had for $6,500, the archbishop advised, perhaps less.[34] The house on Aisquith just south of Orleans was turned into a school, and a convent was built next to it. On September 14, 1831, the nuns took possession of their new home, which they named Mount Carmel after the old.

Archbishop Whitfield finally decided to erect a parish on a stretch of Aisquith Street just below present Eager Street that was still above the settled part of Old Town. But the area gave promise of rapid development as the population pushed out Harford Road. Because he bought the land and would build the church from his own personal fortune, there would be no need for trustees. On May 1, 1833, he laid the cornerstone for the church of St. James the Less, his patron, and exactly a year later performed the consecration. Rev. Louis Regis Deluol, superior of the Sulpicians in Baltimore, recorded in his diary that the rector of the cathedral parish, Rev. Edward Damphoux, preached on the latter occasion from a platform outside the church for the entire two and a half hours the ceremony was proceeding within. It also snowed and thundered that day, Deluol observed, and a Mr. Mills went up in a balloon to a height of two miles.[35]

JOHN BAPTIST GILDEA

Archbishop Whitfield, according to Father Deluol's diary, appointed Rev. John Baptist Gildea pastor of St. James on June 11, 1834.[36] This future pastor of St. Vincent de Paul was, in many ways, an excellent choice. Born in Baltimore on February 2, 1804, of parents who had emigrated from Ireland only a few years before, he had been sent to Mount St. Mary's College in Emmitsburg at the time of the War of 1812. At the end of his college years Gildea entered the seminary run in conjunction with the college but transferred to St. Mary's Seminary in Baltimore a year before his ordination by Archbishop Whitfield on March 25, 1829. He was sent immediately to take charge of the congregations and dependent missions of Martinsburg and Harper's Ferry, (West) Virginia, where he completed the church begun at Martinsburg and built another at Harper's Ferry.

For five years Gildea labored in Virginia "with the most commendable zeal and most beneficial results," his obituary would claim. "Not all the terrors of a raging and desolating pestilence [the cholera epidemics that devastated the C&O Canal construction workers] could withdraw him, for a moment, from the theater of his labors; thrice was he prostrated by the cholera, and thrice did he rise from the bed of sickness to dispense again the consolations of religion to his scattered flock."[37] In the fall of 1832 Gildea informed the archbishop that he had become so worried and worn down that "I could scarcely sit upon my horse or drag my legs after me." Many of his parishioners had urged him to desist but "the idea of those poor souls dying without the benefits of religion was worse to me than death."[38]

Soon after being told of his appointment to St. James, the priest wrote the archbishop that it "would be a blessed retreat after five years of hard labour . . . where I could devote more time to study & my own improvement, whilst I would attend to the care of souls." But he would like to stay in Virginia for about a year more in order to free himself of financial

Rev. John Baptist Gildea (1804–45), a native of Baltimore, founder and first pastor of St. Vincent's. He was a man of great zeal and vision but of poor health.

and other responsibilities he had incurred there.[39] A compromise was evidently worked out: occasional visits to St. James for baptisms, marriages, and burials until he was free to relocate permanently. The first such ceremony—the marriage of Bernard Milloy and Anne Griffin—was performed July 4, 1834. The first baptism—Catherine Ann, the daughter of George Leo and Ann Clarkston—took place on September 20. On May 14, 1835, Father Deluol recorded in his diary: "Mr. Gildea arrived from

Harper's Ferry too late for dinner." His return may have been hastened by an alarming turn of events in Old Town.

A REAPPEARANCE OF ANTIPOPERY

Deluol wrote that he met Gildea at Mount Carmel, "where the Sisters are very frightened, because during the night people came into their yard to taunt them. Sr. Isabella is insane."[40] Maryland Catholics had since the American Revolution enjoyed cordial relations with their Protestant neighbors. In 1830, however, a journal, *The Protestant,* was launched in New York to alert the nation to the dangers of popery. The crusade it called forth won few recruits in Baltimore until the burning of the Ursuline convent-school in Charlestown, Massachusetts, in August 1834.[41] In October rumors began to circulate that the convent-schools of the Carmelites and the Oblate Sisters of Providence, a black community founded in Baltimore in 1829, were targeted for a similar fate.[42] The following May an unfriendly crowd gathered at Mount Carmel. On the eighteenth Gildea reported to Deluol that the situation was truly menacing. He had posted several gentlemen around the convent. "Mr. Boarman," wrote Deluol, "was armed with two pistols and was in favor of going right at it."[43] The determined efforts of Gildea, Deluol, and the new archbishop of Baltimore, Samuel Eccleston, prevented any harm to the Baltimore convents in this troubled period.

On a Sunday in August in 1839, however, Sister Isabella "escaped" from the Carmelite convent. Since the publication of *The Awful Disclosures of Maria Monk* in 1835, ardent nativists had taken up the cause of "escaped" nuns. Rev. Robert J. Breckinridge left his Presbyterian pulpit in Old Town to go to the aid of the unfortunate woman, and a crowd quickly gathered. For three nights angry mobs threatened to destroy the convent. A contingent of the City Guard and a round of judges who tried offenders on the spot forestalled any damage.[44] At least until the 1850s the majority of Baltimoreans deplored the actions of the rabble-rousers of Old Town and other parts of the city.

A FRIENDLY RIVALRY

Louis Deluol was not only the Sulpician superior in America but also vicar general to the new archbishop, his former student at St. Mary's Seminary. He prided himself on the number of penitents he attracted and people he counseled. Among them were members of the Catholic elite of Old Town. Deluol was also appointed extraordinary confessor for the Carmelites. Gildea was their ecclesiastical superior. A friendly rivalry developed between the two for the control and affection of the nuns.

"It appears that Mr. Gildea cannot bear anyone hearing confessions there but himself," Deluol confided to his diary in 1838, "and he is a great bother to the religious in that matter." The Sulpician continued to go to the Carmelites to hear confessions and Gildea would often arrange to be there at the same time. In July 1840, after questioning Gildea's plan to borrow money from the Carmelites, Deluol accompanied the archbishop to the annual distribution of prizes at their academy. "Mr. Gildea insisted upon doing everything by himself, without help from the Religious, or anyone else, and there was some confusion." Together, however, the rivals worked to secure a site for the Sisters of Charity for a hospital in Old Town.[45]

ACTIVITIES PAROCHIAL AND EXTRAPAROCHIAL

One of the early actions taken by Gildea as pastor of St. James was to purchase on March 19, 1835, for $110 a tract of two acres and forty-one perches, a part of "Hanson's Wood Lot" between Aisquith Street and Harford Road, for a cemetery.[46] Gildea was also concerned with the physical improvement of the church building. Among the renovations he directed, and may have designed, was a steeple placed over the sanctuary of the church in 1837.[47]

At the time of Gildea's pastorate (rectorship) at St. James, the Catholic Church in Baltimore began in earnest the organization of charitable and mutual-aid societies. As early as 1827 the Charitable Relief Society had been founded for Catholic women "to unite the piety of Mary and the activity and zeal of Martha" and in 1828 the Tobias Society for "the decent burial of Catholic coloured persons." Between 1831 and 1838 were established five other mutual-aid or beneficial societies, most at the cathedral.[48] Gildea, however, was founder and chaplain of the Calvert Beneficial Society. In 1838 he organized at his own parish the St. James Indigent and Sick Society "to relieve the wants of the poor and sick."[49] About the same time, the prospect of a Catholic society for founding and funding an orphanage for boys—there had been one for girls since 1818—was germinating in the fertile mind of the pastor of St. James.

Before then, however, Gildea breathed life into another project. On

September 1, 1839, two weeks after the nunnery riot, Gildea held an organizational meeting for the purpose of founding the Catholic Tract Society of Baltimore. At the second meeting a constitution and bylaws were drawn. The goals of the society were "to encourage virtue, to expose misrepresentations, and to give a more extensive circulation to the doctrines of the Roman Catholic Church." A board of solicitors was created, an executive committee, a finance committee, and an editorial committee of three clergymen.[50]

Gildea was president of the Catholic Tract Society and one of the three members of the editorial committee. Parishioners of St. James were conspicuous among the committee members and solicitors. A year after its founding Rev. Charles Ignatius White, rector of the cathedral and a member of the editorial committee, would report that "upwards of 1200 individuals" had enrolled.[51]

PLANS FOR FRONT STREET

In 1839 two other decisions were also made: to erect an orphanage and to build a church. It is not clear which came first. On December 20 Deluol recorded that he had gone to the archbishop's after dinner to talk about the "plans Mr. Gildea has for Front Street." A month before, on November 23, George Carter of Loudoun County, Virginia, and his wife "did demise, grant, lease and to farm let" to Samuel Eccleston the Lot 10 that had been laid out as part of Jones Town in 1732 plus a narrow strip designated Lot 116 between Lot 10 and the Jones Falls.[52] On January 2, 1840, were recorded the minutes of the first meeting of the St. Vincent of Paul Benevolent Association. "On this day a meeting . . . took place at the house of John I. Gross, Esq.," the minutes began, "for the purpose of forming an association for the purpose of erecting a male orphan asylum in connection with a Catholic church on a lot of ground recently leased for the purpose." Fifteen of Old Town's leading residents were present.[53]

On February 5 Archbishop Eccleston negotiated a renewable ninety-nine-year lease of Lot 10, subject to a ground rent of $500, with the members of the Benevolent Association and "such others as may unite with them . . . for the purpose of erecting and constructing on said ground a Church or House of Worship, and a Male Orphan Asylum, and School-House for the instruction of indigent youth." The association had agreed to contribute and raise a fund sufficient for this purpose by issuing interest-bearing certificates, or stock, that could not be redeemed for fifteen years. The interest would be paid from pew rents and donations.[54]

That the idea of an orphanage preceded that of a church is suggested by the name of the patron for both orphanage and church: St. Vincent de Paul. Most Catholics knew something of the life of this remarkable French priest (1581–1660), the apostle of charity, the saint of the disadvantaged—the poor, the sick, the orphan.[55] Statues of St. Vincent de Paul almost always showed him with one or more children in his arms or clinging to the skirt of his cassock. Such a statue would later appear in a niche over the main entrance of the church on Front Street. The parish would be one of the first, perhaps the second, in the United States to be named for St. Vincent de Paul.

The decision to create a second parish in Old Town was due in part to the fact that the English-speaking Catholics of Old Town had by 1840 outgrown St. James. The church was also too distant for the residents of the lower part of Old Town, some of whom could have walked to the cathedral or to St. Patrick's in Fells Point in less time than it took to trudge (or

St. Vincent de Paul (1581–1660), patron of the parish, as portrayed on the cover of a brief biography written and published by the eleventh pastor in 1943.

ride) the ten or more blocks to St. James. Most of the wealthier Catholics of Old Town lived in its southern half.

Then there were the Germans. German Catholics east of the Falls, who were accustomed to attending services at St. John's on Saratoga Street, were also growing rapidly, especially after 1834, when even Bavarian Jews began to settle on High, Aisquith, Exeter, and Lombard streets.[56] The German Catholics of Old Town needed their own church. In 1840 the Congregation of the Most Holy Redeemer, or Redemptorists, at Archbishop Eccleston's invitation, agreed to take charge not only of St. John's but also St. James and to make Baltimore their national headquarters. St. James would, in fact, be their principal residence until a new and imposing church to be called St. Alphonsus would replace the old St. John's.[57]

When he moved to Front Street in 1841, John Baptist Gildea would take with him the parish registers. The congregation of St. Vincent de Paul would be the same English-speaking community that had worshiped at St. James since its founding, the same people but in a new home.

FOUNDATION

1840–1846

On May 4, 1840, the Whig Party held its national convention in Baltimore. Its supporters paraded through Old Town to Canton to hear the rousing speeches of Daniel Webster, Henry Clay, and other Whig leaders. "The assembly was one of much show, flying banners, clashing cymbals, restive horses, pretty girls, whole-souled politicians, log cabins, and hard cider." It nominated Gen. William Henry Harrison. On May 5 the Democratic party, mired in depression politics, held a dispirited convention, also in Baltimore. It nominated Martin Van Buren for a second term. Although Baltimore went for Van Buren on November 2, Maryland and the nation chose Harrison. The day after the election a riot occurred in Old Town that caused bodily injury to Dr. Edward Deloughery, a member of the new parish of St. Vincent de Paul.[1]

THE CORNERSTONE

Twelve days after the nominating conventions the American bishops met in Baltimore for their Fourth Provincial Council. On May 17 Father Deluol wrote in his diary: "At the Cathedral, the procession began at 10.30 and everything ended 2.45. . . . I was assistant-priest and archdeacon." In the procession were also twelve bishops, one a visiting Frenchman, and twenty-one priests, the superiors of religious orders or council officials and theologians. After a long description of the banquet held on May 21, Deluol added: "Around 5 P.M., the Archbishop blessed the cornerstone of the church of St. Vincent on Front St. All the bishops were present as well as a few priests. Dr. England preached, but rain interrupted him, and he finished his sermon in the evening at the Cathedral."

The *United States Catholic Miscellany* of Charleston, South Carolina, was more generous in its coverage. Bishop John England of Charleston himself or one of his subalterns was probably the reporter. Under the date May 22 he wrote:

The hour fixed for the ceremony in Front street, yesterday afternoon, was five o'clock. Long before that hour thousands had surrounded the large cross erected on the site of the altar. A heavy shower of rain fell but very few left their places. Soon after five the Archbishop and bishops with a goodly retinue of priests came on the ground in procession from a neighbouring house. The ceremony occupied more than an hour.

A large scaffold covered with drapery and rising two stages had been erected on one side of the square; the bishops occupied the upper floor, the preacher in front, on the understage a large number of ladies took their places. The congregation consisting of very little under 10,000 persons of all ages and denominations of religion, occupied the ground, several carriages filled with ladies lined the street, the windows on every side were occupied, and a pyramid of heads was seen on a scaffold to one angle of the area whilst the roofs of the builders' sheds were all covered. To a spectator at the South Eastern angle in the street the scene was quite imposing.[2]

The *Baltimore American* claimed that "the Reverend gentlemen" came upon the site at half past five chanting the "Gloria in Excelsis." After some prayers the archbishop and his attendants "proceeded to the north west corner, where, with appropriate and solemn ceremony, the foundation stone was laid." From the platform Bishop England "enchained the attention of his immense auditory by a most eloquent, argumentative and practical address," the "gifted divine" having selected as his text, "And Jacob rose early in the morning, and took the stone that he had put for his pillow, and set it up for a pillar, and poured oil upon the top of it" (Gen. 28:18).[3]

A little more than half an hour into his discourse the noted orator had to stop because of rain. Despite Father Deluol's notation, both the *Miscellany* and the *American* agree that the discourse was resumed the following evening. In a crowded cathedral the bishop recapitulated what he had said the previous day, spoke for more than half an hour on "the nature of that relative holiness found in beings rational, animate and inanimate," and then "upwards of an hour" declaimed on the primacy of the pope.[4]

The *American* ended its account: "The Church of St. Vincent de Paul is to be erected, we learn, under the supervision of the Rev. Mr. Gildea, who is to have spiritual charge of the congregation when the edifice is finished."

INCORPORATION

The gentlemen who had gathered at the home of John Ignatius Gross on January 2, 1840, to organize the St. Vincent of Paul Benevolent Association were, in addition to the pastor and the host, Commo. John Daniel Danels, Andrew Cleary, Frederick Crey, Patrick McKew, George C. Collins, Capt. Charles Pendergast, John McColgan, Dr. Charles Maguire, James Roche, Benedict J. Sanders, Thomas C. Dunlevy, John Fox, and James Fortune. Gildea was elected president, Danels vice-president, Cleary secretary, and Crey treasurer.[5] When the archbishop negotiated the ninety-nine-year lease with the members of the association on February 5, Dr. Charles Maguire and Thomas Dunlevy were no longer on the list. By then it was clear that the members' responsibilities had expanded to include the construction of a church, orphanage, and school for the poor. The Benevolent Association had become a parish board of trustees.

On March 1, 1841, the body was legally incorporated under the title "The Association of the Church of St. Vincent de Paul in the City of Baltimore" (see appendix B). Eleven of the original fifteen members of the benevolent association were among the twelve board members or incorporators: John B. Gildea, Frederick Crey, Benedict J. Sanders, John D. Danels, Patrick McKew, John I. Gross, Charles Pendergast, John McColgan, George C. Collins, John Fox, and James Fortune. The twelfth was Daniel Conan.[6] The board would have not only fiscal but a large measure of administrative control of the parish. Whether Gildea, a priest accustomed to making decisions, had any misgivings on this score is not certain, but he clearly recognized that the goals he had set himself demanded more resources than he alone could muster.

St. Vincent's would be the last parish in the archdiocese to be incorporated in the Carroll tradition. At the same time, other parish vestries were surrendering control of properties to the archbishop in his capacity of corporation sole. The trustees of St. Patrick's of Fells Point, for example, readily surrendered in 1844 the powers granted them under the general incorporation act of 1807.[7]

There were some differences between St. Vincent's act of incorporation and earlier ones. The board of trustees was a self-perpetuating body. No vacancy was to be filled among the eleven lay trustees until their number was reduced to five, and then by the remaining members them-selves. There was no provision for parish elections of any other sort. When all debts were paid, the association should "for the time being" cease to exist "as a body corporated," conveying all rights and titles to the archbishop according to the act of 1833. All income deriving from pew rents should be applied to the liquidation of the debt and then to the support of the school.

THE DEDICATION

By December 15, 1840, the church building was well enough along to be visited by Father Deluol with Bishop John Hughes of New York in tow. "Mr. Gildea kept us too long," Deluol complained, "over my protests, and we arrived too late at the Archbishop's for dinner." By spring it was ready for use. On May 23, 1841, John, the son of Francis and Ellen O'Neal, was the first to be baptized there. On the feast of St. Vincent de Paul, July 19, 1841, Deluol blessed the new orphan asylum, said mass, and preached for the fifteen Sisters of Charity and some 200 others present.[8] On August 12 the sisters chosen to conduct the asylum moved in.[9]

The church was to have been dedicated the first of November, but the ceremony was postponed to the next Sunday to allow the repetition of an oratorio, Haydn's *Oratorio of the Creation* performed by Prof. Henry Diel-man, director of St. Vincent's choir. So successful was the second perfor-mance that a third was held on November 5. Tickets at fifty cents, admit-ting a gentleman and a lady, were sold at several music and book stores and at the door of the church.[10]

On Sunday, November 7, the church of St. Vincent de Paul was finally dedicated by Bishop John Chanche of Natchez, former president of St. Mary's College in Baltimore. "The Archbishop attended, vested in cope," wrote Father Deluol. "I assisted him in shoulder-cape and rochet, with Mr. Schreiber. There were ten priests and twelve seminarians, and eight altar boys. Dr. Moriarti [Patrick Moriarty, superior of the Augustinians of Philadelphia] preached for an hour and 20 minutes, poorly. The cere-mony began at 10.30, ending at 1.30. A large crowd."[11]

The next day the pews were sold at auction, John Ignatius Gross the auctioneer. About a third, the choicest, were bought that day, realizing some $12,300. "The bidding was lively, and the sale was closed only when the lateness of the hour made selection difficult to the purchasers." Those who paid the highest prices were Col. Solomon Hillen $610, a Captain

O'Neill $600, Frederick Crey $510, George A. Heuisler $490, John McColgan $420, and Commo. John Danels $400. Most of the rest in the middle of the church went for $100 and up, those in the side aisles and galleries from $25 to $50.[12] There were three free pews. The second gallery was for the slaves of the parishioners or free blacks. A second sale was held the following Monday. Among the subsequent purchasers was Richard Caton, who acquired Pew No. 2 for the use of his wife and daughter.

The total cost of the church was $61,502.91.[13] The sale of pews reduced this by perhaps a third or more. Despite the initial cost, pewholders were still obliged to pay a yearly rent in four installments. Although the major part of the proceeds from pew rents went to liquidate the stock issued for construction, as the articles of incorporation directed, some was used to defray ordinary parish expenses—the salaries for pastor and assistant, sexton, choir director, and custodians, as well as the upkeep of the church. One of the custodians, Hugh Salley, received $25.50 for blowing the bellows of the organ for thirty-three Sundays and eight festivals and another $25.50 for making the fires at the orphanage for three and a half months.[14] But most of the revenue for parish expenses came from the offertory (Sunday) collections, the sale of graves, donations, and bequests. Once constructed, the orphanage and school would be sustained entirely by charitable contributions. From time to time the trustees would issue additional certificates or stock to cover extraordinary expenses.

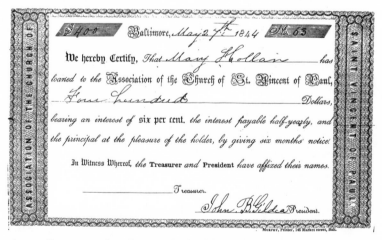

Stock certificate issued to finance the building of St. Vincent's church and orphanage. This was one disallowed by the parish corporation because it was not signed by the treasurer. SULPICIAN ARCHIVES OF BALTIMORE

For the first year, however, expenses were met by short-term loans to the board from the pastor and certain parishioners. Gildea himself lent the largest amount—$3,210—and Frederick Crey, treasurer, the next—$1,000. Then were issued the certificates of stock at 6 percent interest to be paid twice a year. Instead of waiting the fifteen years stipulated in the act of incorporation, however, stockholders could, with six months notice, be repaid upon demand. Over the next three years $19,943 in stock was purchased by fifty-three individuals. The most generous investors were Peter Schreiber (the assistant pastor) $2,500, Thomas P. Jenkins $2,234, William Pendergast $1,200, John B. Gildea (the pastor) $1,168, Benedict J. Sanders (a trustee) $1,026, Frederick Crey (a trustee) $1,000, and Mary A. Hutchinson $1,000. The last was the widow of wheelwright John Hutchinson encountered in the first chapter.[15]

THE PARISH ELITE

Mrs. Hutchinson made no pretense at belonging to the upper class, but most of the others were wealthy enough to move in the right circles, though, with the exception of the Catons, hardly of the first rank. St. Vincent's elite was, nevertheless, an interesting lot.

The man who purchased the most expensive pew, Col. Solomon Hillen (1810–73), was elected mayor of Baltimore the next year, the youngest in its history. The Hillen family had lived in Baltimore County for several generations. Solomon, the grandfather, had been one of the group of Catholics who erected St. Peter's Pro-Cathedral. An aunt had married Michael Jenkins, and their daughter Mary Ann had married Capt. William Kennedy, a wealthy pewholder of St. Vincent's. His sister Jeanette, the wife of John Hunter, was one of the most active members of the parish. Solomon himself, "handsome, accomplished and popular," lived next to his sister two doors down from the church. He had been a member of the Maryland Assembly and U.S. Congress before serving as mayor from 1842 to 1845, when he resigned for reasons of health.[16] On September 29, 1845, Father Deluol administered the last rites but on October 6 recorded: "Went to St. Vincent's and to Colonel Hillen's, who is much better. At his door I met Colonel J. Davis [Jacob Davies], the mayor of Baltimore."[17]

The Caton women on the corner of Lombard and Front were members of the parish until the death of Richard Caton in 1845. His wife and his daughter Emily MacTavish, the only one of four daughters who had not gone to England in search of a titled husband, would then move to

Three buildings on Front Street, the nearest the home of Col. Solomon Hillen, a parishioner and mayor of Baltimore. The middle one is St. Vincent's Male Orphan Asylum and the farthest the church. The Hillen home would become in 1884 a residence for Catholic working girls.

their country estate.[18] With her mother's death in 1846, however, Emily would inherit the Caton pew at St. Vincent's.

Capt. Charles Pendergast (1794–1867) came from Dublin with his father to make a fortune in the quarries at Port Deposit, Maryland. In 1838 Charles moved to North High Street in Old Town and established a shipping business at Smith's Wharf. In 1838 his three oldest children were baptized at old St. James. One of the daughters would enter the Carmelites on Aisquith Street. By the outbreak of the Civil War, Captain Pendergast would be sending a small fleet of ships to Southern ports, but after that to South America.[19]

Another mariner, who lived on Front Street, was Capt. Thomas Peter Jenkins (1816–99), a representative of the prolific Jenkins clan whose ancestor had settled in Charles County in 1670. In 1844 he would marry at St. Vincent's Mary Euphemia Deronceray, the daughter of Charles Deronceray, a musician and composer as well as pewholder. Captain Jenkins' sister Elizabeth married at St. James in 1838 Samuel Brown, the son of Mayor John Riggs Brown. His sister Margaret would conduct the orphanage at St. Vincent's until she entered the Visitation nuns.[20] The captain himself would become one of the leading trustees of the parish.

The valorous Commodore Danels was not a Catholic at the time of incorporation, in fact not until May 24, 1851, some ten months before his wife's death. Eugenie Caze Danels was noted for having "spent her entire life assisting the poor and the needy of Baltimore." The children were as devout as their mother. The boys were sent to St. Mary's College. So also were two adopted children, Emmanuel and Thomas Paez, until their guardian, Commodore Danels, was asked to remove them from the college because they were "colored."[21]

The Danels children would also lead interesting lives. John Daniel Jr. (1812–73), the oldest of five sons, all with Daniel as their middle name, would marry Eleanore Beall Clagett, a sister of the brewer William Clagett, and become a partner in the Clagett and Danels Brewery on East Baltimore Street. Louis Daniel (1815–56) and Simon Bolivar Daniel (1826–73) would become lawyers. Bolivar, who would be married in 1855 at St. Vincent's to Maria Replier of Philadelphia, would serve as delegate to the Maryland Assembly, consul of Venezuela, and judge of the Orphans Court. In 1862 he would be mobbed as a secessionist.[22] Joseph Daniel (1827–65), a graduate of the Naval Academy at Annapolis, would marry Juliana Carroll Paca, granddaughter of William Paca, signer of the Declaration of Independence and third governor of Maryland, and serve the Union cause with distinction.[23] A daughter, Eugenia, would have a granddaughter married in 1913 in the cathedral by Cardinal James Gibbons to the Duc de Richelieu in an international wedding described as the most spectacular in Baltimore since Betsy Patterson had married Jerome Bonaparte.[24]

Another parishioner, and a resident of Front Street, was Martin J.

Kerney (1818–61). A graduate of Mount St. Mary's College in Emmitsburg, he conducted for a time a "classical academy" in Baltimore before giving himself to literary pursuits, authoring a number of texts for schools and a popular *Compendium of History*.[25] In the 1850s he would be editor of the *Metropolitan*, a Catholic monthly with literary pretensions, and the *Catholic Youth's Magazine*. In the early 1850s he would also, as a member of the Maryland Assembly, introduce a bill for the public funding of Catholic schools that would touch off a period of intense anti-Catholicism. Kerney would often volunteer his pen to St. Vincent's Parish as secretary of one or other organization. Two friends also active in the parish were Patrick J. Hedian and Owen O'Brien, who would in 1850 begin a publishing house to put out the first diocesan weekly, the *Catholic Mirror*, under the editorship of a man who would be St. Vincent's third pastor, Rev. Charles I. White. Owen O'Brien would also serve as a trustee.

The original trustees not yet identified were likewise men of substance. Frederick Crey (1777–1854) of Madison Street was a master paver and banker. John McColgan, whose brother Edward would be the long-lived pastor of St. Peter the Apostle, was a liquor dealer and distiller with a home on Front Street. James Roche was a baker and flour dealer on Gay

William Clagett (1812–68), co-owner of Clagett's Brewery (where Brewer's Park now stands), and a parishioner. He was a generous benefactor, especially of the parish schools.   COURTESY OF BRICE M. CLAGETT

Street, James Fortune a grate manufacturer who in 1840 lived outside the parish. Benedict J. Sanders and George C. Collins were both grocers and commission merchants who lived respectively on East Fayette and South High streets. John Fox and Patrick McKew were both grocers and liquor dealers who resided and ran their businesses respectively on the corner of Hillen and Front and on North High Street.[26]

Fox, who died in 1849, was probably the father-in-law of Arunah S. Abell (1806–88), who had moved to Baltimore in 1837 and to Front Street to begin a newspaper on Gay Street that would revolutionize the newspaper world, *The Sun*.[27] Although in later years he would refer to himself jocosely as a Hard-Shell Baptist, A. S. Abell was married in 1839 in Philadelphia by Bishop Francis Kenrick to the widow Mary Fox Campbell, a devout Catholic. While they lived on Front Street, their children were baptized at St. Vincent's.[28] Other parishioners of note were Luther A. Schoolfield, also a resident of Front Street, whose wife was godmother for one of the Abell children. He ran the Lottery and Exchange Office at Baltimore and Gay. James Whiteford, a produce and commission merchant and future trustee, lived on Aisquith and conducted his business at Exeter and Hillen. Isaac Hartman, another future trustee, was a merchant tailor with a home on North Gay and his firm on South Gay. He would become president of the Metropolitan Savings Bank as well as the parish treasurer. William Clagett, the brewer of Baltimore Street, probably a convert, would also become an active member of the parish.[29]

A NOT QUITE ELITE

An elite represents a fraction. Not quite elite but far from destitute were many of the Irish who lived in Old Town before the coming of the famine Irish. John Moore FitzPatrick, the horseman, we have already met. Thomas Gibbons, a salesclerk, lived within the parish boundaries, on Gay Street north of Lombard. There his son James was born in 1834. Thomas Gibbons returned to Ireland to operate a grocery store until his death in 1848. The widow returned with her children to New Orleans. James Gibbons (1834–1921) as archbishop of Baltimore would be the second citizen of the United States to wear the red hat of a cardinal.[30] Hugh Keane, a tailor, of Ballyshannon, county Donegal, would bring his family to Baltimore in 1848 by way of Canada. He lived first on East Fayette and then North High. He was prosperous enough to plan a Jesuit education for his son, but the son, who had made his first communion at St. Vincent's in 1849, chose to work a few years after graduating from Calvert Hall and then enter the seminary. John Joseph Keane (1839–1918) would go on to become the first rector of the Catholic University of America, archbishop of Dubuque, and one of the closest friends of Cardinal Gibbons.[31] Another friend, William Gross, a nephew of John Ignatius Gross, would become archbishop of Oregon City.

Middle-class status could also be claimed by other sons of Irish parents who would make a name for themselves as Catholic clergymen. Monsignor James F. Mackin (1838–1925) would be baptized at old St. James and Bishop Owen B. Corrigan (1849–1929) at St. Vincent's. Monsignor William E. Starr (1840–1921), not Irish, would be baptized at St. Vincent's at age 7. A cardinal, two archbishops, a bishop, and two domestic prelates was a list any Catholic parish would be proud to display.

At the same time, St. Vincent's could claim a number of "free colored" as parishioners, apparently prosperous enough to be a part of the African-American middle class of Baltimore. Sometime before 1840 the Tobias Society lent Gildea a sum on which he paid a substantial interest.[32] Not long before 1843 the St. Vincent's Mutual Relief Society of Colored Persons was founded, Emily Oliver president. On May 8 of that year the society opened an account with Gildea and over the next three years deposited $171.25.[33] On May 27, 1844, Mary F. Hollan, possibly as president or treasurer of the Tobias Society, purchased from the Association of the Church of St. Vincent of Paul a certificate of stock for $400. After Gildea's death the board would refuse to honor the purchase, claiming that Gildea had borrowed the money in 1835, some years before the association was founded, and that the certificate had not been signed by the treasurer, indicating that the money had never entered into the funds of the corporation. The executor of Mary Hollan's estate sued, and the case was submitted to an arbiter, the outcome of which does not appear in Gildea's papers.[34]

THE CHURCH OF ST. VINCENT DE PAUL

Pastor and parishioners alike were proud of their church, their home, whose unique features are described in part 2. If Gildea himself was not the architect, he took an active part in every phase of its construction. The building sat back from the street just far enough to allow only a set of steps and close enough to the Falls to rule out the possibility of a garden, which most residents on the west side of Front Street planted. A few feet separated the church from the presbytery to the north and orphanage to the south. With its soaring tower it was a landmark of the neighborhood.

St. Vincent's Church could boast a grander organ than the cathedral. Even before the church's dedication a choir was organized by Prof. Henry Dielman. "The choir of this beautiful church," reported a visitor from Boston in the fall of 1842, "although yet in a comparative state of infancy, have executed several difficult masses. Mozart's and Haydn's compositions are taken up by them with but very little difficulty."[35]

Gildea and the rector at the cathedral, Charles White, were probably instrumental in convincing the Jesuits in 1842 to conduct Lenten retreats at St. Vincent's and the cathedral. The first, directed by John McElroy, SJ, was held at St. Vincent's, February 13–20, the first parish retreat ever held in the city. It packed the church. On the last two days 1,300 received communion, this at a time when even the most pious approached the altar rail no more than six or seven times a year.[36]

St. Vincent's was seen in its early years as doing for the English-speaking Catholics east of Jones Falls what the cathedral was doing for them west of it. In one area they split responsibility for all of Catholic Baltimore, the cathedral parish sponsoring the orphanage for girls, opened in 1818, St. Vincent's erecting one for boys twenty-three years later.

ST. VINCENT'S MALE ORPHAN ASYLUM

The St. Vincent's Male Orphan Asylum, as a later secretary of its board would recall, was created to care for "neglected and orphaned boys who were gathered in from the damp cellars and convenient store boxes and were given shelter from the inclemency of the weather in clean, warm beds."[37] They were also fed and clothed and, more important, educated. By the end of 1841 twelve orphans lived in the three-storied building that served as orphanage and school under the care of three Sisters of Charity, Sr. Ann Alexis Shorb the "sister servant," as the superior was called. By the end of 1844 there would be thirty orphans.[38]

The Benevolent Association continued its supervision, but from the start laywomen played as important a role in the support and management of the orphanage as laymen. In time, but perhaps not in Gildea's years, a board of "lady managers" would also be created. The chief funding came from the annual subscriptions, but there were donations of many sorts and proceeds from various types of entertainments. The support was citywide. In the long list of benefactors women's names outnumbered men's. Among the most generous and most active were Mrs. Robert Goodloe Harper and Mrs. Emily MacTavish, members of the Carroll clan, Mrs. William George Read, daughter of Gen. John Eager Howard, Mrs. John D. Danels Sr., Mrs. John Hunter, Mrs. Pierre Chatard, and especially the Misses E. M. Landry, Rebecca Hillen, and Harriet Spalding.[39]

A SCHOOL FOR THE POOR

Gildea had envisioned from the start a school for poor boys run in conjunction with the orphanage. The sisters in charge of the orphanage taught the younger boys, laymen the older ones. It would not be thought of as a parochial school for nearly a decade. In the *Catholic Almanac* it would be listed under "Charitable Institutions," and data on the school would in the 1840s be included under that of the orphanage.

On April 21, 1842, Gildea wrote to the mother superior at Emmitsburg telling her that the boys' school had succeeded "almost beyond our expectations." There were then 16 orphans and 260 day scholars. "Sister Ann Alexis is all I could wish her, and her sisters with her." The basement of the church was now completed, and the parish was ready to begin a day school for girls, about which he had already spoken with the mother. The school for girls run in conjunction with the orphanage at the cathedral could accommodate but one-fifth of the girls who should be in Catholic schools, most of whom were in the public schools. "My object in the contemplated school is to hold out inducements to take these poor children from these schools that they may be brought up in the fear of God and be taught the principles of their holy religion."

Gildea wanted two sisters immediately for the girls' school, which he expected to number from 150 to 200, perhaps 300. In time he would want three or four sisters. "I know you will think me extravagant, and will say we have not got the Sisters, but *I do beg you strain a point* to let us have them." The late retreat had convinced him even more to press the matter, for many young women and young men had come to him afterwards begging for the instruction in their faith they had never received. The debt on church and orphanage, he added, was being arranged in such a way that he hoped the sisters' request for a salary could soon be met. Although the debt was heavy, "be assured it shall be attended to."[40]

The sisters' response was apparently all the pastor could wish and more. By the end of 1843 ten sisters were living at the orphanage and 500 pupils attended the day school, 220 of whom were girls. "All branches of a plain and useful education are taught," the *Catholic Almanac* announced, "and the religious education of the scholars is particularly attended to."[41]

Gildea was both founder and president of a Sunday School Association that included among its active members Martin Kerney, Owen O'Brien, and Bolivar Danels. On the feast of St. Aloysius Gonzaga in 1843, nearly 800 children from the Sunday school, day school, and orphanage "marched two by two in bands conducted by their respective leaders" through the streets of Baltimore to "a very pleasant country retreat" to spend the day "in innocent amusement, under the supervision of the ladies and gentlemen of the Sunday school and the sisters of charity."[42]

A SEARCH FOR BROTHERS

It was Gildea's hope, nevertheless, to have religious brothers in charge of the orphans and the boys' school. In 1841 he and Charles White, rector of the cathedral, tried, through the archbishop, to induce the Christian Brothers in Canada to send teachers for the boys' schools of both parishes. The brothers there, the archbishop was told, had not enough members, but would train candidates sent to their novitiate and return them to Baltimore. In 1842 Gildea and White made the long journey to Montreal with three boys from St. Vincent's and two from the cathedral. Only one would persevere, but he would return to Baltimore with a Canadian brother in 1845 to take over the new school called Calvert Hall, built for them on the site of old St. Peter's.[43]

In the meantime Gildea became impatient. Learning from the Redemptorists of a newly founded congregation of brothers in Bruges, Belgium, the Xaverian Brothers, who were training members to teach the deaf and mute, Gildea wrote to the founder and superior, Brother Theodore Ryken, at the beginning of 1844. Specifically he wished his brothers to take over the orphanage, to teach the older boys in the day school, and to undertake the instruction of deaf-mutes. In the late summer Brother Ryken wrote that he was unable to send anyone for at least another year. Before the year passed Gildea was dead, and the invitation was forgotten.[44]

THE CATHOLIC TRACT SOCIETY

The Catholic Tract Society that Gildea had founded in 1839 continued its periodic meetings and its literary offerings for most of the years left him. In 1842 Rev. Peter Schreiber, assistant pastor of St. Vincent's and member of the editorial board, gave the address at the second annual meeting. In it he revealed that the treasury was empty. Tracts of about twenty-five pages each continued, nevertheless, to appear monthly throughout 1842 and with less frequency thereafter. They treated such subjects as the nature of religion, the Scriptures, the rule of faith, the sacraments, and religious life. Reflecting a growing defensiveness on the part of the Catholic Church in America, their apologetic character is indicated by such titles as "Faith and the Catholic Church: Unchanged and Unchangeable" and "The Catholic Church Is the Sole Depository of the Doctrine of Jesus Christ" (in two parts).[45]

Gildea and White, the other member of the editorial board, were perhaps the authors of most of the unsigned tracts until White became involved in other publishing ventures that will be described later. In 1844 the society was renamed the Metropolitan Tract Society. As such it put out six more tracts. And that was all. By then Gildea's health was precarious.

A PASTOR OF PARTS

The tract society revealed but one facet of a man of many parts. The tastes and interests of the first pastor would be indicated by the inventory of his personal estate taken after his death. His most valuable effects, aside from his library, were a horse and buggy ($325), a piano ($175), a chalice and plate ($60), fourteen paintings representing the Stations of the Cross ($35), a portable cupboard ($30), a cooking stove ($29), and a cask of Lisbon wine ($16.50). Undoubtedly the personal property he treasured most was the library, which consisted of over fifty titles, many of them multivolume works. Among the mostly theological and apologetical treatises, sermons, biblical studies, and histories, there were, however, bound volumes of the *Rambler* and the *Spectator*.[46]

On October 1, 1842, Gildea himself purchased the house built on Lot 9 of the 1732 survey from the widow Ann Campbell for a rectory.[47] It was a brick structure considerably older than the church. Typical of many residences on Front and nearby streets, it had two stories and a garret under a gabled roof in the main building and a two-story annex at the back. On the first floor was a narrow hallway on the church side and two parlors each with a fireplace and mantle. On the second floor were two bedrooms. In the "back building" were two more bedrooms. The second parlor apparently served as a dining room. The garret was used for storage for everything, including saddlebags, a barrel of sugar, and the cask of Lisbon wine already mentioned. A housekeeper undoubtedly lived in one of the bedrooms of the back building.[48] The other occupants of the presbytery were the assistant pastor and a dog.

If one can judge from the welter of documents he left behind, Gildea's greatest talent was not in the field of finance. A number of creditors, the *Baltimore American* and the Carmelites among them, declared that they had never received "any part, parcel, security or satisfaction" for sums owed them by the pastor.[49] Even on the rectory was an unpaid mortgage owed the widow Campbell. This and Gildea's handling of some of the stocks issued by the association would later involve the trustees in a number of suits. St. Vincent's first pastor had too many irons in the fire.

FRIENDLY RIVALRY: PART TWO

The friendly rivalry between the Sulpician superior and pastor of St. Vincent's continued throughout the latter's pastorate. With the exception of one year, Gildea continued to serve as director of the Carmelites and Deluol continued to visit them to hear confessions. On October 28, 1844, Deluol recorded a meeting with Mrs. Emily MacTavish, one of his lay "penitents" of Old Town. When he told her that the church forbade the indiscriminate reading of books by Protestant authors, she refused to believe it. "I told her just about everything that can be said on the subject, but it was in vain. She wept bitterly, and told me that she was going to go to Mr. Gildea. I answered: Very well, and she left. Heavy rain with thunder and lightning." The last allusion was apparently to the weather and not the meeting. Gildea's direction was of short duration, less than four months. Nine months after his death Mrs. MacTavish would ask Father Deluol to become again her spiritual director. With appropriate promises made, he consented. The next day Deluol would dine at Mrs. Caton's with Father White, now pastor of St. Vincent's, Mrs. Harper, and presumably Mrs. MacTavish.[50]

THE PASSING OF THE FIRST PASTOR

Gildea, who had no assistant at St. James, was given one at St. Vincent's, probably for two reasons: the added burdens of a larger parish and orphanage and his failing health. The first baptisms performed by Peter Schreiber were in December 1841. Gildea had carried to Baltimore the effects of his bouts with the cholera in Virginia. Through most of his four and a half years at St. Vincent's he was probably in the last stages of consumption. A tradition says that it was because he lived in an unheated room.[51] A spell of bad health in 1844 incapacitated him, but he seemed to recover. Toward the end of January 1845, however, Deluol spoke to Schreiber about the way the pastor was "managing his spiritual and temporal affairs: a great confusion in everything; a great help to his parents who are personally in bankruptcy." He added, "Mr. Gildea is ill as they ask me to go hear the confessions at Mount Carmel."[52]

On February 18, sixteen days after his forty-first birthday, Gildea drew a will. He bequeathed his personal property to his two sisters, his house to the parish if the trustees paid his sisters $1,000 apiece, and the cemetery on Harford Road, now used by St. Vincent's Parish, to the archbishop.[53] That same evening Deluol wrote in his diary: "I got to Mr. Gildea's at 9.30; he died at 11.30, while I was saying the prayers for the dying at his bedside." The next day Deluol returned to see that everything was done properly and found "a tremendous crowd." On the twentieth he recorded, "The Archbishop sang the High Mass and I preached for an hour and a half at Mr. Gildea's funeral. It began at 9.30 and ended at 11.45: large attendance."[54] The first pastor was buried, as he requested, in the basement of the church beneath the altar.

At the next meeting of the Sunday School Association, its members were moved to speak of "his kindness of heart, his gentleness of manners, his paternal admonitions, and the many amiable qualities which truly entitled him to the fond and affectionate title of *Father Gildea*." In a series of resolutions they also alluded to "that disinterested zeal and unbounded charity which rendered him emphatically the friend of the poor, the consoler of the afflicted, the father of the orphan."[55] The Calvert Beneficial Society passed similar resolutions, and a J. Augustus Shea was moved to write a poem, two of whose ten stanzas ran:

> In him the virtues three,
> Faith, hope, and charity,
> Found illustration of a holier world;
> And when thy love he spoke
> The trump of heaven awoke,
> Hope filled the air, and faith her flag unfurled.
>
> Well may we weep for him;
> But, Lord! we must not dim
> One moment of his glory with our grief;

> Better that he should see
> Our hearts thus turned to thee,
> The Way, the Truth, the Life, the sole relief.[56]

THE PASSING OF THE SECOND PASTOR

The archbishop appointed Gildea's assistant his successor. It was not then apparent that the assistant's health was almost as precarious as Gildea's. Peter Stanislaus Schreiber was almost a year older then Gildea. Born in Baltimore May 29, 1803, he was raised by a widowed mother, a convert. She had sent him to Mount St. Mary's College in Emmitsburg, where he was Gildea's older classmate. There he also entered the seminary and returned to St. Mary's Seminary in Baltimore two years before his ordination on August 26, 1827. In Richmond and at St. Peter's on the Hill in Washington he proved an able pastor, but in 1833 he was recalled to Baltimore as assistant pastor at the cathedral. There he would stay until named assistant pastor at St. Vincent's.[57]

On April 30, 1845, the archbishop appointed Schreiber pastor and sent him Rev. Charles C. Brennan as his assistant. On September 6 the newly ordained William Dent Parsons was sent to replace Brennan. A few days later Schreiber fell seriously ill. Deluol went to visit him and "found the house full of all sorts of people, mostly women. Mr. Schreiber is very sick." The doctors were baffled. "Some think that he has asthma," Deluol confided, "which would be a good sign; others say that the lungs have apoplexy, which would be very bad." On September 15 Schreiber's horse was brought to Deluol to take him to St. Vincent's. "I found Mr. Schreiber close to death; however he was still conscious. I spoke to him, and he understood me; we prayed together. Finally he expired at 8 o'clock sharp." St. Vincent's second pastor was buried the next day. Deluol sang the mass. The archbishop gave the eulogy. As he had requested, the second pastor was buried with the Sulpicians at St. Mary's Seminary.[58]

THE THIRD PASTOR

Charles Ignatius White was appointed pastor of St. Vincent's October 23.[59] Like his two predecessors he had been born in Baltimore, on February 1, 1807, but he attended St. Mary's College in his native city. Then he entered the seminary there. In 1828 he went to the Sulpician seminary at Issy, France, and was ordained in the Cathedral of Notre Dame by the archbishop of Paris on June 5, 1830. After serving as assistant at St. Patrick's, Fells Point, he was called to the cathedral, along with Schreiber, in 1833. There he became acting pastor in 1839 and regular pastor in 1841. In the latter capacity he cooperated with Gildea on the projects already described. In 1843, after having launched the year before the *Religious Cabinet,* which became in 1843 the *United States Catholic Magazine,* he went to St. Mary's College to teach moral philosophy.[60]

White was initially delighted to succeed his two friends. The third pastor liked to entertain. In January he held a dinner to which he invited the archbishop, the other pastors, several priests, and some of the leading laymen, although none, it would seem, from the parish, to honor the famous convert Orestes Brownson, in town for a lecture.[61]

Something was amiss. On August 6, 1846, the archbishop went to the seminary to seek the advice of his Sulpician confreres about the parish. He wanted to send there the pastor of St. Matthew's in Washington, John P. Donelan, and "get rid of Mr. White in any way that he can," Deluol recorded. At a dinner given by the pastor of St. Patrick's a month later,

Rev. Charles Ignatius White (1807–78), third pastor but soon removed by the archbishop for reasons not clear. Eccentric and gifted, he was later pastor of the future St. Matthew's Cathedral of Washington, D.C.

the archbishop told White "that he must absolutely leave St. Vincent's."[62] The reason for the removal Deluol did not reveal. Fr. John Sinnott Martin, a future historian of the parish, would claim that White was unpopular with both parishioners and trustees.[63] Such a relationship with the latter is suggested by the fact that he had editorialized in the *Religious Cabinet* on the evils of the trustee system while pastor of the cathedral, where the trustees had even greater power than at St. Vincent's.[64] The number of trustees at St. Vincent's had fallen to six: Capt. Charles Pendergast, Frederick Crey, Patrick McKew, Daniel Coonan, George Collins, and John Fox.

Upon the third pastor, moreover, devolved the problems arising from the settlement of Father Gildea's estate.[65] In early 1846 he was obliged to call upon the trustees to repossess the rectory by paying off the mortgage. In so doing they became the legal owners of the pastor's home. They also acquired title to the ground on which it stood.[66]

White was temperamental at best, eccentric at worst, a not uncommon condition of the truly gifted. Whatever the cause of his removal, he was sent first to the small parish at Ellicott Mills, then was allowed to live with one or other wealthy Catholic family in the country. During this virtual banishment he would create a small parish, St. Charles Borromeo at Pikesville.[67] The leisure allowed him to indulge his literary bent. By 1848 he would be back in the archbishop's good graces. In June he would sing a mass in the cathedral, preach, conduct vespers, and then read portions of his biography of Mother Elizabeth Seton.[68] By then he would be recognized as one of the leading Catholic writers in the country. In 1857 he would be named pastor of St. Matthew's in Washington. There he would die in 1878, after having achieved the distinction of being the oldest priest in the archdiocese and the only one to have known personally nine of its archbishops.[69]

The leavetaking of the third pastor spelled the end of the first phase of the parish's development, a period dominated by descendants of the Catholic gentry and merchant princes accustomed to an easy exercise of power. While he may have contested this exercise of power, Charles White perpetuated in other respects the Carroll church, particularly the interfaith harmony and the social, civil, and cultural engagement that would be modified substantially by an immigrant influx of unprecedented proportions that began about the time of White's removal.

❀ 3 ❀

TRANSFORMATION

1846–1873

In 1845 Baltimore's first horse-drawn omnibus carried passengers outward. A burst of home building, 2,006 in 1847, some for the well-to-do at the edges of the metropolis, some for workers closer to the center, was accompanied by the conversion of older residences into multifamily dwellings in such parts of the city as Old Town.[1] In 1847 the famine Irish began to arrive in Baltimore in frightening numbers. Germans soon followed but for different reasons.

The railroads attracted alien labor to the city. In 1850 the Philadelphia, Wilmington & Baltimore (later the Pennsylvania Railroad) built its terminus, the President Street Station, at the southern end of St. Vincent's Parish while the Baltimore and Susquehanna (later the Northern Central Railroad) built another, called Calvert Station, near its northern end. The Irish who had settled first in Fells Point pushed west into the neighborhood of the Mount Clare B&O railroad yards or north into Old Town, where a large number huddled around Hillen Street. Still others followed their compatriots westward as construction workers on the B&O (Baltimore and Ohio) Railroad or C&O (Chesapeake and Ohio) Canal.[2]

As the immigrants moved in, wealthier members of St. Vincent's moved to more fashionable parts of the city, to country villages, or to rural estates, like the ones around Pikesville for whom Father White created the parish of St. Charles Borromeo in 1848. Col. Solomon Hillen moved from his residence on Front Street. Mrs. Emily MacTavish moved from the Caton mansion to Folly Quarter in Howard County.

THE NATIONAL PARISH

The transformation of the parish from elite to immigrant was a gradual process. Although a lap or two behind other large urban sees in the east, the archdiocese of Baltimore was shaping to its own "immigrant church." A very different church from that fashioned by John Carroll, its energies were directed more each day to filling the spiritual, psychic, and even material needs of a very different constituency, in the process raising walls against an increasingly hostile environment. The national parish was the principal building block. But there was also the school, the orphanage, the hospital, the mutual-aid and fraternal societies, and a militant press. The immigrant church in Maryland took shape under the leadership of a most unlikely architect, a product of the gentry of the Eastern Shore. Gracious, frail, enigmatic, Samuel Eccleston had an intuitive appreciation of the needs of the Irish and German newcomers that his Sulpician confreres lacked. He would march in their parades, preside at the founding of their societies, seek the personnel needed to serve them, speak to them in terms they understood.[3]

Neither St. Joseph's in South Baltimore, founded in 1839 near the future Camden Station, nor St. Peter the Apostle in West Baltimore, dedicated in 1844 near the Mount Clare shops, was originally created for the Irish, but both rapidly became identified with them. From the start St. Alphonsus, which replaced the old St. John's in 1845, was a national or ethnic parish, the national center, in fact, for the Redemptorist outreach to urban Germans.[4]

Like the archbishop, St. Vincent's fourth pastor, John P. Donelan, was attuned to the needs of the immigrants. He won, in fact, the affection of both the merchant aristocrats and the growing number of impoverished Irish who crowded the back, the balconies, and the empty pews at the early masses. Under his direction the immigrants would begin, in effect, to steal the parish from its middle-class proprietors. St. Vincent's in time would be identified as the leading Irish parish in the city. But always with a difference. For one thing, it would count as many pastors of German as of Irish descent. For another, it would retain for most of the century a small core of old families.

THE FOURTH PASTOR

In the marriage register the fourth pastor wrote, "This day, Sept. 14, 1846, the undersigned took possession of the Church of St. Vincent de Paul as Pastor and Ass[istan]t Past[or]." The undersigned were John P. Donelan and Michael Slattery. Slattery signed for himself. Quite often they were referred to as "the pastors." Donelan was born in Boston April 18, 1813, but in the 1830s the two Donelan brothers, John Philip and James Benedict, entered St. Mary's Seminary and were ordained for the archdiocese of Baltimore, John on July 24, 1836. Both were talented and attractive. John was chosen in 1837 to be the first pastor of St. Matthew's Parish in Washington. When John was sent to St. Vincent's, James took his place at St. Matthew's. It is not known where or when Michael Slattery was born, only that he entered St. Mary's Seminary in 1841 and was ordained in 1844. He was a hard worker, "a man of action rather than thought."[5]

The fourth pastor's first task was to bring to a successful conclusion

Rev. John P. Donelan (1813–66), fourth pastor, was like his predecessor removed by the archbishop for unspecified reasons. He was, however, eloquent and well liked by the parishioners.

the suits that had resulted from the settlement of Father Gildea's estate. The six remaining trustees did not help much. Mr. Collins was out of the city and Mr. McKew was ill, Donelan explained to a lawyer in March 1847.[6] The irksome litigation and financial affairs of the parish apparently persuaded the old trustees to resign in favor of a new and younger board.

PARISH FINANCES

A methodical approach to parish finances with a built-in system of checks and balances was soon worked out. In 1848 a "financial department" under Frederick Crey and Fathers Donelan and Slattery "as treasurers" drew up a financial statement that was first examined by a special committee composed of George Collins, John McColgan, and Thomas Jenkins and then "approved and adopted by a committee of clergymen and the Most Rev. Archbishop, as their report will show by reference to the books of the Church." The financial statement was again reviewed on September 8, 1850, in a report of the "financial committee," which the board of managers then "respectfully submit[ted] to the stockholders and friends of the Church."[7]

Appended to this report was another dating from the appointment of a new treasurer on April 15, 1849. The board of trustees now consisted of Rev. John P. Donelan, president, John F. Connolly, William Johnson, Thomas P. Jenkins, and James H. Bevans. The new treasurer was Isaac Hartman. The next year Hartman would be added to the board and would retain both positions throughout Donelan's and the next two pastorates. The appended report showed that the debt on the church had been reduced from $35,411.68 in May 1845 to $32,369.25 in September 1850.[8] This was not an overly impressive reduction, but responsibility for the debt was a way the board of trustees had of maintaining control of parish affairs. They were in no hurry to erase it. The cathedral trustees would not pay off their debt until 1876.

The report estimated yearly parish receipts at $6,100, of which $4,700 was expected from pew rents, $1,200 from the Sunday collections, and $200 from the cemetery. Pew rents for the next two years and four months, however, totaled scarcely $5,200 while total expenses for 1852 alone reached nearly $9,000. To cover expenses the parish was obliged to issue $2,006 worth of new stock and borrow an additional $1,243. In 1854, however, pew rents brought in $4,296.07, not far off the original estimate.[9]

Pew rents remained an unpredictable source of income. By 1852 there were 228 pewholders, all but a few of them on the books since February 1, 1849, when a new ledger was begun.[10] There were thirty-eight pewholders who paid $30.00 a year in four installments ($37.50 after 1850). Thirty-six paid $25.00 a year, sixty-six $20.00, twenty-four $15.00, twenty-two $10.00, and the remaining few different amounts. Only three of the pews in the "Coloured Gallery" were purchased by parishioners for their slaves, namely, by Capt. William Kennedy, Mrs. Mark Jenkins, and Mrs. Mary Burke. Apparently only one "free colored," Anthony Calath, rented there.

The number of delinquents was a source of concern. Over thirty pewholders by 1852 were marked "hopeless." The person responsible for collecting the rents was the sexton, who in the late 1840s and most of the 1850s was Thomas Walsh. He also had to admonish those who transferred their pews to other people without obtaining the consent of the board. One, in 1852, was Mrs. Emily MacTavish.[11] For all his troubles—he was also responsible for the upkeep of the church property—the sexton received $500.00 a year.

ORPHANAGE, SCHOOLS, AND RECTORY

The report on parish finances was always accompanied by a separate one on the orphanage. That of September 1850 confessed to "many anxious days." When the sisters withdrew from the orphanage in 1846, Father Donelan persuaded the Christian Brothers to take charge. For want of members, however, they left after two months. Miss Margaret Jenkins took over until October 1848 and then Miss Sarah Griffin, but pastor and parish both wanted the brothers back. Finally in August 1849 three Christian Brothers returned with Brother Ambrose (James Rourke) as director. The board of lady managers was pleased; friends of the orphans were encouraged to visit the fifty boys on Thursdays to see for themselves "the cleanliness, order, and regularity observed." The lady managers in 1850 were Jeanette H. Hunter, Elizabeth McKew, Margaret Crey, Rebecca Fry, Theresa Johnson, and Sarah A. Connolly.[12] The lady managers were, more often than not, wives of the parish trustees.

Voluntary subscriptions, donations, fairs, and sales were still the principal means of support. These usually produced enough to cover the annual expenses but rarely more. The St. Vincent's Male Orphan Association and Sewing Society was founded in 1849.[13] Brother Elisee, a young

Canadian, became a successful mendicant. On market days—three times a week—he went with basket in hand from stall to stall, two orphans at his heels dragging a hand cart.[14] The report of January 1852 showed an increase of thirty-five orphans over the fifty in 1850. Twenty, however, had been bound out, leaving sixty-five at the orphanage. In October 1853 one of the "orphans" was bound to St. Mary's Seminary as a servant for $3.00 a month. He left in April with a balance of $5.06 in his account, which was paid to his father.[15] A number were actually those with one parent or simply boys whose parents were unable to support them.

The Christian Brothers had also assumed charge of the boys' school in 1848. Two brothers from Calvert Hall, the *Catholic Almanac* announced, "daily repair to St. Vincent de Paul's Church, in the basement of which they conduct school, containing 200 children."[16] When the brothers took charge of the orphanage the next year, they established their second home in Baltimore at St. Vincent's. The first report on the "Male school" in 1850, when there were "upwards of 500 boys" in five classes, boasted that it had "more than realized the most sanguine expectations of the Congregation and Pastor." The boys were taught "the usual branches of an English education, from the lowest to the higher classes in Mathematics, Mensuration, Algebra, &c., together with French." The parishioners were proud of the new boys' school, which they saw as contributing to "a new era in the history of the Catholic youth of Baltimore."[17]

The "nearly 200" in the girls' school, still taught by the Sisters of Charity, were offered "the usual branches of English education, tapestry, needle work, &c." Income at the school, said Sister Fidelis, the sister servant, in her report of 1850, was barely enough to support three sisters. It was "highly desirable" that the sisters have a house of their own instead of paying $200 a year rent. Their house on Front Street was too small to accommodate a larger student body. The sisters themselves had just affiliated with the Daughters of Charity in France, and the people of St. Vincent's would soon accustom themselves to the distinctive white cornettes they wore. By 1851 St. Vincent's with its 608 students—453 boys and 155 girls—was far ahead of the other six parishes of Baltimore that had schools.[18] The *Catholic Almanac* of 1852 also revealed that Sunday schools were conducted in most of the parishes, those of St. Vincent's (the only one mentioned by name) counting 900 children. The boys were taught by the brothers and the girls by young ladies.[19]

On December 11, 1848, a meeting was held for the purpose of raising a fund to purchase the rectory from its trustee owners, who had apparently neglected its upkeep. The next month another meeting was held to create a fund association. The house could be purchased for $5,183.04 (the amount originally expended by the trustees) if it were paid off in three years. After a motion of Father Donelan that the pastors not be elected officers, Capt. Richard Lilly was voted president and Martin J. Kerney secretary. A subscription was taken on the spot, each of the six trustee owners pledging $100. Some sixty men and thirty women pledged lesser amounts, aggregating a total of $1,610.[20] An appeal was also made in March 1850 to the people at large in the confident expectation that "ere long the present unsightly barn, miscalled a house," may belong to the congregation and "bear a pleasing exterior, and afford a comfortable residence to the Clergymen laboring with zeal for the good of others." A fair raised $1,200 for the "presbytery."[21]

In 1854 the original six trustee owners, with the consent of the new trustees, deeded the rectory and grounds to Archbishop Francis Patrick Kenrick of Baltimore in his capacity as corporation sole.[22] An annex was soon built that provided a dining room and kitchen on the first floor with a guest room and housekeeper's quarters above. A passageway was also constructed between rectory and church.[23] When the improvements were completed, St. Vincent's rectory was all that pastors and parishioners alike could wish.

THE PARISH SOCIETIES

In his first year as pastor Donelan founded the St. Vincent's Indigent and Sick Society—"to relieve the wants of the sick and the poor," the *Catholic Almanac* explained in case there was any doubt. The Young Catholic's Friend Society had been organized in Baltimore in 1842 by young men of good families to afford the opportunity to meet periodically to hear lectures and concerts and, at the same time, collect clothes for poor children so that they could attend Catholic schools.[24] Donelan organized a branch at St. Vincent's. These societies for the relief of the helpless poor, as with the Male Orphan Association and Sewing Society already mentioned, sprang from a sense of *noblesse oblige* characteristic of the Carroll church.

Of a different order were the mutual-aid and mutual-support societies associated with the immigrant church. In 1846 the *Catholic Almanac* told its readers that there were "several Temperance associations in the diocese and various other societies for the promotion of piety among the faithful."[25] The year St. Vincent's created its first temperance society is not known, but when it sold an organ in 1850 to Frederick Crey, the proceeds were divided "between the Male and Female Junior Temperance Societies."[26] Of the societies for the promotion of piety there is no doubt. On July 18, 1847, after administering confirmation, the archbishop installed the Sodality of the Blessed Virgin Mary at St. Vincent's. There were actually separate sodalities for the ladies (counting 170), for men (76), for the children (200), and for the "colored of both sexes," for which no number was given.[27]

The "beneficial" or mutual-aid societies of the immigrant church enabled those of modest means to assist one another and thus maintain a measure of independence. They also served a social need for those excluded from the purlieus of the elite. At St. Vincent's, however, the beneficial societies often enrolled representatives of good families. In 1849 or 1850 Father Donelan organized the St. Vincent's Male Beneficial Society and the St. Vincent's Female Beneficial Society.[28] On July 19, 1850, the nearly 200 members of the St. Vincent's Male Beneficial Society held its annual meeting and elected Rev. John P. Donelan president, Martin J. Kerney vice-president, and James Hasson Jr. secretary.[29] A paucity of records allows little more than speculation on the genesis and development of many of these early societies at St. Vincent's.

THE CHANGING POPULATION

What can be said with greater assurance is that the parish population was growing by leaps and bounds. The number of baptisms, one of the most reliable indices of growth, rose from 144 in 1846 to 600 in 1851, the highest in its history. The number of marriages that year (201) was also the highest. The 600 may have been, for reasons not clear, abnormal. The number of baptisms fell back to 497 in 1852, about where it was in 1850. A conservative estimate of the parish population at this time, however, would be from 15,000 to 20,000.[30] Whatever the number, it represented numerically the peak years of the parish. But it was a parish that stretched from the waterfront to the northern edge of the city. That would soon change.

That the increase was due mostly to an Irish influx can also be demonstrated by an examination of baptisms. In the first six months of 1842 approximately 45 percent of the children baptized, judging from surnames, were of British (English, Scots, and Welsh) origin, 35 percent Irish, 9 percent German, and 11 percent of other or undetermined origin. In the first six months of 1851, however, almost half were of Irish extraction, a third

British, and the rest others. The percentage of Irish would continue to increase at the expense of other national groups but never to their complete exclusion. In the baptismal register covering October 1845 to December 1855 the eleven names that appear most often are Smith (43), Murphy (34), Byrne (27), Murray (27), Jones (26), O'Neill (24), Ward (24), Green (22), Reilly (22), Connolly (19), and Walsh (19). It was not a very stable population in this decade. Of twenty-seven couples named Smith, for example, only seven had more than one child baptized at St. Vincent's and only two had more than two.

A SAD LEAVETAKING

Father Deluol, to judge from his diary, had little to do with St. Vincent's under its fourth pastor. On July 11, 1848, however, he wrote: "Mr. Donelan came to tell me that the Archbishop wants him to prove to me that his administration of the finances of the asylum is good. None of my business. However, since he insisted, I told him what I had heard." Less than a month later Deluol recorded that the archbishop had appointed another Sulpician, Gilbert Raymond, to examine Donelan's books and report to him.[31] The suspicions of archdiocesan officials undoubtedly had much to do with the method of strict accounting worked out about this time at St. Vincent's. Whatever doubts the archbishop may have entertained, however, he allowed Donelan to remain as pastor.

On April 2, 1851, Samuel Eccleston died and was succeeded as archbishop by Francis Patrick Kenrick, former bishop of Philadelphia. Kenrick was unable to abide priests guilty of financial irregularities or of insobriety. In December, two months after his arrival in Baltimore, he sent Donelan to St. Charles College. The departure was a matter of great regret to his "numerous friends, but he must yield to religious obedience," the *Catholic Mirror* said only by way of explanation.[32]

On January 20, 1852, a delegation of the St. Vincent's Male Beneficial Society presented their founder with a series of resolutions on parchment in a gilt frame expressing their affections and respect. To these former parishioners Donelan acknowledged his physical and spiritual decline and confessed that he had forgotten the most important duty, his own sanctification. "Obedience is the only safeguard to the priest," he agreed. But when his superiors called him back, he hoped to return "with renewed energies—a stronger—a wiser—and a better man." The "consoling recollections of days gone" would sustain him. "I can say no more—God bless you all—and believe the heart feels most when the lips move not."[33]

The unhappy priest never returned. He would be sent to serve the country missions of southern Maryland until about 1855, when he and his brother moved west. John Donelan would die July 15, 1866, in Rockford, Illinois, having built there a church that would be a cathedral. Some seventy-five years later Monsignor James Mackin of St. Paul's Parish in Washington would recall that, as a teenager, "I sat upon the altar steps and listened to his wonderful eloquence. He was my ideal and, next to God, I worshipped him. But he was called away and died far from the place he loved."[34]

THE FIFTH PASTOR

Rev. Leonard Ambrose Obermeyer arrived at St. Vincent's on December 20, 1851, a week after he had written the archbishop that he would accept the pastorate.[35] He was born December 5, 1807, near Conewago, Pennsylvania, where many German Catholics had settled in the area opened by the same John Digges who had in the 1730s laid the wagon road to Baltimore. His father owned a papermill near Emmitsburg. He would enter Mount St. Mary's College and then the seminary, which he served in several capacities before his ordination on December 8, 1837.

Obermeyer replaced Fr. Henry Myers at St. Mary's in Cumberland in 1841 at an important point in that city's history. The B&O Railroad and C&O Canal would leave a sizable residue of Irish construction workers. Obermeyer worked well with these sons of Erin. He built for them a magnificent church to replace the old St. Mary's and named it St. Patrick's. It was dedicated a month and six days before he arrived in Baltimore.[36]

A priest-historian later associated with St. Vincent's would remember Obermeyer:

> He was a man of profound and exact learning. His personal characteristics were eminently social. He was a high-toned courteous gentleman; learned rather than refined; admired rather than loved; popular, in a sense, with those who were not afraid of him; reverenced as a good priest by all. He was very firm, and stood like a rock against every form of levity, and every encroachment of the spirit of the world on his congregation.[37]

His assistant was John F. Hickey, a Sulpician. Hickey would remain with Obermeyer until November 1855, when William Parsons, Father White's assistant, returned. He was followed in 1858 and 1859 by Fathers John Byrne and George Flaut.

THE NEW PARISHES

Flaut and Byrne had tried in succession in 1853 to create a new parish in the northern part of St. Vincent de Paul Parish called Gallows Hill. The health of both proved unequal to the strain, and Father Hickey went up on November 27, 1853, to bless the temporary church called St. John the Evangelist on Valley Street, halfway between the penitentiary and St. James Church. In short order it could accommodate no more than a fourth of the burgeoning population that crowded it. Rev. Bernard J. McManus was sent as pastor to erect a new church on Valley at Eager Street.[38] The Catholics in that part of town were too poor, the *Catholic Mirror* announced, to build their own church. An appeal was therefore made to "the good people of Baltimore."[39] Those of St. Vincent's contributed generously to the new St. John's, dedicated June 15, 1856.

A month later the wealthier Catholics to the north also had a church. Its beginnings went back to 1851, when the Jesuits were looking for a place to build a college. One proposal, frowned upon by the new archbishop, was to give St. Vincent de Paul to the Jesuits so that they could erect their college on Front Street. Frederick Crey of St. Vincent's suggested the Carmelite convent-school on Aisquith, thinking that the nuns would move to a more secluded part of the city when Archbishop Kenrick persuaded them to close their academy.[40] Although this suggestion was also rejected, Crey would help determine the location by offering the Jesuits a chapel that he had built in his mansion on Madison near Beuren Street just east of Jones Falls for the Catholics of the neighborhood.[41] In 1853 the Society of Jesus decided to build both college and church at Madison and Calvert streets just to the west of the Falls. St. Ignatius Church was dedicated August 15, 1856.[42] Although it took fewer parishioners from St. Vincent's than did St. John's, it took the best. Bolivar Danels, who shepherded the act of incorporation for the college through the House of Delegates, Francis Neale, Francis Elder, Nicholas Woodward, William Clagett, and others had at least pews there, even if they remained on the rolls of St. Vincent's. While the First Plenary Council of Baltimore of 1851 provided for territorial parishes, it allowed the purchase of pews in parishes other than the one in which the pewholder resided.

Other parishes were created in the 1850s to absorb the stream of immigrants—Immaculate Conception in 1850, St. Brigid in 1854, and St. Lawrence O'Toole in 1859 to accommodate the Irish, St. Michael the Archangel in 1852 and Holy Cross in 1858 to welcome the Germans. In 1856 the *Catholic Mirror* estimated on the basis of baptisms that the three largest parishes were St. Alphonsus with 14,310 parishioners, St. Michael's with 12,782, and St. Vincent's with 12,451. St. John's, the daughter parish, was estimated at 5,213.[43]

In 1853, following the decrees of a diocesan synod called to implement the legislation of the First Plenary Council of Baltimore of 1852, the boundaries of the Catholic parishes of Baltimore were precisely drawn for

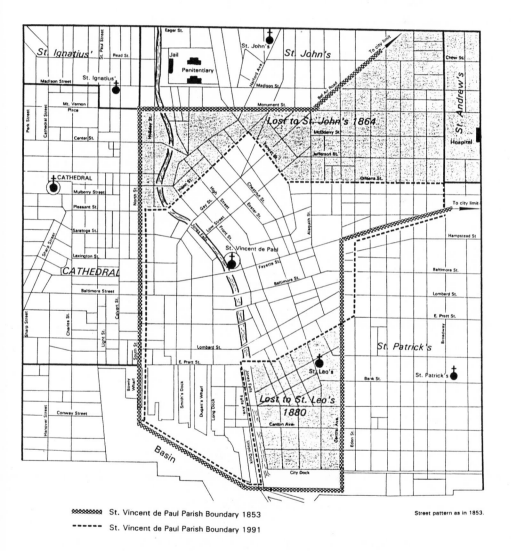

St. Vincent de Paul Parish Boundary 1853

St. Vincent de Paul Parish Boundary 1991

Street pattern as in 1853.

Parish boundaries of St. Vincent's drawn in 1853 when St. John's Parish was created and St. Ignatius Parish planned. The portions indicated would later be lost to St. John's and the future St. Leo's Parish. JAMES DILISIO

the first time. Those of St. Vincent de Paul were described as running along South and North streets (now Guilford Avenue) on the west, Pratt Street to Bowley's Wharf and then along the water line on the south, Canal Street to Fayette Street on the east, and Monument Street and Belair Avenue on the north. Between Belair and Fayette the parish ran to the city limits.[44] The cathedral parish to the west, St. Ignatius and St. John's to the north, and St. Patrick's to the southeast were all territorial parishes. The national, or German, parishes had their own boundaries. Parts of St. James and St. Michael's overlapped St. Vincent's.

THE NEW CEMETERY

In 1853 the Association of the Church of St. Vincent de Paul purchased from Johns Hopkins, Miles White, and Robert Purviance five acres at $1,350 for a new cemetery. The old cemetery on Harford Road had been condemned so that new streets could be run through and new homes built. The new cemetery was at the end of Mine Bank Land (now Rose Street) a little west of Belair Road and a half mile north of the then city limits (now North Avenue). On May 19, 1853, the cemetery was blessed by the pastor with Fathers Hickey, Flaut, and Byrne assisting. Many of those present selected their lots then and there.[45]

The total debt incurred by the new cemetery was $3,129, which, besides the purchase price, included adjustment of claims against the old cemetery, removal of bodies, fencing, and construction of a vault. It was soon paid for by the sale of gravesites and of town lots from the old cemetery. A square (16 by 20 feet) in the new cemetery cost $40.00, a lot (8 by 10 feet) on the broad walk $12.00 (later $18.00), a lot on the narrow walk $10.00 (later $15.00), a single grave for an adult $4.00 and for a child under ten $2.50. To have a grave dug cost $2.00 for an adult and $1.50 for a child.[46] The records show that wealthier members of the parish often provided for the burial of the poor. From July 3, 1853, when the first burial took place, until December 26, 1854, sixty-six were buried. Half of them were children, mostly babies. Many died of the cholera.[47]

THE SCHOOLS AGAIN

Despite Father Gildea's promise the parish paid nothing to the sisters, or the brothers who conducted the parish schools, a condition that would continue as long as they taught there. Partly the teachers were subsidized by their religious orders; partly they were compensated by the parents who were able to pay. The brothers had less of a problem. They lived with those who conducted the orphanage, which was sustained by its benefactors. In 1855, however, they apparently attempted an arrangement similar to that of the brothers at the cathedral, who conducted an academy for the middle class, Calvert Hall, which supported the brothers teaching at the parish school. The *Catholic Almanac* of 1856 shows two schools for boys at St. Vincent's: St. Vincent's Academy with 120 pupils and the "Common School" with 170 boys. The term "parochial school" appears for the first time for the parish schools at the cathedral, St. Peter's, and St. Alphonsus, all taught by the Christian Brothers.[48] At St. Vincent's it was usually called the Male Parish School. As late as 1861 the financial report of the orphanage spoke of an excursion of "the Academy" for the benefit of the orphanage.

The school for girls conducted by the Sisters of Charity at St. Vincent's was listed with the girls' academies from 1850 to 1853, when four sisters taught some 200, all but 50 of whom were paying students. In June 1853, however, the convent-school was moved from Front Street to a larger home on Fayette a few doors west of Gay. While the rent was higher, the sisters hoped for a greater number of paying students as well as free ones. The next school year five sisters taught 250 pupils. It was not enough; the sisters withdrew from St. Vincent's in 1854.[49]

In an attempt to lure them back the parish acquired a building on Front Street for $3,800, and St. Vincent's Female School was incorporated in May 1856. None of the eight incorporators belonged to the parish board of trustees. Gen. William Clagett was the guiding spirit and treasurer.[50] The sisters were apparently reluctant to be under the control of trustees. Lay teachers were employed at St. Vincent's Female School until Father Obermeyer persuaded the trustees to give the sisters a ninety-nine-year lease.[51] The Sisters of Charity returned on September 26, 1858. By 1861 daily attendance at the school averaged 235, of whom 139 were unable to pay anything.[52]

Ownership of property was also complicated by ground rents. On February 9, 1857, the lot on which the church stood was conveyed by the owner to the archbishop as a corporation sole subject to a ground rent of $285.28 a year while the lot on which the asylum stood was conveyed to the St. Vincent of Paul Benevolent Association subject to a ground rent of $214.72. The ground rent of $240.00 a year on the girls' school would not be bought out until 1879, for $4,000.[53]

THE SIXTH PASTOR

Father Obermeyer's health began to fail. Perhaps as early as 1858 he tendered his resignation to the archbishop. His "voluntary retirement" because of "shattered health," however, was not announced until the beginning of 1860. The leavetaking of January 29 was "a deeply affecting scene," according to the Catholic weekly, his farewell address leaving "the whole congregation, with scarcely an exception" in tears. Father Obermeyer would retire to the "cherished home of his early manhood," Mount St. Mary's College and Seminary.[54] There he would do some teaching; there he would die March 16, 1865.

It was probably at Obermeyer's suggestion that his friend, Rev. Henry Myers, was named his successor. Obermeyer had succeeded Myers, his senior by almost two years, in Cumberland. Born February 1, 1806, Myers was, like Obermeyer, a native of Conewago, Pennsylvania, and of German stock. After four years at St. Mary's Seminary in Baltimore he was ordained September 3, 1831. After a pastorate in Garrett County he accepted that of St. Mary's in Cumberland in 1836. In 1841 he continued his eastward progression, first to St. Mary's in Hagerstown, then to the parish founded by Father White, St. Charles Borromeo in Pikesville, and finally to St. Vincent's, where he began his pastorate February 15, 1860.[55]

Temperamentally Myers differed from Obermeyer. He was kind, friendly, mild-mannered, well liked. Less domineering, he apparently worked better with the trustees. But he does not appear to have gotten along as well with the women in the parish. "I am sorry," he wrote Archbishop Martin John Spalding, archbishop since 1864, "you are so tormented by the complaints of women regarding the asylum. I have long since experienced that women, especially widows, are very annoying to clergymen."[56]

A WELL-CONDUCTED PARISH

As administrators Obermeyer and Myers were much alike. They addressed the problems of church, orphanage, and two schools to the satisfaction of most. With the cooperation of the trustees Obermeyer was able to reduce the debt on the church from about $31,000 at the beginning of 1851 to $17,000 at his retirement. Father Myers erased it entirely shortly before his death in 1873. St. Vincent's and the Cathedral of the Assumption were the only parishes to publish annual financial reports.[57]

They were also the only two parishes in Baltimore to have active boards of trustees.

Parish finances remained, nevertheless, unpredictable, being dependent on the punctuality of the pewholders in their payments and the whim of the stockholders in their demands for redemption. Income from pew rents dropped, inexplicably, from $5,211 in 1851, Obermeyer's first year, to $1,286 in 1852, his second. It generally averaged about $3,500. In 1856 over $8,000 in stocks were redeemed but in 1861 only $775. Whenever stockholder demands for payment were excessive, new stocks were issued in order to balance the books. As a result, parish income and expenses ranged from $5,000 one year to $9,000 another.

St. Vincent's Male Orphan Asylum made a great leap under Father Myers. With nearly 100 orphans in November 1860 a grand fair was held to finance another school building behind the orphanage. The building was constructed and equipped at a cost of $5,200, partly to house shops to teach the orphans trades and provide additional income for the orphanage, an idea suggested by an industrial school opened by the Holy Cross Brothers at St. Patrick's. In 1861 over $2,000 was derived from the tailoring and shoemaking departments.[58]

The number of orphans dropped as soon as the Civil War was over. In 1866, when there were, according to Father Myers, forty (but according to the *Catholic Almanac* sixty), the pastor complained to Archbishop Spalding that only six of them were from St. Vincent's. While the asylum took boys from every parish except St. Patrick's, little help came from these parishes other than the annual subscriptions that brought about $500. At Archbishop Kenrick's orders the treasurer had drawn upon an endowment during the war years, of which little was left. "By my office of 2d. [?] President of the Board, I have nothing to do with the spending of the monies." Myers suggested that half the orphans be returned to their parents.[59] At Archbishop Spalding's request the state appropriated $1,500 for St. Vincent's Male Orphan Asylum in 1868.[60]

The fairs, entertainments, raffles, and excursions for the benefit of the orphanage not only helped to keep the orphanage afloat but also enhanced the social life of the parish. The great bazaar to fund the new building in 1860 was "the first time in ten years the ladies of this congregation have undertaken a fair," the *Catholic Mirror* reported. Two tables of "fancy and useful household articles," two tables of "Christmas notions," a table of "choice confectionaries," and a supper table were run by matrons of the parish. There was also a "post office" with Miss Barringer as postmistress and a "soda fountain" run by Mr. Fowler.[61] Whatever the sixth pastor may have thought of the active role of the ladies of the parish, they would represent an increasingly important part of it financially as well as socially.

POLITICS, RELIGION, AND NATURE

As the social life of the parish intensified, the political life of the city approached the frenetic. In 1853 the avowedly anti-Catholic Know Nothings, officially the American Party, appeared in Baltimore to battle the Democrats. In the fall a pitched battle in Old Town at Fayette and Exeter proved the first of many in that part of the city. Political clubs with such terrifying names as the Rip Raps, Plug Uglies, and Blood Tubs (Know Nothings) pitted themselves against the Bloody Eights and Butt Enders (Democrats). For six years at every election Catholics and foreigners were terrorized by Know Nothing gangs. Only the Eighth Ward, or "Old Limerick," with St. John's at its center returned in kind.[62]

Abhorrence of the Know Nothings was soon eclipsed in the Catholic community by an almost equal detestation of abolitionists and the Republican Party that replaced the American Party nationally. On June 18–23, 1860, the Democratic Party reassembled at the Front Street Theater, two blocks up from the church, to conclude a national convention that tore it apart, thus assuring the election of Abraham Lincoln. On April 19, 1861, parishioners of St. Vincent's joined the mob that assaulted Union troops on Pratt Street as they tried to march from the President Street Station to Camden Station.[63] A number of Catholics were arrested as secessionists, including the publishers of the *Catholic Mirror*. In 1864 at the Front Street Theater Abraham Lincoln was nominated for a second term.

St. Vincent's parishioners were distracted by different events in the postwar years. The Second Plenary Council drew forty-seven bishops to Baltimore in the fall of 1866. In 1870 a magnificent procession was staged for the return of Archbishop Spalding from the Vatican Council, at which he had played a prominent role. In the line of march the St. Vincent's contingents were conspicuous.[64]

On June 17–21, 1871, the celebration in Baltimore of the twenty-fifth anniversary of the coronation of Pope Pius IX proved a "most extraordinary affair," one that would "long be remembered by the rising generation of the city." Each parish tried to outdo the other in its decorations.

Bird's-eye view of 1869, showing the heart of St. Vincent's Parish. On a diagonal can be seen the Front Street Theater, St. Vincent's Church, and the Shot Tower. MARYLAND HISTORICAL SOCIETY

Above the main entrance of St. Vincent's was emblazoned in gas jets "Long Live Pius IX," and on the upper portion of the façade beamed a multicolored globe. On the twenty-first a torchlight parade made its way from Central Avenue to the cathedral, "in point of numbers and brilliancy of design . . . one of the grandest that has ever passed through the streets of Baltimore." St. Vincent's marched in the division of Irish-American societies, Henry S. Buckless, a parishioner, the marshal. In a "fine barouche" Father Myers and his two assistants preceded the parish float with large pictures of St. Peter, Pope Pius IX, the Blessed Virgin, and St. Joseph surmounted by a statue of St. Vincent. On one of its sides was the inscription, "Let us from henceforth call Pius IX Pius the Great, for he alone is the greatest successor of St. Peter."[65]

The floods and droughts of the postwar years were the worst ever visited upon the city. Although the summer floods of 1858, 1866, 1868, and 1869 flushed the Jones Falls, into which 20,000 privies drained illegally, they wreaked tremendous havoc. The basement of St. Vincent's Church was seldom dry. A drought in 1872, however, reduced the Falls to a trickle and dried up the city pumps, as well as the basement. City planners bewailed the "silly, unreflective, procrastinating, impracticable, and perverse" citizens of Baltimore who refused to accept their remedies for the alleviation of such natural disasters.[66]

A MEASURE OF STABILITY

Under Father Myers the parish achieved a measure of stability. Outward migration slowed and the parish population remained about the same, the number of baptisms some 250–265 a year from 1862 to 1872. The school population also held steady: 300 boys and 250 girls in 1860 but 250 boys and 300 girls in 1872. A sizable number of well-to-do families, perhaps a slight majority non-Irish, still provided the leadership that kept the parish in the public's eye. Isaac Hartman remained a trustee and the treasurer throughout Father Myers' pastorate. Thomas P. Jenkins was for almost as many years the secretary. Other trustees of long tenure under Obermeyer and Myers were William Johnson, John F. Connolly, Owen O'Brien, Peter A. Magers, and Denis Kavanagh. Elizabeth Kennedy Fitz-Patrick still lived across the street from the church with her daughter and son-in-law, John J. McWilliams, inspector of the city's boilers and a member of the Maryland House of Delegates. Even the newcomers from Ireland enjoyed, perhaps, a greater degree of economic well-being at St. Vincent's than in any of the other parishes identified as Irish. A measure of this prosperity was reflected by the parish collections taken for the pope, the seminary, and other worthy causes.[67]

But as St. Vincent's—and St. Patrick's—stabilized, surrounding parishes expanded. St. John's, the daughter parish to the north, had by 1873 twice the population of St. Vincent de Paul. Several of the surrounding parishes now counted larger school attendance and more societies and sodalities—at least until the advent of Rev. Edmund Didier as assistant pastor.

Father Myers was fortunate in his assistants. One was Rev. John J. Dougherty, later vicar general of the archdiocese. Another was Rev. Thomas Sim Lee, a true aristocrat and later the builder of the present St. Matthew's Cathedral in Washington, D.C. In 1871 came Fr. Michael Dausch, who later that year was joined by Father Didier.[68]

Father Myers was given two assistants partly because of his failing health. He died in the parish rectory on July 21, 1873. Fr. Charles White returned to deliver the eulogy. Over 100 carriages and a long line of mourners on foot processed to the cemetery outside the city. "Seldom has so large a funeral cortege passed through our streets," the *Catholic Mirror* claimed.[69] Henry Myers was the only pastor of St. Vincent's to be buried in St. Vincent's Cemetery.

❊ 4 ❊

ZENITH

1873–1892

The new archbishop's attempt to bring a greater degree of order and regularity to parish reporting and recordkeeping was partially successful, a notable achievement in a diocese long resistant to standardization. The aristocratic James Roosevelt Bayley was installed as eighth archbishop October 13, 1872, about a year before he named Edmund Didier the seventh pastor of St. Vincent de Paul. As bishop of Newark he had worked wonders with the same business methods that were transforming northern cities. Catholic Baltimore did not embrace these methods with the same enthusiasm, however.[1] Most pastors initially made an effort to answer in full the printed forms with the word "Notitiae" at the top, which they first received at the end of 1873. Thereafter, the responses to these annual reports were uneven at best.

THE NOTITIAE

Father Didier was among the most conscientious in filling out the Notitiae. The first, dated January 1, 1874, covered the year 1873. On the first page he filled all the spaces on parish statistics. There were about 3,000 Catholics in the parish, he recorded, of whom about 800 were men, 1,200 women, and 1,000 children. About three-fourths of the parishioners had made their Easter duty (yearly confession and communion). About 75 of the children not enrolled in the parochial school attended the catechism classes on Saturday and 175 attended on Sunday. There were 250 in the boys' school and 275 in the girls'.

For the confraternities and religious societies and their numbers Didier listed the Male Beneficial Society with 130 members, the Female Benefi- cial Society 100, the Temperance Society 250, the Sodality of the Blessed Virgin Mary 100, and the Apostleship of Prayer with 1,100. He also listed, but without numbers, the Young Catholic's Friend Society, the St. Vincent de Paul Conference, and the Sodality of the Sacred Heart. In the year 1873, there had been 263 baptisms, of whom 19 were adults; 67 marriages, of which 18 were "mixed"; 77 deaths, of whom eight were children; and 247 confirmations, of whom 34 were adults.

The second page was devoted to administrative questions. "Have you the [sacramental] registers required by Statutes?" it asked. "We have them," the pastor answered. "Are they properly kept?" "Yes," he assured his new ordinary. "Have you made any additions to the property of the Church during the past year?" The parish had bought a new organ worth $6,000 and had painted the rectory and orphanage.

"What is the amount of Insurance on Church?" $32,500. "On Parochial House [rectory]?" $5,000. "On School House?" On the sisters' school $8,000 and on the orphanage $9,000. "In what Companies are you in- sured?" The Queen, National, Howard, and Equitable insurance compa- nies. "State Amount of Premium on each Policy." On the church $83.00, the rectory $15.00, and the orphanage $9.00. Nothing was paid on the sis- ters' school, the pastor explained, because Equitable did not require a yearly payment. "It is a joint concern." "Have the Premiums been regu- larly paid?" Yes. To the next question—"Have you made in accordance with the Statute of the Diocese, an Inventory of any articles of Church or House Furniture belonging to yourself, and had it inserted in the Book of Church Records?"—Didier penned his only evasive response: "All the fur- niture, pretty much, belongs to Church."

The third page was the financial report. Receipts for the past year had totaled $8,058.27, not counting a collection of $219.31 for the organ and $200 for the seminary (no explanation of why they were not included in the total). Pew rents had brought in $4,048.97, offertory collections $2,117.30, the cemetery $262.50, and donations $1,157 and $472.50 (no ex- planation for the two different sums).

Under expenditures the pastor's salary was given as $950 and the assis- tants' as $607 ($550 for the regular assistant and $57 for a part-time one). Nothing was listed for teachers' salary since, as Didier noted, the brothers and sisters asked none. The sexton earned $600 plus a 2.5 percent com- mission on pew rents, which in 1873 had amounted to $101. For the cathe- draticum, or archdiocesan tax, the parish paid $181.51. Except for the choir ($400) Didier ignored the next several categories—ordinary church expenses, improvements and repairs, amount of debt paid, insurance, and extra—and created his own. "Insurance, Ground Rent &c" took $383.34, the furnace $92.70, cleaning the church $107.61, candles $203.60, "Wood &c" $149.75, furniture $396.04, plumbing $136.34, "Repairs &c" $56.00, Father Myers' funeral $146.79, and "Gas, Water, Wine, &c" $535.02. Total expenditures amounted to $5,046.92, considerably less than total receipts.

The section on debts showed also a healthy state of affairs. There were no mortgages. Under "Bills due" only $125 was owed for the melodeon and $100 for the organist's salary. On deposit in the bank were $973 and three notes to pay for the organ at six-month intervals amounting to $2,500.[2] The archbishop was probably pleased with the report overall.

The Notitiae that arrived at the end of 1874 contained a few additions. One informed the pastor that the reports were due at the chancery the first of February "sub poena suspensionis ipso facto incurrendae." This intimidating prod, which was doubtless needed in a few cases, would be dropped by Archbishop Bayley's successor. Except for this omission, however, and an addition that first appeared in 1891 requiring auditors to sign the financial report, the Notitiae would remain substantially the same for the next eighty-three years.

THE NEW TRUSTEES

The most significant addition to the second Notitiae was a set of questions relating to the tenure of church property. They required Didier to rethink the changes he had contemplated in the trustee arrangement. In a space provided in the first Notitiae for "Statements or suggestions" Didier had written that the trustees of St. Vincent's had held their annual meeting January 7, 1874, and "considering the state of the finances, so healthy," and the fact that all the old trustees but one had moved away from the parish, it was "unanimously resolved to deed the Church &c over to the Most Rev. Archbishop." A committee of three was appointed by the chair (Didier) "to wait upon his Grace."

The archbishop did not approve this attempt to discard the trustee system at St. Vincent's, but the second Notitiae revealed that he had required an important modification. "The old Board of Trustees having removed from the Parish some years ago," Didier repeated, "a new Board has been lately organized according to the letter of the Act of incorporation—with the Pastor of the Church as Treasurer, according to the instructions of his

Grace." At a meeting of the board in late January 1875, Didier was "elected" treasurer as well as president and Arthur V. Milholland secretary. The other members of the board were John F. Hunter, William J. Kelly, Joseph Cassidy, and John Brooks. Milholland was chief clerk of the First Branch of the City Council. Hunter, president of the board of directors of the Maryland Penitentiary, would in 1882 be elected sheriff and in 1884 appointed fire commissioner.[3] He would also be president of the Broadway Savings Bank. This board remained intact for most of Didier's eighteen and a half years at St. Vincent's. The trustees would continue to play an indispensable role in the organization and financial administration of the parish. Didier worked well with the board, assuming the new role of treasurer when matters of financial import arose.

For the rest of Archbishop Bayley's administration, the annual reports would note that church property was vested in the board of trustees. For 1878, however, the first year of the administration of Archbishop James Gibbons, Didier recorded that ground rents had been deeded to the archbishop and for 1880 all property. Ground rents for the church land, he also noted in this last report, had been bought out with legacies belonging to the orphan asylum in 1876, and ground rents for the girls' school in 1879 from a sinking fund he had organized in 1876.

TO THE MANOR BORN

Edmund Didier had inherited wealth, which he was not reluctant to use in the material development of his parish. He was, as we have seen, a descendant of the merchant Henry Didier who had come to Baltimore in 1774 and son of Dr. Franklin Didier of Old Town, where he was born on December 20, 1832. Educated in private schools, he had worked in the office of his uncle Edmund Didier, president of Mutual Fire and Marine Insurance Company, and after a year as bookkeeper in the drygoods firm of Hammond, Pollard, and Lawrason had decided to enter the seminary, having developed a vocation to the priesthood as an altar boy at the Carmelite convent on Aisquith Street. His few years in the business world would render him a more competent administrator than most pastors. Didier entered St. Charles College at 18 to begin eight years of study there and at St. Mary's Seminary. He was ordained July 28, 1858. His pastoral experience was varied; he had served as assistant or as pastor of the missions of Montgomery County, the parish at Hagerstown, and the parishes of St. Peter's, St. Joseph's, and St. Vincent's in Baltimore.[4]

Edmund Didier (who pronounced his name as if it rhymed with tidier) was a well-traveled man, a friend of artists, writers, and statesmen. He had an attractive personality in a rather formal way. One clerical admirer recalled that because of his "priestly bearing, patriarchal appearance, his shock of snow-white hair, his universal kindness and charity to all classes, he became well known and actually venerated." Parishioners would record in 1891 the "numerous acts of kindness and charity that cost him many a hard ride."[5] Later reminiscences would be more specific. The unscrupulous knew how easily he was lured on errands of mercy always with money in his pockets for the taking.

IMPROVEMENTS, RENOVATIONS, AND A CONSECRATION

The pastorate of Edmund Didier would be the most fruitful and in many ways the most significant historically at St. Vincent de Paul. It would be the most productive certainly in terms of improvements, renovations, and enlargements of the several buildings owned by the parish as well as in the number of new and different institutions and organizations Didier would found to serve the changing population.

Rev. Edmund Didier (1832–1903), seventh pastor and representative of an aristocratic family of Baltimore. Under him St. Vincent's would be the most productive parish in Baltimore in the number of institutions and organizations it created.

Before his advent, there had been, as far as is known, only painting and fresco additions. Didier began his pastorate with a new organ. This and the extensive renovation of the church in 1876, a set of chimes in 1883, a skylight in 1887, and a baldachino in 1890 will all be described in part 2. The basement of the church was enlarged in 1874 and made into a chapel.[6] In 1875 he put up a new building at the cemetery and a third floor, with other improvements, at the rectory, the last made possible by the donation of a Mrs. Mary Dowling. In 1876, in addition to renovating the church, he built a new school house for the sisters, and in 1877 had the exterior of the church patched and painted from the tower to the ground.[7]

Not only had Didier managed all the additions and improvements up to 1879 with ease but had also paid a standing debt of $13,000 on the church. Debt free, the church could now be consecrated. This occurred March 25, 1879, the Feast of the Annunciation. The solemn consecration of a Catholic church was not an everyday event, partly because the bishop, in this case Archbishop Gibbons, had to prepare by a "black fast" and then with a small army of attending clergy endure a three-hour ceremony in which twelve small crosses (which are still in place) on the four walls were blessed. The throng inside the church and out was swelled by members of all the parish societies.[8]

In 1879 Didier also purchased a mansion on Baltimore Street and organized the St. Vincent Hall Association for the purpose of raising a home next door for the parish societies and a meetingplace for other Catholic organizations of the city. Carroll Hall was built in 1880. Its career will be considered in connection with the societies it housed.

To round out his catalogue of achievements Didier furnished the rectory in 1881 with a new parlor and furnace and in 1885 added what he called "a large and commodious back building" for $2,348. In 1886 he provided sizable additions to the two schools. In the summer of 1891 he had the exterior of the church painted again and the dome gilded in anticipation of the celebration of the fiftieth anniversary of the church.[9]

Throughout his pastorate Father Didier sought to make St. Vincent's "a model church in every respect." His tastes in church architecture were, for his age, as good as any Catholic pastor's. Vivid frescoes bathed in the glow of iridescent glass and a superabundance of gilt characterized Didier's St. Vincent. Yet in comparison to other Catholic churches of the city, its architectural features were fairly restrained.

Effortlessly, it would seem, the seventh pastor paid the bills for all im-

St. Vincent's chimes, installed in 1883, were one of the many additions and improvements Father Didier made to the parish plant.   SUNPAPERS

provements. Didier knew better than most pastors the value of a dollar. His business acumen was respected by parishioners, merchants, and bankers alike. In 1888, when the trustees assumed the debt on the girls' school, the bank refused to extend the note without raising the interest. Didier persuaded several of the bank's best customers to withdraw money that was earning 3 percent with a promise of 5 percent that he himself would pay. Then he marched to the bank with the depositors' books and withdrew enough to cover the debt on the girls' school.[10]

THE BENEFICIAL SOCIETIES

More important, however, than his contributions to the business affairs and physical improvements of the parish was Didier's response to the needs of his parishioners in the form of the parish organizations and institutions he created and sustained. He also directed more vigorously than had his predecessors the already existing societies. In August 1875 he revised the constitution of the St. Vincent's Beneficial Society and negotiated its incorporation. Applicants must now be residents of the city, not over 45, and possessed of certificates from their spiritual directors stating that they were practicing Catholics. By 1875 it was one of the most flourishing Catholic societies in the city, claiming 160 or more members. On July 25, 1876, it ran an excursion for 1,200 people to Walker's Pavilion. "Rev. Fathers Didier and Dausch," the *Catholic Mirror* reported, "took great interest in the pleasures and amusements of the excursionists. It is understood that a very handsome sum was realized."[11]

Didier's association with the Father Myers Beneficial Society was initially not so close. Founded on March 18, 1874, by a group of young men who had been much under the spell of the sixth pastor, it filled the need for a more congenial group their own age. Rev. Joseph Andreis, one of the assistant pastors, when approached to be chaplain, advised the body not to have one. Didier, however, accepted the position of honorary chaplain as well as honorary president. William Murphy was elected first president and John Gildea Hook, perhaps the leading spirit in the venture, the recording secretary. The benefits and social features were similar to those of the St. Vincent's Beneficial Society, but all members had to vote on anyone who sought admittance in the 35-to-40 age group, and no one older need apply. The Father Myers Beneficial Society refused to affiliate with the Irish Catholic Benevolent Union, as the St. Vincent's Beneficial Society had done, perhaps because it thought the union's membership too old or too Irish.[12]

BUILDING AND LOAN ASSOCIATIONS

Akin to the beneficial societies were the building and loan associations found especially in the ethnic parishes of Baltimore. They allowed the less affluent to own their own homes. St. Vincent de Paul apparently had two in the Didier years but neither was initially his creation. In 1886 he complained to the archbishop that his assistant, Rev. Joseph A. Gallen, had established a building and loan association without consulting him. Another such association, he revealed, had ended some years before in losses and lawsuits, and this one was already arousing dissension. At Didier's insistence the curate was removed, but he continued to operate the association. In 1889 Didier asked Gibbons, now a cardinal, to compel Gallen to dissociate himself from it entirely before trouble and scandal resulted.[13]

In March 1891 Didier presided over the incorporation of the St. Vincent's Perpetual Building and Loan Association with a capital stock of

$130,000. It was probably the same organization but now totally under his control. It would continue to appear on Gay Street near High in the city directory until 1914.

THE TEMPERANCE SOCIETIES

As assistant pastor Didier had founded the St. Vincent's Temperance Society, on February 11, 1872, when fifty-four pledged total abstinence. It soon attracted some 250 members. In the role of temperance advocate, in fact, Didier would surpass Fr. Edward McColgan of St. Peter the Apostle, the first noted Catholic of the temperance crusade in Baltimore. In 1880 parish affiliates of the Catholic Total Abstinence Union met at St. Vincent's rather than St. Peter's to elect delegates to the national convention. The St. Vincent's Temperance Society was the most prominent at a great temperance rally staged at the Maryland Institute in 1886.[14] While St. Vincent's was no exception to the general decline of temperance societies in the depression years of the 1870s and beyond—down from 250 members in 1873 to 100 in 1883—it was at the center of a movement in the late 1880s to reclaim "the low and degraded" of that part of the city, of which more will be said in the next chapter.

At a meeting of the St. Vincent's Temperance Society the first Sunday of 1874, the Cadets of Temperance were formed. Fifty-two "manly boys" took the pledge. Among the speakers on the occasion was Capt. Matthew Clark, a pioneer in the cadet movement.[15] Temperance cadets were teenagers, too young to join the adult temperance societies but old enough to be the targets of temptation. Cadets, as at St. Vincent's, were usually uniformed as an inducement to join.

At a meeting in 1878 Didier urged the cadets "to shun all evil places of amusement, corner loafing, and bad associations" and announced for the coming week a debate on which locale was the most beneficial: the theater, the corner, or the cadets' hall. The hall, of course, won hands down. The next "debate" was on "Alcohol and Tobacco."[16] The cadets counted about 200 the first year but between 50 and 75 per year thereafter. In the 1880s they disappeared from the annual reports. Yet the corps had a longer life than other such junior organizations created in Baltimore at the time.

THE LYCEUM MOVEMENT

Under Didier, St. Vincent's would not only have its first young men's literary association but would take the lead in the lyceum movement. In the 1870s and 1880s the Catholic literary associations assumed increasingly the character, as well as the name, of the lyceum movement in America, copying its programs for self-improvement and enrichment.[17] St. Vincent's Lyceum was founded August 28, 1878, with Father Didier both "originator and manager." Called originally the St. Vincent's Literary and Dramatic Institute, it was open to young men 18 to 30. In less than a month it had sixty members and a hall at 42 E. Fayette Street. On September 24 it adopted a constitution and elected its first officers.[18] On November 21 the institute held its first monthly entertainment. There were solos, duets, a trio, a quartet, recitations, and a humorous reading. In April it offered at the Concordia Opera House a historical drama, "The Midnight Watch," and a comedy, "Toodles," at fifty cents for reserved seats and twenty-five for all others, for the benefit of the orphanage.[19]

Archbishop Gibbons paid a visit two and a half years after the founding and congratulated the lyceum on its flourishing condition. It then had about 180 members. By the fourth year it was publishing an annual called *The Souvenir* and conducting a hop to mark its anniversary that went into the "wee sma" hours. Among the constitutional changes proposed in 1883 was the creation of a Catholic historical society "to promote the study of the primitive records of this state," wherein were buried a glorious history of the church.[20] By 1884 St. Vincent's Lyceum had, with 140 active members and 540 volumes, the second largest membership and library of all the literary societies in the archdiocese, being surpassed only by the Carroll Institute in Washington.[21]

Sports were an increasingly popular feature. In 1883 St. Vincent's Lyceum bowed to St. John's Institute 15 to 12 in baseball. In 1886 it formed a stock company to build a gymnasium. At the same time it created an endowment fund for the burial of members "to increase the lyceum's popularity"![22] In 1885 the annual hop was replaced by a quadrille with a grand promenade, an indication, perhaps, of the upward social mobility that kept pace with the athletic prowess and intimations of mortality of its members.

In 1887 Mayor Ferdinand C. Latrobe dropped in on one of its weekly meetings, and a banquet was held for Peter J. Campbell, a former president and member of the Maryland General Assembly from the Fifth

Ward (St. Vincent's), who thanked the members for their support during the last session. The social whirl, sports, and politics notwithstanding, St. Vincent's Lyceum did not forget its original purpose. When Didier addressed its 200 members in 1889, the *Catholic Mirror* noted that it had as fine a library as a gymnasium.[23] At its monthly receptions songs continued to be sung and recitations rendered.

CARROLL HALL

It was the founding of St. Vincent's Lyceum that spurred Didier to take upon himself a project long debated—the erection of a hall large enough to accommodate the many Catholic societies of the city. At the beginning of 1879 Archbishop Gibbons had asked the Consolidated Board of Catholic Beneficial Societies of Baltimore why its metropolis did not have a large Catholic hall like other great cities. Three months later Didier purchased for $7,000 from his own pocket the McKim mansion on Baltimore Street between Exeter and Lloyd. On May 29 he organized a hall association, with himself as president and treasurer and Henry S. Buckless as vice-president, for the purpose of building an adjoining hall. At $50 a share, the association expected to raise $20,000. Eighty-two purchasers took one to fifty shares each, Didier the fifty. At the fall meeting of the Consolidated Board the pastor displayed his plans for a three-story hall with an auditorium for 1,000 and urged support. By the beginning of 1881 Carroll Hall was ready for renters. It contained not only an auditorium but four other large lecture rooms, offices, a bowling alley, and a billiards room. The purpose of the building, it was explained, was to provide a pleasant place to spend the evening away from streetcorners and saloons. When the first dividend was paid, Didier devoted the greater part of his returns to a soup kitchen for the poor behind the hall.[24]

Although most of the societies of St. Vincent's moved their headquarters there, Carroll Hall did not attract the anticipated number of other Catholic societies, who expected accommodations for nothing or considerably less than what they paid for Raine's Hall or the Concordia Opera House. The hall association, therefore, had to rent the facilities "for political meetings, worldly concerts, dancing schools, objectionable soirees and the like." Didier found these events so distasteful that he persuaded the shareholders to rent only to "first-class concerts, lectures, fairs, and other innocent amusements." With a drastic decline in income, Didier was compelled to sell Carroll Hall in early 1888 to four members of the parish for $18,750, considerably less than the $25,000 it had cost.[25] St. Vincent's Lyceum continued to use the hall until 1890, when it moved its headquarters to a building at 11 N. Front Street nearer to the church.

LITERARY SOCIETIES UNITE

By this time another young men's literary society had been founded in St. Vincent's Parish: Brownson Institute. Organized at the end of August 1888 and named for the famous convert Orestes Brownson, it was apparently the work of Fr. Thomas Stapleton, assistant pastor at St. Vincent's, a "prime favorite of young men," or at least the work of those attracted to him. Stapleton was its chaplain. There was no hint of rivalry between the lyceum and the institute. Didier publicly congratulated the new society, located at 506 E. Baltimore Street, and assured its members of his full support.[26] The two apparently appealed to different age groups and interests.

Brownson Institute was also more disposed to affiliate with the diocesan union of literary societies. A movement toward union at the diocesan level, as with the temperance and beneficial societies, had gathered momentum under Bayley. Under Gibbons a pattern of combination, dissolution, and a new aggregation of young men's literary societies occurred with some regularity. A Young Men's Catholic Association was organized in 1872, renamed the Catholic Library Association in 1877, and disbanded in May 1879 for lack of leadership and interest only to be followed by the Young Men's Catholic Union, or sometimes Union of Catholic Literary Associations, organized in November.[27] This latest attempt at union was inspired by a desire to affiliate with the Catholic Young Men's National Union, which was planning its sixth annual convention for Washington in 1881. Founded in 1874, the CYMNU, the Catholic answer to the Young Men's Christian Association (YMCA), had attracted only one affiliate in the archdiocese of Baltimore, the Carroll Institute in Washington, prior to 1880. That year St. Vincent's Lyceum and four other literary societies of Baltimore also affiliated. On January 10, 1881, these six bodies met at Carroll Hall to adopt a new constitution. Didier was one of the speakers. As special goals the delegates agreed to work for justice to the Indians, a free night school, and Catholic chaplains for the army.[28]

By 1883 this new diocesan union claimed eight societies, Carroll Institute of Washington and St. Vincent's Lyceum having over 200 members each, the others 30 to 80 each.[29] In 1886, however, St. Vincent's Lyceum disappeared from the list of affiliates. In 1890, as a consequence of the many meetings required to organize a mammoth torchlight parade to commemorate the centennial of the American Catholic hierarchy in 1889, another regrouping occurred, this one called the United Catholic Literary Associations (UCLA).[30] The Brownson Institute joined right away. Seven of some twenty, including St. Vincent's Lyceum, did not. The next year, however, it did, and its president, Joseph J. Maguire, was elected president of the UCLA.[31]

Among the young men's literary societies, St. Vincent's Lyceum was remarkable for its staying power. Pastors grumbled about them, one saying that there was no more "arrant humbug" than the societies that masqueraded as "literary." Yet even he admitted that the hops they enjoyed were no more than "saltatorial." Didier was as insistent as any pastor that liquor be excluded from their gatherings. In 1883 the *Catholic Mirror* characterized the young men's societies in general as "utopian" and a $1,000 donation of the union for a convention of the CYMNU in Baltimore as "a lavish, wasteful, and sinful generosity."[32] Whatever their shortcomings, the young men's literary societies were important for the measure of culture and refinement, as well as self-confidence and self-esteem, they imparted to the sons of immigrants striving to enter the middle class. St. Vincent's Lyceum proved also a training ground for a number who would enter the political arena.

THE KNIGHTS OF ST. VINCENT

Father Didier, although well aware of the advantages of literary societies, was not so quick in appreciating the needs that Catholic knighthoods filled. The knightly societies were a product of the Bayley years. The first in the archdiocese were the Knights of St. Patrick, founded at St. Patrick's in Washington in March 1871.[33] It was a model for the others that followed. In 1877 a Grand Union of Catholic Knights of Baltimore was formed with Archbishop Gibbons as its chaplain. In 1879 the Baltimore union, counting some ten commanderies with an average of sixty uniformed knights each, called a convention in Baltimore for the purpose of establishing a national union. The union evolved into the Knights of St. John.[34]

The knighthoods, besides their social and often insurance features, served a craving among Catholics, especially immigrant Catholics, for greater visibility. The knights were the most enthusiastic marchers of all the different societies. The considerable expenditures for badges, sashes, swords, capes, and plumes were gladly borne.

Only when Carroll Hall was ready for occupants were the Knights of St. Vincent organized. On November 14, 1880, at an organizational meeting chaired by Didier, thirty-five signed up at once. In early January the Knights of St. Vincent held their first election, and a "handsome uniform" was adopted. Didier was their chaplain, Peter J. Campbell chief knight. The next summer the knighthood sponsored an outing at Schuetzen Park, which featured a flag presentation and sports. In 1887 it was one of nineteen knighthoods in the long parade that welcomed James Gibbons, now a cardinal, back from Rome. Only two others, however, counted fewer than the forty-two knights in St. Vincent's contingent.[35] By then it had already disappeared in the listing of societies in the Notitiae of St. Vincent's Parish. St. Vincent's lack of enthusiasm for the trappings of knighthood may have reflected the large percentage of old and assimilated families in the parish. The rolls of knights in the ethnic, or national, parishes were significantly larger.

THE CATHOLIC BENEVOLENT LEGION

Almost as eager for parades as the knightly societies were the national insurance and fraternal organizations that appeared in Baltimore and Washington in the Gibbons years, all forerunners of the Knights of Columbus. Not only did they offer better economic benefits than the old local beneficial societies that they often displaced but also a greater esprit de corps, prestige, and many of the accoutrements of the knighthoods. The Catholic Benevolent Legion (CBL), founded in Brooklyn, New York, in 1881, proved the most popular by far in Baltimore.[36] The first branch of the CBL in Maryland was established in 1882 at St. Joseph's Parish by Frederick A. Lucchesi, a former parishioner of St. Vincent's and the principal promoter of the new organization. The second was founded at St. Vincent's itself, also in 1882, and called the Father Myers No. 15, the fifteenth branch established in the United States.[37]

Although parish based, the CBL branches were more oriented toward national affairs and goals than parochial ones. At the same time, they had greater success in forging a stable and productive interrelationship between the many units at the regional level by the frequent banquets, smokers, and entertainments to which all members in the city were invited. The Father Myers No. 15 grew from about 100 to 150 members and was still going strong at Didier's retirement, with James J. O'Connor as president.

PIOUS SOCIETIES

The number of pious societies doubled under Didier while the old sodalities continued strong and active. Of the latter the Sodality of the Sacred Heart, the women's sodality, fluctuated between 200 and 400 per year, that of the Blessed Virgin Mary, the men's sodality, between 100 and 200. The League of the Sacred Heart, or Apostleship of Prayer, established by Didier as assistant pastor, averaged 1,200. The large number was due not only to Didier's promotion but also to the fact that its members, although obliged to say set prayers, were not required to meet in church at set times to say them. Didier was a promoter of the league citywide.

The pious societies, of course, did more than pray. The Sodality of the Sacred Heart in 1889 introduced reading circles of ten to fifteen each who met weekly in private homes in the parish for reading, discussion, and singing, "a feast of reason and a flow of soul" (but no refreshments).[38] The men's sodality sponsored a winter lecture series. Its prefects in 1891 were Adam Deupert and Charles J. Murphy, its spiritual director Father Stapleton, the assistant pastor.[39]

To the pious societies already at St. Vincent's when he became pastor, Didier added probably four others. One was the Nocturnal Adoration Society. Begun in the archdiocese at St. Ann's in 1883, it was quickly copied by other parishes. By the fall of 1885 St. Vincent's adoration society numbered 140 ladies and 45 gentlemen. Beginning at 9 P.M. on Thursday, the men prayed in shifts until 6:00 A.M. and then the women until Benediction at 9 P.M. on Friday. The same James O'Connor who would serve as president of St. Vincent's Lyceum and the CBL was also the adoration society's president.[40]

Didier founded at St. Vincent's the first branch of the Confraternity of the Holy Face in Baltimore. Although one of his favorite devotions, he listed it only once in the annual reports, that of 1888, when he recorded 400 members. Possibly in existence before, it certainly was for the remainder of his years at St. Vincent's. Didier had a side altar in the church dedicated for its use and upon it placed a perpetual light for the sins of blasphemy, the elimination of which was the confraternity's object. There the members gathered weekly to pray. In 1889 a fresh impetus was given the confraternity by the presentation of diplomas obtained from France to the twelve most active women promoters.[41]

For two years the Bona Mors Society appeared in the annual reports from St. Vincent's. In 1888 it had 300 members and in 1889, 200. It was probably in existence for some years, but there is no other record. As the name suggests, its principal purpose was to pray for a peaceful death. There is also reason to believe that Didier established the Confraternity of the Holy Thirst in his parish even though it never made the Notitiae. Founded in 1875 by Father McColgan at St. Peter the Apostle Parish, it had spread throughout the archdiocese and even the nation. Its purpose was to pray for those afflicted by the curse of drunkenness, one of Didier's principal preoccupations.

CHARITABLE ORGANIZATIONS

A spin-off of the women's sodality was the Ladies' Relief Society, a charitable organization. While most of the beneficial, temperance, and literary associations of the parish engaged in some form of charity, those with specific charitable goals now had a new addition. A Conference of St. Vincent de Paul had been organized in the parish of St. Vincent de Paul in 1866, the second in Baltimore.[42] This small corps of dedicated men, averaging only about fifteen at St. Vincent's, as in other parishes, continued the special services to the poor for which the St. Vincent de Paul Society had become famous. So also did the Young Catholic's Friend Society continue its distribution of clothes to poor schoolchildren along with its somewhat elite tradition, about 75 gentlemen in Didier's first five years, about 40 thereafter.

The Ladies' Relief Society would soon become the most active of the charitable organizations at St. Vincent's. It was organized March 8, 1875, by Didier himself in response to Archbishop Bayley's appeal for women's associations devoted to works of charity. Didier appointed the officers. Its active members attended monthly meetings, at each of which they paid twenty-five cents dues "to be expended for the poor of Christ." Honorary members paid according to their means. From October until April the active members visited and helped needy families (53 in the season ending April 1887), distributed clothes (120 pairs of shoes and 400 other pieces of clothing in the same period), and conducted a sewing class. Each summer the women's sodality of St. Vincent's organized a "grand moonlight excursion," the proceeds of which went for the clothes distributed by the Relief Society.[43] Although the activities of the Ladies' Relief Society were well covered in the Catholic weekly up through 1882, when the pastor staged a reception and supper at Carroll Hall to honor it and other groups, the society as such received not a mention in the Notitiae. From 1890 through 1892, however, Didier listed the Sewing Class with 75 to 80 members.

THE SANCTUARY SOCIETY AND THE CHOIRS

Also honored at the reception and supper above mentioned were St. Vincent's Sanctuary Society and choir. There are few records concerning the Sanctuary Society. It appeared only in the Notitiae for 1889 with 250 members. Presumably its principal task was the same as other sanctuary or altar societies: the care of the sanctuary and the altar linens. Its membership was probably drawn from the women's sodality.

The reputation of St. Vincent's choir continued to grow under Didier. It was as impervious to the attempts of Archbishop Bayley to substitute Gregorian chant for the classical masses of the masters favored in Baltimore as were the choirs of most parishes.[44] At the patronal feast of the church in 1883, for example, when a statue of St. Vincent newly arrived from Paris was installed, Haydn's Mass No. 2 was sung and at the fiftieth anniversary of the church in 1891 Haydn's Mass No. 3 was offered one day and a Beethoven mass with the Sanctus and Benedictus from Gounod the next. The choir was under the direction of Prof. Charles J. Tillman. There were occasional voice solos, duets, and quartets, and organ solos rendered by Prof. James Mallon. On special occasions there was a full orchestra at the mass as in 1883 and at that of the celebration of Father Didier's fiftieth anniversary as a priest.[45]

St. Vincent's had also a schoolgirls' choir and after 1889 a schoolboys' choir organized by Brother Arsenius and coached by Professor Mallon. The boys' and girls' choirs alternated at the 9:00 Sunday mass.[46] The adult choir always sang at the high mass at 11:00.

THE OLD AND NEW INSTITUTIONS

Father Didier saw to it that the boys' and girls' schools were well run and well supported. He likewise took a special interest in St. Vincent's Orphan Asylum, which throughout his pastorate housed 50 to 60 boys a year. Under the direction of the brothers and control of the trustees, it continued to depend upon a body of unfailing benefactors. Didier himself subscribed $100 a year. In 1882, which may be taken as typical, there were on average 52 boys. For them $3,895.06 was expended and $4,343.69 raised, $1,181.00 of it by subscriptions, most of them $5.00. The rest of the revenues came from a sinking fund set up by Didier, a picnic, an entertainment sponsored by the lyceum, an excursion sponsored by the sodality, three sizable legacies, alms boxes installed in ten neighborhood stores, and from "Relatives of the Orphans and Boarders." The sources of income varied from year to year. A decade later $916.67 came from the City Council, $666.66 from a bequest by Miss Emily Harper, and $523.30 from a pound party, the largest three amounts except for the annual subscriptions, which by then were down to $720.00.

In January 1878 the trustees of St. Mary's Industrial School of Baltimore acquired a former hotel and tavern at High and Low streets and opened on July 16 a home for the working boys who had graduated from the industrial school and others recommended by pastors and other authorities.[47] St. James Home, conducted by the Xaverian Brothers, was not officially a part of St. Vincent de Paul Parish but because it was within its boundaries the archbishop sought to place its financial burdens upon Didier's shoulders, a responsibility the pastor sought initially to evade.[48] In 1887 Father Stapleton, the assistant pastor, was placed in charge. In 1890 he began a small publication named *The Home Messenger.*[49]

The success of the working boys' home suggested to Didier a home for working girls, for the "friendless females in a large or a strange city," such as those recently founded in Chicago, New York, and Cincinnati.[50] In 1884 Didier purchased the former three-story home of Mayor Solomon Hillen next to the orphanage. "A generous benefactor of the deserving poor," the *Catholic Mirror* reported—Didier himself, of course—had donated $10,000 to erect and furnish a large building to the rear.[51] The following summer a board of twelve lady managers was created to oversee the work of the matron, and on November 1, 1884, the home was dedicated.[52]

Although St. Vincent's Home was originally intended for about 60 servant girls, the 35 or so young women living there in January 1888 worked mostly in the lithograph building, in "sewing houses" (sweatshops), and in nearby stores. Those who could not find a job were taught needlework.[53] The home was supposed to be self-supporting, the girls who could afford it paying $2.50 a week. When the number and quality of the residents declined, however, Didier appointed a new board and replaced the matron with three Sisters of Mercy, who took charge in the summer of 1890. Immediately the situation at St. Vincent's Home improved. The sisters also conducted classes in sewing, typewriting, housekeeping, and cooking. The home contained a library and chapel.[54]

In the spring of 1887 Didier opened a night school for working boys at

Carroll Hall.[55] Toward the end of 1888 he informed the cardinal of a plan to open a home for newsboys and bootblacks too young to be taken in by St. James Home, for which he would donate $10,000.[56] When the committee Gibbons appointed to study the project gave less than an enthusiastic endorsement, Gibbons refused permission, fearful that the expense of Didier's undertakings would eventually fall upon the archdiocese, "which," the cardinal explained, "is already burdened with Houses whose support taxes the efforts of the faithful." At the same time, he praised Didier for his "laudable efforts in the cause of benevolence."[57]

Didier's persistence, however, carried the day. In April 1889 he purchased for $6,000 a building on East Fayette near Holliday. There he moved the night school, which members of St. Vincent's Lyceum volunteered to teach four nights a week from 8 to 9 o'clock, Didier himself teaching religion the fifth. At the home the boys could get three meals for only 20 cents a day and a place to sleep for only 5 cents a night. In warm weather, however, most preferred to sleep around the neighborhood, mostly on cellar doors. Lest one might think it was simply a way to avoid the instructions, the *Catholic Mirror* assured its readers that the twenty-five boys at the home in March 1890 were "eager to learn." In the meantime the Young Catholic's Friend Society opened a Sunday school in the northern part of the parish for the boys "growing up in vice and ignorance."[58]

A PARISH UNEXCELLED

St. Vincent's in the 1870s and most of the '80s was unrivaled for its many institutions and organizations, which often served as models for other parishes. In the many Catholic parades to which the city was treated, its units continued to be the most conspicuous. For the centennial celebration of 1889 it had a large float with a gilt cross surrounded by the orphans preceded by 150 men of St. Vincent's (Catholic women never marched) and four open carriages bearing the pastor and other prominent parishioners.[59]

The Third Plenary Council of Baltimore had decreed in 1884 that in all dioceses of the nation a certain percentage of pastors be designated irremovable. At the clergy retreat in September 1887 Gibbons finally named three (far from the percentage required): the pastors of St. Patrick's in Washington and of St. Patrick's and St. Vincent de Paul in Baltimore.[60]

A FRUITFUL RETIREMENT

On the second Sunday of January 1892 Father Didier, despite his irre-movability, surprised everyone by announcing his retirement as pastor of St. Vincent de Paul. "He gives as his reason for resigning from the rector-ship," the *Catholic Mirror* explained, "that he wants to take a needed rest."[61] This was not the real reason, for Didier refused to slacken the pace he had set himself early in life. The mystery of his retirement must remain so until the next chapter.

From St. Joseph's Hospital on Caroline Street, where he lived and served as chaplain, Didier became an even more energetic promoter of pious societies—in the city, the archdiocese, the nation. By the spring of 1894 he had enrolled 10,000 in the Confraternity of the Holy Face. A new interest was the Society for the Poor Souls, for which he offered special beads to the people who recruited the largest bands of those willing to pray for the release of the suffering souls in Purgatory.[62]

In December 1892 Didier purchased a building on Centre Street near Charles as a permanent home for the United Catholic Literary Associa-tions. As its treasurer he remained active in the affairs of the UCLA. In 1899 the UCLA was replaced by the Baltimore Grand Council of the Young Men's Institute, another national union, with Father Didier as head of the board of directors.[63]

In December 1898 Didier bought for $8,000 a building at Biddle and Caroline streets and created a board of directors to oversee St. Anne's Home for Aged Ladies. Over the next several years twelve to twenty-five residents paid $3.00 a week. Young women out of work, probably resi-dents at St. Vincent's Home, were hired to do the housework.[64] In 1900 the chancellor of the archdiocese informed Didier that the cardinal had given earnest consideration to his proposal for a home for aged and in-firm priests but that the consultors found it not feasible. Instead they sug-gested that he donate a handsome sum to the Clerical Beneficial Society as the Father Didier Foundation.[65] The retirement home in which Didier doubtless wished to spend his last days never materialized.

THE END OF AN ERA

Didier died at St. Joseph's Hospital on May 18, 1903, and was buried from St. Paul's Church nearby, not St. Vincent's, whether of his own choice is not known.

Edmund Didier had reigned in Old Town at a time the Catholic Church in the United States was spawning its greatest variety of institu- tions and organizations to meet the growing needs of a largely immigrant population. In the process St. Vincent de Paul Parish, under his zealous stewardship, had few equals. Yet the remarkable achievements that piled one upon the other so rapidly in his eighteen and a half years as pastor obscured a darker side of the parish's history: the ominous forces that were tugging it downward. A few perceptive minds were beginning to wonder how many years the parish might outlive the century that was rushing to a close.

DECLINE

1885–1912

From the day he became a cardinal in 1886 until the day he died in 1921, Baltimore-born James Gibbons was the most powerful man in Catholic America and Baltimore the center of Catholic affairs. It was a power that derived from the personality of the man, however, and not the base from which he operated. As Gibbons grew in stature, his archdiocese shrank in relative strength.[1] In many ways the course of St. Vincent de Paul Parish mirrored that of the premier see. Under Didier's energetic pastorate its reputation was sustained as the wellsprings of its greatness dried.

ENCROACHMENTS

St. Vincent's was one of the earliest parochial victims of Baltimore's Industrial Revolution, of the encroachment of the central business district and of demographic deterioration. Its life blood was drained by the exodus that gathered momentum in the last fifteen years of the nineteenth century and reached near fatal proportions in the first fifteen years of the twentieth. That part of the parish west of the Falls was surrendered entirely to business and municipal buildings.

East of the Falls a large number of the well-to-do Irish and old-stock families still filled the two- and three-story houses of Old Town in the mid-1880s: the Deuperts, Milhollands, Dunns, Tierneys, and Cains on Front Street, the Adamses on Pratt, the Keanes (parents of Bishop John J. Keane) on High, the Quinlans on Saratoga, the Lapourailles on Exeter, the Tighes on Orleans, the Ryans on Hillen, the Grosses on Caroline, and a few just outside the parish like the Hunters on Broadway.[2]

THE ITALIANS

The first threat to the parish, as perceived by many of its Irish and old-stock members, was the growing number of Italians. The baptismal registers reveal that of the 225 baptisms in 1880 137 fathers were born in Baltimore, 38 in Ireland, and 21 in Italy. A few Italian families, middle-class and from the north of Italy, could be found in the sacramental registers from the start: the Maffeis, Lucchesis, and Pessagnos. Even the majority who came in the 1870s and '80s were from Genoa and other northern towns.[3] The largest colony of Italians could be found in the southern part of the parish, especially on President Street. Many were laborers, hucksters, and peddlers; some were substantial businessmen. Carlo Rettaliata ran a restaurant, Angelo Baccigalupi a confectionery, and John Cuneo a grocery, all on President Street. To name but a few of the Italians scattered throughout the parish, Antony Rettaliata, a saloon keeper, could be found on Gay Street, Frank Crovo, a shoemaker, on Low, and Angelo Grossi, a ballet master and later costumer, on High.[4]

By the time Didier became pastor in 1873, the Italians were numerous enough for Rev. Joseph L. Andreis, a priest from the area of Turin, Italy, to be sent as his second assistant to serve them, not only the Italians of St. Vincent's Parish but also those found near the markets in St. Joseph's Parish to the southwest and St. Patrick's Parish to the southeast.

St. Vincent de Paul was the fountainhead of all future Italian parishes in Baltimore. The Italians gathered in the basement chapel at St. Vincent's for their own services every Sunday and holy day. In 1879 Archbishop Gibbons asked Andreis for a report on the Italians of Baltimore. There were about 500, he responded. Many had returned to Italy, but many more were expected. It was time the Italians had their own church, he suggested.[5] Gibbons agreed. On September 11, 1880, he laid the cornerstone for the church of St. Leo the Great at Exeter and Stiles streets. A year later it was dedicated with Father Andreis as pastor.[6]

In the annual report for 1880 Didier observed that his parish was flourishing. The Italians had a church of their own, to the great relief of St. Vincent's. The priest there, however, should "confine himself to his legitimate work, and not preach in English or interfere or mix up with the American & Irish population." Some three months earlier Didier had informed the archbishop of Andreis's efforts "to attach the best and most respectable families" of St. Vincent's to himself, "by assiduous visiting, attentions & the like." He feared that if Andreis was not restricted to the use of the Italian language at church services St. Vincent's would be "in a constant turmoil." He reminded Gibbons of his promise that St. Leo's be strictly an Italian parish. Some of his best families passed St. Vincent's to walk the half mile to worship with the Italians. Four months later Didier reported that Andreis was still reading the gospel and making announcements in English. The remedy, he now insisted, was to assign a "real Italian" to St. Leo's who would "hunt up" and attend those Italians who were sadly neglected.[7]

Andreis apparently stopped his attempts to attract the Irish and Americans but told Gibbons a year later that St. Leo's had not the resources to continue as an Italian parish. Non-Italians were barred from his church by causes "too unpleasant to mention." The parish must fail if the archbishop did not come to its financial assistance.[8] In less than a month St. Leo's became a "mixed" congregation, non-Italians constituting the great majority of the congregation.[9] That section of St. Vincent's below Pratt Street was detached to form St. Leo's, now a territorial parish.

In his report for 1882 Didier characterized St. Vincent's: "It is going down—having been crippled & broken to pieces, by the most *populous* section, having been tacked on, to an Italian Church. The only remedy is, to give back to the 'old Parish' what was detached some eighteen years ago, and tacked on to St. John's." Most of the Catholics in that section still came to St. Vincent's, Didier claimed. But the suggestion went unheeded. The previous year Didier had complained of St. Vincent's being hemmed in by the Bohemians (St. Wenceslaus), Italians, and Africans (St. Francis Xavier). In the report for 1884 he suggested that St. Leo's be given to the Italians of the whole city and the territory lost to St. Vincent's be restored. The Italians were much neglected, he reiterated. Many of them still came to St. Vincent's.

FINANCIAL WOES

For a time Didier gave up. In the Notitiae for 1886 he admitted that all would be well if the intruders could be kept out. Although small, the parish could be held intact with careful management. But it was "barely large enough" for "first class Institutions." The next year, however, he again suggested that the parish be awarded more territory, admitting that it was a recommendation not likely to be honored. "One half of our people lie beyond the Borders. . . . We have not elbow room." Finally in the Notitiae for 1888 he had to confess to financial difficulties. Extravagance on the part of the sisters, he claimed, had caused a debt of $4,000 on the girls' school, and there was a $500 debt on the asylum. On the second Sunday of April 1888 Didier surprised his parishioners by telling them that the revenues of the parish were not equal to its expenses. Contributions had slackened since the long-standing debt had been paid off. The institutions for which the parish was responsible were too extensive for the size of the parish. The pastor urged his flock to pay their pew rents regularly and contribute to the collection basket.[10]

From a high of nearly $9,000 in 1875, parish income fell to $5,718.24 in 1884. Although revenues would rise again to over $7,000 in 1890, they would fall back in 1891, Didier's last year, to $5,871.70.[11]

DETERIORATION

Diminishing revenue was largely the consequence of a greater concern for the seventh pastor: the deterioration of the neighborhood. Income actually rose in the depression years of 1873–78, as the economic pinch probably retarded the pace of leavetakings from the parish. But Old Town was greatly shaken by the Great Railroad Strike of July 1877, which began when workers stoned the Sixth Regiment Armory near the Shot Tower. Fathers Didier and Dausch performed the requiem for at least two parishioners felled by army bullets.[12] Thereafter movement from the parish accelerated.

More important was the urban growth and industrialization that touched the parish. West of Jones Falls, federal and municipal buildings, including City Hall, the U.S. Post Office, and police headquarters, vied with some of the city's largest business firms and banks in displacing homeowners from that corner of the parish that lay in the Ninth Ward. East of the Falls, in the Fifth Ward, the contractors of the city's largest occupation, the clothing industry, were appropriating basements, lofts, and even living quarters in residential districts for sweatshops while impoverished immigrants moved into the area to find ready employment within walking distance. The greatest number after 1880 were Russian Jews, but Bohemians, Austrians, Lithuanians, and later Italians could also be found in the sweatshops of Old Town.[13] Increasingly single-family homes were subdivided for a half dozen families. A growing number of African Americans penetrated the northern part of St. Vincent's Parish.

By the early 1890s, sawmills, furniture factories, box factories, steam laundries, tanneries, and meatpacking plants crowded former residential

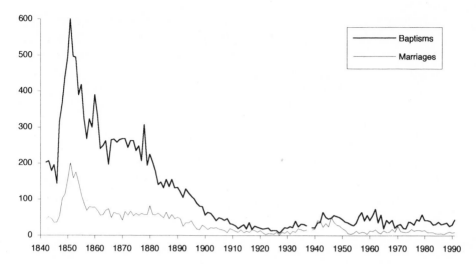

Baptisms and marriages (1842–1991) illustrate graphically the numerical decline that overtook the parish. Until the 1880s the decline was due largely to the loss of portions of the parish, after that to an exodus of the Catholic population. A revival of the 1920s is not reflected because many of the Italian parishioners chose Italian parishes for marriages and baptisms. ANDREW TOMLINSON

streets.[14] Gay Street, with its many retail stores, was the principal business thoroughfare. Their proprietors in 1884 created the Old Town Merchants and Manufacturers Association. Not many of St. Vincent's parishioners could be found on its board of directors.[15]

PARISH POPULATION AND HEALTH

In Didier's eighteen and a half years the parish population fell from about 5,000 to 2,000 or less. In the annual report for 1880 he counted 6,423—2,000 men, 3,000 women, and 1,423 children (although only 750 were under instruction in the boys' and girls' schools and the Sunday school). This was probably inflated. The 4,867 the year after—1,500 men, 2,500 women, and 867 children—was perhaps closer to the fact. The largest drop occurred in 1882, from 4,000 to 2,800 when St. Leo's was detached from St. Vincent's. Didier apparently never took a complete census. For some years he gave an exact number for men, or for women, or for children, but never at the same time.[16]

A better indicator of parish health was the number of baptisms, which fell from 263 in 1873 to 121 in 1891. The 307 counted in 1878 included 59 adults baptized at the end of a parish mission, the only one for which there is any record in the Didier years. Otherwise adult baptisms (converts) averaged about 12 a year. Marriages declined from 67 to 46 in the same period. The average number of "mixed" marriages a year was about 15.

The southern reaches of Jones Falls became more unhealthy each year. By the 1870s the Falls had become a great open sewer, "discharging its malodorous contents into the inner harbor." Baltimore had a higher incidence of typhoid fever than any large American city.[17] Consumption, however, was the most dreaded disease. Sixteen of the 114 deaths in St. Vincent's burial register for the period July 1870 to July 1871 were from consumption and only three from typhoid fever.

SALOONS AND POLITICS

"This part of the city," Didier wrote in the annual report for 1890, "is going down—people are moving out into the more salubrious borders. Hence there is a great falling off in works & finances. The only thing that succeeds hereabouts, are the saloons; they increase in number and mischief every day." With 2,100 saloons in 1880, Baltimore had the largest number of such establishments of any southern city and one of the largest in the nation.[18] The greatest concentration could be found in St. Vincent's Parish. Many of the leading parishioners ran them. The Roddys owned so many in the northern part of the parish that it was called Roddyville. George W. Trumbo, a marshal in the Catholic centennial parade of 1889, strung a banner from his saloon at Front and Plowman to the Central Theater across the street proclaiming: "Jumbo House. The Largest Glass of Beer in Town."[19]

On the third Sunday of July 1887 the pastor of St. Vincent's delivered a sermon that startled the city. It was a scathing denunciation of the violation of the Sunday liquor laws not only by members of his own parish but even more so by the officials who allowed the laws to be flagrantly abused. The latter included the marshal, the police commissioners, and the grand jury. Beer and whiskey ruled the city, Didier declared, chiefly through the bosses and ward politicians, who were fattening on the poor working man whose votes they needed to stay in power.[20]

Less than a year later a "great indignation meeting" was held in the basement of St. Vincent's Church to protest the "dives" that infested East

Baltimore. Didier presided, but in attendance were ministers of different denominations and prominent citizens from all parts of the city, including the president and secretary of the Society for the Suppression of Vice. Didier anathematized the "immoral, disreputable houses, dives, midnight dancing saloons, etc." that had brought down property values and driven respectable residents from that part of the city. The audience adopted a resolution protesting the city's licensing of such "dives" on Baltimore Street in the area of the Falls.[21]

Unlike many teetotalers, Didier did not want to ban all saloons but to reduce their number to a respectable few by a license fee of $1,000 for whiskey and $600 for beer. The "high license" movement he promoted, to which even Cardinal Gibbons and the *Catholic Mirror* lent their support, was one of the earliest stirrings of reform in Baltimore. But in 1890 it wrung from the legislature only a watered-down version of the bill the reformers sought.[22]

Catholics before the impact of the Progressive Movement proved less than enthusiastic supporters of antidrinking and antigambling laws. In 1889 the *Mirror* decried a growing tendency among Catholic societies to indulge in tippling and gambling and even hinted that there were pastors who countenanced such activities. Two years before, the *Baltimore Methodist* had remarked upon the number of ads for distilleries carried by the *Mirror* itself while the *Catholic Citizen* of Milwaukee, taking note of a dispute in its pages in 1888, observed: "The *Catholic Mirror* will go on advertising prayer books and whiskey—piety and punch—and sedulously guard itself against the danger of intolerance."[23] Even the printed program for the fiftieth anniversary of St. Vincent's in 1891 carried more ads for breweries than for any other business.[24] But Carroll Hall failed, as already noted, because Didier refused to rent for any event that featured a bar.

SONNY MAHON

There can be no doubt that one of the principal targets of Didier's jeremiads was John J. "Sonny" Mahon. A member of St. Vincent's Parish, he was the political sachem of the Ninth Ward and the chief lieutenant and heir apparent of Isaac Freeman Rasin, boss of the Democratic machine that had held the city in an iron grip since the 1870s.[25] That the Rasin machine commanded the unwavering allegiance of working-class Catholics was due in no small degree to Sonny Mahon.

According to the baptismal record at St. Vincent's, John, son of James and Anne Mahon, was born August 2, 1851.[26] The birth occurred in a little house on Frederick Street between Lombard and Pratt. "About the first thing I remember," Sonny recalled in his autobiography, "was St. Vincent's School on Front street. That school was run by the Christian Brothers and those Christian Brothers certainly did use[d] to whale the life out of you. They were good men all right, but they didn't stand no foolishness." They used a strap the boys called the Blackbird. "Playing truant and fighting, as I recall it, were the principal reasons why the Blackbird and I saw so much of each other."[27] According to his autobiography, the seven years at St. Vincent's, which he quit at age 14, was the only schooling he ever had. He never knew much about books, he boasted, but did know "considerable about men." In his first biography, however, in 1879, John J. Mahon claimed to have gone on to St. Francis College in Loretto, Pennsylvania, for three more years.[28] He ran away to

John J. "Sonny" Mahon (1851–1928), a power in the Democratic machine of Baltimore and its boss from 1907 until his death, was a parishioner of St. Vincent's. An active benefactor of St. Vincent's Orphanage, he died as president of its board of directors.

marry at age 19 and lived in a flat over "old Mrs. Roach's store" on Lombard Street near Frederick.

As a boy Sonny had learned politics in his mother's boardinghouse. Politics in those days, he recalled, "was rough, and we were as rough as you make them." Quite early in his career his political skills were recognized by "old man Rasin," who began to groom him as his successor, an event that would transpire at Rasin's death in 1907. In the meantime, Mahon devoted every waking hour to the well-being of the Democratic machine of Baltimore, among whose goals, although not the principal one, was the preservation of the compensations of the working class: drinking, gambling, and prostitution.

Father Didier would also have listed Sonny's brother James among the wardheelers who were carrying the city to ruin. "Col. Jimmy" Mahon, a sports figure known at every track from New York to New Orleans, ran the biggest "policy shop" in the city on Frederick Street. In 1908 he would be shot near City Hall by "Big Bill" Harig, an investigator for the Society for the Suppression of Vice, whom Mahon had accused of "squealing" to the police.[29]

The political principles of Sonny Mahon were, of course, often at odds with the moral principles of his church. "But there are two things," he boasted, "I haven't forgot how to do, and I'm glad of it—one is to say my prayers and the other is to blush. So long as a man prays regular and can feel ashamed of himself once in a while there is hope for him. Most of those Maryland Club fellows stopped praying when they joined the club, and never did blush."

Sonny's early training at St. Vincent's showed in other ways. He had many charities; St. Vincent's Orphan Asylum was his favorite. His name appeared among the annual subscribers and frequently among the benefactors. In 1898, for example, Mr. John J. Mahon treated the orphans to an oyster supper, ice cream, and cakes. Mrs. James Mahon, his sister-in-law, donated clothing.

TROUBLESOME ASSISTANTS

While the political, economic, and moral health of his parish and his city were taking their toll, Edmund Didier had to contend with other tribulations closer to home. He seemed always to be at odds with his assistants. First, Michael Dausch, whom he had inherited from Father Myers, was given to fits of depression. This "habitual insanity," Didier explained to Archbishop Gibbons, was the result of his being passed over when it came to building new parishes. Dausch was given a parish in 1878 and replaced by a priest who should, Didier complained to Gibbons, take the pledge because he was often "hors du combat."[30]

In September 1880 Didier demanded a first-class assistant without delay. Andreis was paying too much attention to the better part of the congregation and the other assistant took little interest in parish affairs, leaving Didier "with too much care on my mind." In their places came two assistants; one refused to teach catechism and the other created a building and loan association without Didier's approval. The pastor wrote his archbishop: "I have worked, as you well know, faithfully & constantly for the Diocese & for this Parish; and I think I deserve, if not honors & favors, at least a congenial and considerate Assistant." Gibbons assigned to the parish the newly ordained Thomas E. Stapleton, who apparently won the hearts of all but the pastor. At the beginning of 1892 Didier complained with an edge of bitterness about the permission Gibbons had granted another popular assistant, James A. Cunningham, to travel south. "If you wish, by such treatment of the Pastor, to force him to resign, and will make suitable arrangements for the future, I will be happy to consider them."[31]

The inability of pastors and curates to work harmoniously was nothing new in the oldest archdiocese, and Didier had undoubtedly been asked to take his share of the more troublesome priests. But there was apparently a touch of envy in his relationship with the popular Andreis, Stapleton, and Cunningham. That Didier was not totally out of sympathy with the younger clergy, however, is indicated by the fact that he was one of only two pastors chosen for the six-member board of examiners that periodically interrogated the newly ordained.

THE HONORS WITHHELD

The same diocesan synod that had decreed the board of examiners, however, also required a board of consultors to be chosen from the outstanding members of the clergy. Didier was not one of the six chosen in October 1886.[32] The slight to which he alluded at this time with regard to "honors and favors" could only have been intensified in December with the choice of Rev. Bernard J. McManus of neighboring St. John's as the second monsignor of Gibbons's creation (the first being Edward McColgan, his vicar general, in 1885). By the late 1880s St. John's was beginning to surpass its mother in the number of organizations and activities it could boast. The status of irremovable rector in 1887, already noted, was not enough to assuage the resentment.

THE RESIGNATION

Irremovability suggests that it was never Gibbons's intention to pry Didier from his parish. At the same time it may be doubted that the cardinal argued long against the second proffered resignation in 1892. Didier had mentioned resigning in 1890. The immediate cause was not suggested in the letter itself, although it followed an interview with the cardinal. The terms of resignation, however, he did put down: the chaplaincy of a hospital with board and lodging but no salary plus the chaplaincies at the girls' home on Front Street and the boys' home on High. It would be an honorable position, he claimed, and the archdiocese would not be "accused by the Community, of any unfair dealings in my regard."[33]

For whatever reason, the resignation was deferred until offered again in the letter of complaint of January 1892. On the surface it was an amicable leavetaking, but Didier's presence was never noted in accounts of the few great moments left to the parish to which he had devoted so much time, energy, and personal wealth.

THE EIGHTH PASTOR

The eighth shepherd of the flock of Front Street was Rev. John Daniel Boland, former pastor of St. Thomas Aquinas at the outskirts of the city. The 36-year-old priest was Baltimore born. He was probably delighted with his new assignment until he came to know the problems. The parishioners were certainly delighted with their new pastor. A priest who knew him well, Rev. Thomas J. Stanton, would later characterize Boland as a "magnetic fascinating man," a man of good sense and sound judgment. "He was a man of frankness, openness of character, honest, cheerful, joyous in disposition, almost boyishly happy. In his character there was a rare blending of manliness and gentleness." He was also an eloquent preacher. "Everyone loved him."[34]

For a time all went well. In 1895, in fact, Boland undertook another extensive renovation of the church, which will be described in part 2. The church was reopened the second to the last Sunday in October with a show of pomp and pride reminiscent of the halcyon days. Fifty little girls from the sisters' school dressed in white scattered flowers as they marched down the center aisle. A choir of eighty voices sang Gounod's *Messe Solonelle.* "You see what has been accomplished by the proceeds of the fair," Father Boland told his audience, "one of the handsomest churches today in Baltimore."[35] It was, however, the last event at St. Vincent's to win a column or more in the Catholic weekly for almost half a century. The cost of the renovation according to the annual report was $9,221.60.

The Notitiae for 1895 also recorded the greatest annual income to date—$11,836—as well as the largest expenditures—$13,231. Father Boland had indeed an extraordinary talent for loosening purse strings. That same year, however, pew rents fell below $2,000, and below the Sunday collection, for the first time. In the ten and a half years Boland was pastor, pew rents went down as offertory collections went up. The unpredictability of extraordinary sources of income, often lacking in specificity in the Notitiae, produced unaccustomed fluctuations in revenue, $4,564 in 1897, for example, compared to the $11,936 of 1895 and $7,663 in 1902, Boland's last full year as pastor. The last sum, however, was made possible by the sale of the school property for $2,846.50.

THE LOSS OF INSTITUTIONS

The loss of the school was, perhaps, the last of a series of setbacks that convinced Father Boland he should not go down with a sinking ship. At the end of the 1898–99 school year, the Sisters of Charity withdrew from the girls' school, which was then closed. The girls were sent over to the boys' school at the orphanage to be taught by the Sisters of Mercy, who had agreed to replace the Christian Brothers.[36] In 1901 the one school counted only 155, down from 419 for the two schools in 1894. In 1902 the parish school was closed. The number of Sunday school pupils likewise declined, from 400 in Boland's first year to 150 in his last.

The Christian Brothers also left the orphanage in 1899, and the Sisters of Mercy took charge there as well. Both the orphanage and the school were closed a few months that year for renovation, the orphans being lodged with charitable families.[37] The orphanage was still in a fairly healthy state since it drew from all parts of the city and remained a well-supported charity. (Sonny Mahon was now vice-president of the board of directors.) But the deterioration of the neighborhood placed its continuance in Old Town in doubt. The same was true of St. Vincent's Home for working girls next door, still run by the Sisters of Mercy. The home for newsboys did not survive the death of Didier, if it lasted even that long. Institutions did not close their doors with fanfare.

DECLINE OF THE PARISH SOCIETIES

Parish societies and sodalities also became shadows of their former selves. In his first annual report Boland listed only the Sodality of the Sacred Heart for women, the Sodality of the Blessed Virgin Mary (also called of the Rosary) for men, and the Nocturnal Adoration Society. Overlooked were the St. Vincent de Paul Conference and the Young Catholic's Friend Society, which he included in the next reports, the latter society, in fact growing to 85 members by 1898. The Adoration Society disappeared in 1893 and the men's sodality in 1895. The women's sodality declined in membership from 250 in 1892 to 100 in 1901 and then disappeared temporarily, leaving only the St. Vincent de Paul Conference with five members and the Young Catholic's Friend Society with 40 in 1902. St. Vincent's Lyceum and the Catholic Benevolent Legion continued a tenuous existence, the Father Myers No. 15 of the CBL, in fact, holding on to its place in the city directory until 1926. With neither, it would seem, did the eighth pastor have much to do. The decline in parish societies may have been the result of Boland's lack of interest in them as much as of a dwindling population. The only new association formed in the Boland years was the Holy Name Society, which was spreading rapidly throughout the city, and this from 1896 through 1898 with only 70 to 80 members a year.

THE EXODUS

The most distressing downturn was the parish population. For his first year Boland estimated "about 2800" and then blanks until 1896 and 1897, when he put down 2,000. And then there was nothing in this crucial space in the Notitiae for the rest of his tenure on Front Street. The precipitous decline that followed would be indicated by the 400 for 1903 recorded by his successor. Some parishioners were kept in place by their attachment to the popular pastor. When he left, many followed him. Boland was given only one assistant. Stapleton remained four years; then two more came in rapid succession.

At his own request Boland was transferred to St. Pius V on Schroeder

Street and Edmondson Avenue in a neighborhood that was still fashion-able. One of the parishioners who followed him was Adam Deupert. Born in Germany in 1849, Deupert was brought to Baltimore as an in-fant. From a newsboy he became a goldbeater in a workshop near the or-phanage on Front Street and then proprietor of the gold-leaf firm that gilded the dome of St. Vincent's. As a member of the City Council for three terms and clerk of the Court of Common Pleas for eighteen years, he was a friend of Mayor Latrobe and Sonny Mahon. In 1882 he became a member of the board of St. Vincent's Orphan Asylum and its president in 1884, a position he would retain for another fifty-five years. He was also a trustee of St. Vincent de Paul from 1896 to 1903, when he followed Fa-ther Boland to St. Pius. From 1921 until 1934 he would serve as president of the Metropolitan Savings Bank and in 1941 be buried from St. Ignatius, St. Pius having experienced for a decade or two after Father Boland's untimely death in 1908 a decline not unlike that of St. Vincent's.[38] The loss to St. Vincent's of such as Adam Deupert was thought by many a death blow.

THE NINTH PASTOR

To St. Vincent de Paul Parish came Desire (also Desiderius) Constantin DeWulf in the fall of 1903 to preside over its death throes. The ninth pas-tor was born in Roulers, Belgium, on December 24, 1840, and in 1864 was ordained under the title of his patrimony, not of missionary as were most secular priests in America. This meant that he could pick and choose his place of service. The Civil War had prevented his going to the place of first choice, Vicksburg, Mississippi. He stayed in the archdiocese of Balti-more, which he came to love and eventually to know better, perhaps, than any priest or prelate in it. In addition to several parishes in Washing-ton and Baltimore, Father DeWulf labored, often as pastor, in ten other parishes or missions stretching from Oakland to Upper Marlboro, always ready to move where he saw the greatest need.[39]

THE JEWISH INFLUX

"The number of Catholics living within the limits of the parish," DeWulf wrote in his first annual report from St. Vincent's, "is diminishing daily owing to the influx of the Jewish population." The next year he reemphasized the daily loss and added, "The majority of the population is

Jewish. Some Italians live in the parish but few of them can be prevailed upon to come to church."

Old Town by the first decade of the twentieth century was heavily Jewish, largely because of the needle trades located there but partly because of the synagogues left by the German Jews who were moving to other parts of the city. By 1901 there were some 400 sweatshops in East Baltimore. Ship to shop was made easy; a labor center was located at 7 High Street. Settlement houses for Jewish immigrants multiplied in Old Town, Friendly Inn the most famous. Most of the recent Jewish arrivals, some 66,000 between 1880 and 1905, were from Russia, the nation of birth of the second largest number of foreign born in Baltimore (the largest still being German) at the opening of the century.[40]

There was little evidence among the few old families who stayed of an overt resentment of the invasion. Jewish parents, however, complained of a devout Catholic teacher at the public school on High Street not far from St. Vincent's who was teaching her pupils Catholic prayers with instructions to recite them at home.[41]

THE REMNANT

In 1908 there were but ninety-seven "enrolled members or pewholders" at St. Vincent's, a few of the old names—Brooks, Cassidy, Kelly, Roddy, Tighe—among them. About half of the names were Irish, the rest English or German and three Italian—Cutino, Grossi, and Magula. Fifteen lived on Baltimore Street, eleven on Front, counting the six residents of St. Vincent's Home but not of the rectory, and most of the rest on Aisquith, Gay, and High. "Today but little remains to indicate the early glory of the neighborhood," the *Catholic Red Book* lamented.[42] DeWulf could not even find enough members to maintain a board of trustees. After his first year as pastor, he sought only the two auditors required to sign the financial statement.

Although he recorded 400 souls in 1903, he put down 600 in 1904. For the rest of his eight years at St. Vincent's the estimated population fluctuated between the two numbers. The cardinal continued to send an assistant, perhaps because of the pastor's age, but none stayed long.

In 1909 St. Vincent's Orphan Asylum, and with it the Sisters of Mercy, moved to York Road outside the city. Adam Deupert was the prime mover. With the loss of the sisters St. Vincent's Home for working girls closed.[43] The empty buildings next to the church stood like brooding ghosts for the small number of worshipers who passed them on the way to mass.

TWO PLUSES

Although the parish population was pitifully small, Father DeWulf managed to keep parish revenues at the level maintained by Boland but with even less predictability. In 1906 revenues were $7,129, in 1907 $4,850. In 1906 improvements and repairs cost $2,163, but the extraordinary collections had brought in $2,292, more than the offertory collections, the next highest amount. The extraordinary and offertory collections were considerably greater than pew rents. In 1910, DeWulf's last year, pew rents totaled only $639, as compared with $4,049 in Didier's first full year as pastor.

Also on the positive side was the modest revival in parish societies. In 1905 the Holy Name Society and Sodality of the Blessed Virgin Mary reappeared, the latter now a women's sodality, along with the Sanctuary Society. The next year they appeared with numbers in the annual report: the St. Vincent de Paul Conference 10, the Young Catholic's Friend Society 20, the Holy Name Society 25, the Sodality of the Blessed Virgin Mary

Rev. Thomas J. Stanton (1864–1941), "orator of the Alleghenies," helped save St. Vincent's from extinction by his well-attended Sunday sermons.

75, and the Sanctuary Society 75. But the Holy Name Society with six in 1908 dropped off the list in 1909. The sodality was gone in 1910. It was a losing battle.

THE EULOGY

Seriously ill in 1911, DeWulf gave over the business of the parish to his assistant, Fr. John Coolahan, early that year and died a year later, January 11, 1912. During his eight years at St. Vincent's he had worked a minor miracle in keeping a sinking parish afloat. But he died, perhaps, in the belief that his efforts had been in vain, that his successor would have the thankless task of performing the act that he had stayed, the closing of the parish.

At the end of 1911 it was reported that St. Vincent's and St. Leo's Parish would be merged and that St. Vincent de Paul would be abandoned, its site being sought by a corporation. The cardinal's residence said only that "something may be given out a little later."[44] On such matters the cardinal was, fortunately for St. Vincent's, a procrastinator. The fate of the parish would hang fire a few more years.

DeWulf had extended an invitation, probably in his last year, that would have important consequences after his death. Most accounts of the parish tell of DeWulf's inviting Rev. Thomas J. Stanton, the "orator of the Alleghenies," to preach the Sunday masses soon after coming to St. Vincent's because of his own heavy accent.[45] Stanton could not, however, have come to St. Vincent's before 1911, for reasons that will be noted later. The flamboyant speaker undoubtedly accepted the invitation in the belief that his engagement would be short. In 1914 he would compose a piece entitled "Old St. Vincent's" for the Catholic weekly.[46] It was most likely also one of his sermons and sounded very much like a eulogy. It is a fine specimen of the pulpit oratory (or banquet address) that brought tears to the eyes of Catholics at the turn of the century.

"To one who has the seeing eye," he began, "and the story-teller's art as well as a sincere appreciation of the trials and struggles of the parish priest, the history of the pastors of St. Vincent's would be a story as interesting as the fabricated romances of the Arabian Nights." Speaking of DeWulf's efforts in behalf of the parish, he declared:

> Yet he fought the uneven, almost hopeless, battle bravely. St. Vincent's was a dying parish and Father DeWulf was a dying man. . . . He was a man of

strong will, pure soul, lofty character. His works of charity were numerous, but very little was ever known of them. . . . [He] died a poor man.

Stanton continued:

If the parish could talk, the words of affection which a dying mother would be apt to address to her daughters would run: "Hear me, for I am very old. I had grown wise before you learned your first lessons of wisdom. Three generations ago I was on the deck with a hopeful company, when the voyage began. Time passed and the life of a whole generation passed with it. I then found myself in a luxurious cabin with a prosperous throng. Time passed and the craft which held us began to go to pieces. Time passed till a few only were left on the raft, pieced together from fragments. Now the raft has broken and parted. All that remain are floating, clinging to the solitary spars."

Then, as with all his sermons, Stanton ended with a poem.

O God, forgive my raving;
   I'm a mother old and sad.
I know I should rejoice to think
   They walked the fields of gold.
Dear Lord, you'll not forget them,
   And you'll make their dear hearts glad.
But don't let them forget me
   And the love they knew of old.

REVIVAL

1912–1965

When he left St. Vincent's for St. Mary's, Rockville, in April 1912 to take the place of the incoming pastor, Father Coolahan was given a "purse of gold" by the congregation and a "handsome surplice" by the altar boys who idolized him.[1] The new pastor was Rev. Philip Bernard McGuire, 40 years old, born December 8, 1871, in Altoona, Pennsylvania. Ordained by Cardinal Gibbons in 1897, he had served in Washington, Baltimore, and two county parishes, the last being Rockville.[2] If the cardinal intimated that his stay might be short, Father Phil did nothing to show it.

FATHER STANTON'S SERMONS

Father Stanton continued to come down from Catonsville for his Sunday sermons. In no time he filled the church each time he spoke. In 1913–14 the Jones Falls was covered over by a roadway that made it easier for his admirers to come from a distance. It was not the brevity of the sermons, seldom more than ten minutes, but the content and delivery that enthralled them. He had a love of the classics, of history, and of poetry. He had a flair for the dramatic. Young priests and seminarians came to take notes on how to deliver an affective homily.

Born in Oakland, Maryland, the orator of the Alleghenies had labored long in the area of his nativity. He had served as pastor at Lonaconing in Allegany County for thirteen years. In 1900 he published *A Century of Growth*, a two-volume history of the Catholic Church in western Maryland. Called to Baltimore as pastor of St. Joseph's in 1905, his health began to fail in that unaccustomed clime. After nine months at a country parish, he retired in 1908 in order to test the therapeutic qualities of Europe, Mexico, and the South Seas. In 1911 he took up residence at Mount de Sales Academy as chaplain, and there he would remain until he died in 1941.[3] He enjoyed the popularity he won so easily at St. Vincent's. For twenty-five years he would continue to come down every Sunday to deliver the sermon at two masses and say the high mass.[4]

REACTIVATION

While the Stanton sermons drew from outside the parish, the new pastor kept a tenacious few in place. "Father McGuire in the face of the gradual exodus of communicants to other neighborhoods," a local paper revealed, "has gathered around himself a number of men and women who are determined that the church will retain at least a part of its prestige and influence in an environment that has so materially changed." The occasion was a parish picnic, in effect a reunion of parishioners past and present. In addition to an annual picnic at Grieb's Park on Belair Road, where Father Phil himself organized sack, potato, candle, three-legged, walking, and running races, an annual oyster supper and bazaar was also inaugurated at St. Vincent's.[5] Many old-timers came back for the elaborate May procession.

But the most ambitious undertaking was a revival of the St. Vincent's Lyceum in 1915. "The parishioners of St. Vincent's," a local paper explained, "feeling the need for an organization for the welfare of the parish and not having many young men to call on, invited men from other parishes and from the Catholic night workers of Baltimore, and have decided to form an association for the betterment of the church." With the pastor they laid plans for "what promises to be one of the largest clubs in Baltimore . . . open to young men regardless of parish, who are fond of dramatics and athletics." A basketball team was also formed. A dance was held in January and a vaudeville show in February 1916. In October a minstrel and dance at Hazezer's Hall on West Franklin Street attracted a "throng."[6] To many it must have seemed that the good old days had returned.

Among the most active young men from the parish itself were the Wagner brothers and their relative George C. Rohleder. In addition to constituting a loyal core of altar boys, they learned to play the chimes, long silent, a task that George would continue to perform for over fifty years. Every Sunday and holy day thereafter, every local and national hol-

The Wagner brothers, Joseph and Caspar Andrew (with another brother and their relative George Rohleder), constituted the faithful core of altar boys in the early 1900s. ST. VINCENT DE PAUL PARISH

iday, the strains of such religious and national hymns as "We Need Thee, Heart of Jesus," "Like a Strong and Raging Fire," "Holy God, We Praise Thy Name," "Maryland, My Maryland," and "The Star-Spangled Banner" wafted through the streets of Old Town.[7]

THE PRINTERS' MASS

At the *Baltimore American* James Nelson, managing editor of the Sunday edition, was concerned about the gambling and drinking habits of his reportorial and printer staffs. He spoke to William Warwick, a devout Catholic, who rounded up a few other Catholic employees. Together they visited Father McGuire, who initially showed little enthusiasm at the prospect of rising in the wee hours, when the presses stopped at Baltimore and South streets, to say a mass for them. He approached the cardinal, however, who obtained from Rome an indult, permission by way of exception, for a mass to accommodate the night workers of the *Baltimore American* and the *Sun.*[8]

The first "printers' mass" was said at 2:30 A.M. on Sunday, April 11, 1914. Curiosity drew a respectable number to the first mass, but attendance fell off thereafter. To "hold the boys together" Warwick organized a choir. It was a great success. Workers at United Railways and the post office nearby joined the printers. Soon some 200 attended regularly. The count continued to climb as partygoers joined, and soon outnumbered, the workers. Within a few years the printers' mass was a favorite haunt for Baltimore Catholics.[9]

A few months after the commencement of the printers' mass, permission was also obtained for a noonday mass (actually 12:05) on Sunday. Originally intended as a convenience for workers and travelers, it too grew in popularity, especially for those who liked to sleep late on Sunday but avoid the high mass, always the last. Masses at 2:30, 7:00, 9:00, 10:30 (the high mass), and 12:05 on Sunday for a parish with a resident population of about 800 occasioned the boast: "St. Vincent's has now the most unusual schedule of masses of any church in this section of the country."[10] Well aware of the geographic advantage of his church, Father McGuire also devised, probably in 1916, special Lenten devotions on Wednesdays and Fridays for those who wished to walk over from the business district at the noon-hour break.

DIMINISHING RETURNS BUT HOPEFUL SIGNS

While the new masses and Lenten services drew hundreds from outside the parish, the attempts to revitalize within soon experienced, after the initial heartening successes, diminishing returns. The Young Catholic's Friend, St. Vincent de Paul, and Sanctuary societies were replaced in

1914 by the League of the Sacred Heart and the Angels (children) Sodality, which numbered no more than fifty or sixty members each. Neither the St. Vincent's Lyceum nor the Ushers Club organized by Father Phil in 1912 found a place in the annual Notitiae. The lyceum lasted probably no more than two or three years. The Ushers Club, however, played an indispensable role after the launching of the printers' mass. Those who controlled the crowds at the latter became known as the Night Owls.

In 1919 a novena in honor of St. Rita was held when a statue of the saint was purchased for the church. It inspired the St. Rita Society with an initial 200 members. But in 1922 the society disappeared from the Notitiae. In 1922 the Sacred Heart and the Angels sodalities were re-placed by the Sodality of the Blessed Virgin Mary and Holy Name Society, the favorite parish organizations of the new archbishop, Michael J. Curley. They counted even fewer members, with the exception of 1928–29, when, for reasons unknown, the Holy Name Society claimed about 100.

The parish population as recorded by Father Coolahan at the beginning of 1912 was 400, or 150 men, 150 women, and 100 children. Father McGuire doubled the figures in each category in his first report. This count persisted in the Notitiae until 1921, when he conducted a parish

Rev. Philip B. McGuire (1871–1939), tenth pastor, genial and liked by all, began the famous printers' mass at St. Vincent's in 1914. ST. VINCENT DE PAUL PARISH

census. The new archbishop, he doubtless surmised, would be more exacting than the cardinal. At the beginning of 1922 he recorded 1,602
parishioners, 751 adults and 851 children, doubling again the previous estimate. The reason for this surprising increase will become apparent later,
but there was little correlation with the gratifying upswing in parish
revenues.

In McGuire's first year an income of $3,224 fell short of expenses by
$847. As a result of the two additional masses, however, an income of
$4,496 could be reported for 1915. "Beg to remark," the pastor explained,
"that if it were not for the two unusual masses here, this church would
not be able to exist." In 1916 "seat offerings," a set amount collected at the
church door, was inaugurated. At $7,721 they outstripped the offertory
collections in 1921 by $1,758. The total receipts of over $16,000 that year
left a comfortable balance in the bank of $10,278.[11] The new archbishop
must have been impressed.

THE NEW ARCHBISHOP

On November 21, 1921, the chimes of St. Vincent's welcomed the new
archbishop to Baltimore. The Irish-born Bishop Michael Joseph Curley of
St. Augustine, Florida, was chosen to succeed the venerable cardinal, who
had reigned for forty-three years. The *Baltimore American* predicted that
Curley would soon be made a cardinal and that Baltimore would remain
"the true capital of American Catholicism."[12] Neither prediction proved
accurate.

To Curley fell the tasks that the archbishops of larger sees had undertaken almost a generation earlier: centralization, consolidation, and Ro-
manization (a closer adherence to the policies and directives of the Holy
See). From the start he established a reputation as a schoolman. He was
also a battler, generating a militancy rare in the oldest American see.
Through such organizations as the Holy Name Society and Sodality of
the Blessed Virgin Mary he energized his Catholic charges.[13] All of this
would have an impact at St. Vincent's, but its connection with the new
archbishop would be closer than that of any other parish.

Archbishop Curley lived simply. He had no car. He would have in Baltimore only one priest thought to be a close friend. Father McGuire was
tagged to be his chauffeur for trips around town as well as the long and
tiring visitations of the archdiocese. By one estimate Father Phil would
drive the archbishop 200,000 miles.[14] He was also host for the many
times Curley chose to stay in the rectory on Front Street rather than his

own at the cathedral. A room was reserved for the archbishop, who seemed more at home among the poor of Old Town.

THE ITALIANS RETURN

By the time Archbishop Curley came to Baltimore, it was obvious that the demographic base of St. Vincent's was largely Italian. The growing number of Italian immigrants who could not find homes in the overcrowded Little Italy sought them as near as they could. The Fenarolis in 1915 bought a house on Front Street opposite the Furncraft Wholesale Furniture Company, site of the old Front Street Theater. The DaRamo family, in-laws of the Fenarolis, lived across the street from the rectory where the FitzPatricks had lived.[15]

The earliest indication of the Italian influx was a jump in Sunday school attendance in 1917, from the usual 60 to 200. This, the pastor explained, was "due to the fact that we are gathering in Italian children of careless parents." The principal gatherer was Miss Bina Kavanaugh, who marched through the streets each Sunday like a pied piper leading the children to the basement of St. Vincent's.[16] With the jump in parish population to 1,602 in 1921 the pastor observed, "Our people drift into this section when needy—& out again when prospering, excepting Italians." For the year 1924 he distinguished between the Italians—1,962—and others—525. With an additional 441 under five the total parish population came to 2,928. By the end of 1926 it was 3,413, the peak year of the parish's numerical revival. In 1930 it fell to 1,367, a total the pastor would simply copy for the next five years.[17] In 1936 it went up again, to 1,950.

"Looking back over nine years of figures for St. Vincent's, there are some rather interesting contrasts," the archbishop told the pastor at the beginning of 1930. "Today the population is well over 3000, counting of course I am sure our Italians. It is well to regard them as an integral part of the present day parish population." He then continued pointedly: "What surprises me most is the small number of baptisms. It is evident that the Italians carry their babies to some Italian Church for Baptism."[18]

It was true: the disparity between parish population and baptisms was never greater in the history of the parish. From 1912 through 1920, in fact, baptisms averaged 23.7 a year whereas from 1921 through 1928, when the population was two to three times greater, they averaged but 14.9 a year. Until 1928 neither McGuire nor the priests who came on weekends to help him made much of an effort to cater to the cultural needs of the Italian parishioners.

In 1928 St. Vincent's was given a full-time associate pastor, the first in sixteen years. Rev. Angelo Romeo was a native of Italy who had come to Baltimore by way of Providence, Rhode Island. One of the first things he did was to organize the St. Vincent's Society for Italian Fathers and Mothers. The society held socials, a spaghetti dinner in the fall, a Communion Sunday four times a year (sometimes sparsely attended), and a special celebration of the Feast of St. Vincent similar to that of St. Anthony in Little Italy (always well attended). Each July 19 a procession wound its way through the streets with the statue of the patron saint festooned with ribbons to which dollar bills were pinned. There was also a buffet supper and an evening concert of Italian operatic selections rendered usually by musicians brought in from Philadelphia.[19] The number of baptisms rose appreciably.

THE PARISH SCHOOL

In 1928 St. Vincent's could also claim again a parochial school. In 1910 St. Leo's had rented the empty orphanage next to St. Vincent's church for a parochial school in the hope that it would attract pupils from both parishes. But it proved too far away for the children of Little Italy. In 1913 St. Leo's had established an orphanage under the Pallotine Sisters, which in 1914 was moved to the vacant building on Front Street. There the sisters began classes for the orphans and other children of the neighborhood.[20] Father McGuire gave free use of the building and served as chaplain to the sisters, who in return assumed charge of the sacristy.[21] Unhappy with the physical conditions and quality of education at St. Leo's Orphanage and desirous of a parochial school in every parish, in 1927 Archbishop Curley urged Father McGuire to open his own.

In 1927–28 the parish purchased the old Dolley Madison Public School No. 43 on High Street and five rowhouses on the other side of Front Street. The latter were torn down or renovated to provide an entrance on Front Street, a playground, and a convent. The second floor of the school was transformed into a parish hall and the basement into meeting rooms and a kitchen. Proceeds from the parish, a bank loan of $92,000, and a $50,000 gift from the archbishop himself covered most of the cost. At the end of it all the parish had a standing debt of $95,500.[22]

The Franciscan Sisters of Glen Riddle, Pennsylvania, agreed to staff the school. It opened September 17, 1928, with seven sisters, Sister Honorata principal, and 202 pupils in grades 1 through 7. A kindergarten of twenty pupils was taught by Miss Rose Alcarese, who would later be the only vocation to the Franciscan Sisters from the parish.[23] According to Father McGuire's successor, "Discipline was at first a somewhat difficult problem, but after the expulsion of a small group who had plotted the assassination of their teacher, the pupils seemed to grasp the idea that the school, altho free of tuition and any solicitation or other device for raising money, was anything but free of law and order." Academic standards and deportment improved thereafter. "Objectionable language was rarely heard and almost never was it necessary to remove offensive symbols [graffiti] from desk or wall."[24] In 1930 the school had its first graduating class: Lucy Azzaro, Ida Cruciotti, Theresa Minacapelli, Sam Azzaro, and Leo Godfrey. It accepted children from outside the parish and even non-Catholics if there was room. It would reach its peak in 1934 with 357 pupils.

A MONEY PROBLEM

Archbishop Curley urged Father Phil to hold extra collections to pay off the debt, which the pastor seemed reluctant to do. Since the introduction of the special masses and seat offerings, St. Vincent's had had an enviable surplus each year. The pastor was doubtless convinced that the debt could be paid in time with little effort. While income from the offertory collections continued to rise, however, that from seat offerings sank from $12,437 in 1927 to $4,848 in 1933. On May 9, 1933, the pastor received the following peremptory letter from the archbishop:

> The following orders relative to your Church are to be carried out beginning Sunday, May fourteenth, and are to be carried out without question or discussion.
>
> (1) On Sunday, May 14, you shall abolish all collections at the door. Consequently, people going to St. Vincent's Church may enter without paying a dime or anything to anybody.
>
> (2) Consequently on Sunday, May 14th, you shall abolish money changing and money changers at the door.
>
> (3) Announce at all the Masses on Sunday, May 14, the second collection to be taken up in the Church immediately after the Communion of the Mass. This collection will take the place of your door collection, and is to be set aside for the use of the school and for the purpose of meeting your heavy obligations on your school at the present time.
>
> (4) Be good enough to announce to your Ushers that all collections be

St. Vincent de Paul Parochial School, revived in 1928 at the behest of Archbishop Michael J. Curley, continued until 1960, when it became a casualty of urban renewal.   ST. VINCENT DE PAUL PARISH

Graduating class of 1930, the first of the revived parish school. With the principal, Sister Honorata, are Sam Azzaro, Ida Cruciotti, Lucy Azzaro, and Leo Godfrey. A fifth graduate, Theresa Minacapelli, is missing.   ST. VINCENT DE PAUL PARISH

brought back to the Sanctuary rail in the baskets in which such collections are taken up, and all collections thus returned are to be deposited inside the Sanctuary rail or placed in a basket provided by you for that purpose.

(5) These collections are to be taken charge of either by yourself or your Curate or by an agent of your own selection. They are to be taken to your Rectory and counted by yourself and your Assistant.

(6) You are hereby directed to dispense with the services of such Ushers as you may select for retirement and I repeat that these orders are to be carried out without question and without any asking for reasons.[25]

The pastor's reluctance to hold special collections to pay off a debt was not the reason for this, on the face of it, harsh communication between friends. Reports of irregularities had led to an investigation "that established serious and persistent alienation of collection receipts" on the part of a highly trusted member of the Ushers Club.[26] After the directive of 1933, totals from the second collection in lieu of seat offerings (but still listed as seat offerings in the Notitiae) rose, climbing to $12,000 again in five years.

It should perhaps be noted at this point that the last collection of pew rents at St. Vincent's took place in 1934. It brought in $10.00. The installation of a poor box, one of the archbishop's favorite projects, took place in 1923.

ANOTHER CLOSING?

As early as the mid-1920s the question of relocating the central police headquarters near City Hall was raised. The church-rectory-orphanage complex at St. Vincent's was considered a possible site. It was apparently in anticipation of demolition that preparations were made for the removal of the first two pastors believed to be entombed in the basement. The remains of Father Schreiber, however, were not found. They were later discovered in the cemetery of old St. Mary's Seminary in the laity section, without the "Rev." on his stone.[27] In any case, the new police headquarters, completed in the fall of 1926, was erected near its original site on the other side of the Falls.

In 1930 the archbishop wrote the cardinal prefect of the Consistorial Congregation in Rome for permission to abolish three irremovable rectorships of the archdiocese. All were of inner-city parishes that had lost most of their residents. St. Patrick's in Baltimore had become largely Polish and St. Vincent's largely Italian. It was difficult to find priests to accept them.[28] In 1931 the permission was forthcoming.

St. Vincent de Paul had, in truth, begun another downward slide as construction of the Orleans (or Bath) Street viaduct displaced many of the Italian families who had had their stalls at the Bel Air Market. Accompanying the numerical decline of residents was a deterioration in the conduct of the transients at the printers' mass. Father McGuire's successor recalled: "Occasional inebriates and some irreverent night prowlers out 'slumming' had often punctuated Fr. McGuire's sermons with less pertinent interruptions than those customary in St. Augustine's day." Such incidents led to the unkind designation of the printers' mass as "the drunkards' mass."[29]

As the parish declined, so too did the health of the tenth pastor. Although probably reluctant to show favor to a friend, the archbishop petitioned Rome to have Philip McGuire made a monsignor. On June 5, 1939, he was one of nineteen domestic prelates created for the archdiocese, the first and only pastor of St. Vincent's, as it turned out, to be so honored. But he wore his red robes only in his coffin. On October 16, 1939, the archbishop himself closed the eyes of his friend in death. To the funeral of this genial, in some ways enterprising, pastor came over 100 priests. A resident of St. Leo's Orphanage in Father McGuire's last years, Albert "Pete" Puliafico remembered him as "a white-haired gentleman" and "a gentle soul," as kind to all as he was to the orphans in whom he took a special interest.[30] Not the most imposing priest upon the altar, nor the most inspiring in the pulpit, nor the most efficient in an administrative capacity, he was, as all who knew him were prepared to admit, a true pastor of souls.

THE ELEVENTH PASTOR

Father Phil was hardly in his grave when the archbishop was informed that a successor was waiting in the wings. Fr. John Sinnott Martin, pastor of Holy Family Parish in Randallstown, himself told the archbishop that, largely for reasons of health, he would like to be pastor of St. Vincent's, which few other priests did. "This from the flat of my back," responded the ailing archbishop. He would be happy to give the request "every consideration."[31] On May 16 the chancellor informed Father Martin of his appointment.

Born October 13, 1894, in Fairmont, West Virginia, but of parents married in Baltimore by Bishop Owen Corrigan, a product of St. Vincent's, the new pastor was educated in the public schools of Fairmont and of Oakland, Maryland, to which the family moved. His father, an attorney, was descended from prominent Baptist ministers. The son studied for the priesthood at St. Mary's Seminary and the Catholic University and was ordained by Bishop Corrigan two months after the death of Cardinal Gibbons in 1921. There was nothing remarkable about the education he received. The extraordinary competence he acquired in the fields of literature, art, architecture, music, history, and politics was largely the result of a restless and inquiring mind. Until his appointment to St. Vincent's he had little outlet for the interests and the expertise he continued to develop. After having served as curate in both Washington and Baltimore, he had spent five years as pastor at Randallstown and its missions before taking up residence on Front Street on June 1, 1940.[32]

There Father Romeo told him of the strict economies he had practiced as acting pastor to reduce the parish debt to $55,000. He also told him of his failure to induce all but twenty-five of the Italians of the parish to attend a much publicized mission conducted in their own language. Father Martin had no illusions about the state of the parish, having been confessor to the sisters of its school. He came, nevertheless, rich in plans.

THE INITIAL PLANS

The first of Father Martin's projects was a thorough renovation of the church, much neglected in McGuire's later years. The physical transformation of St. Vincent's Church in 1940–41, in anticipation of its hundredth anniversary, will be described in part 2. Suffice it to say here that in the plans he himself worked out in minute detail John Sinnott Martin evidenced not only a remarkable grasp of architectural principles but a liturgical sense well in advance of that of the ordinary Catholic of his day. The baroque encrustations gave way to an almost stark simplicity. One of the medallions in the window of the Eucharist depicted two deacons distributing communion under both species, bread and wine, with the wafer to the hand of the communicant. Some parishioners were not happy with the changes, especially with the disappearance of windows, statues, or other church effects that bore memorial plaques.[33]

For the celebration of the centenary on October 19, 1941, a committee was formed to publish a *Centenary Manual* that contained the best account of the parish to date. Father Martin himself directed the choir for the mass said by Rev. William Sauer, a product of the parish. There was also a banquet attended by the governor, mayor, and archbishop, a procession in honor of St. Vincent, in which the Carroll Mansion Drum and Bugle Corps, the St. Leo's Drum Corps, and the band of Our Lady of Pompei marched, a solemn benediction in the evening, and a concert by the Our Lady of Pompei band.[34]

The archbishop provided Father Martin an opportunity to lay out his other plans by requesting in 1943 that all pastors submit their postwar projects. The first, the pastor revealed, was the eventual retirement of the debt. The second was an expansion of services to Catholics at large by special devotions, confessions, and counseling at any hour. The third was a revival of the kindergarten. The fourth was the acquisition and conversion of the St. Leo's Orphanage to a community center and "hostel for women who find themselves in the city without funds, jobs and shelter."

"We think," the pastor concluded, "that it is a good thing to have a parish like St. Vincent's where people may come who find their own

The centennial celebration, 1941, was attended by Archbishop Michael Curley, Gov. Herbert O'Conor (to his right), Mayor Howard Jackson (to his left), and Congressman Thomas D'Alesandro Jr. (fourth row, center left). Father Martin, the pastor, stands at the governor's right. *CATHOLIC REVIEW*

churches too crowded, the hours of mass inconvenient or who have some complaint, often purely personal or largely imaginary, against some condition or circumstance in their own localities." To the many who came to St. Vincent's out of affection for bygone years, to the transients and workers, could be added those who by means of the confessional returned to the church, "the greatest good we do." Two small study clubs for new-to-town Catholics at the nearby Social Securities offices were also being conducted.[35]

The archbishop responded that the two could talk later of plans 2 to 4. The first, retirement of the debt, was "a *now* plan and a *must* plan," not a postwar plan. Father Martin succeeded in erasing the debt in three years. In congratulating him for the second year's reduction, Archbishop Curley repeated a suggestion he had made in 1942, that St. Vincent's create an endowment fund.[36] Despite the parish's substantial income, Martin did not add this recommendation to his list of projects. As it turned out, plans 3 and 4 had to be abandoned because the orphanage was not quite ready to close its doors.

There were other disappointments. The Italians had not participated in the centenary celebration to the extent Martin had wished. Membership in the St. Vincent Society had dropped almost at once. The annual procession was soon discontinued. The Ushers Club suffered a similar fate as a result of the pastor's assumption of what the members had considered their right to choose the ushers for particular masses, this on the order of the archbishop.[37] Societies that Father Romeo had created—the Altar Boys Society, Young Women's Social Club, Alumni Association, Athletic Association, and Boy Scouts—disappeared from the annual reports with Father Martin's advent.[38] By 1943 both Sodality and Holy Name Society were recorded as "inactive." The disappearance of parish societies may not have been a source of great grief to the eleventh pastor.

WARTIME GROWTH

The rationing of gasoline and tires occasioned by World War II caused many to discontinue the long ride to St. Vincent's, but this was more than offset by the influx of war workers into the city. It was, in fact, for the latter that Father Martin was granted permission in 1941 for a midnight mass (actually 12:15 A.M.) on Sunday. Attendance at this and the printers' mass increased to such an extent that the basement was converted once more into a chapel, the Good Shepherd Chapel, with the cast-off furniture of other parishes to accommodate overflow crowds.[39] As many masses were said as were needed. From 1944 the stipends paid the priests who were brought in to help out on weekends and holy days were more often than not larger than the salaries of the pastor and his assistant combined. Father Martin himself policed the parking lot, church, and chapel during 12:15 A.M. and 2:30 A.M. masses. It needed only a flick of the finger to rid the congregation of the inebriates who had given Father McGuire such grief.

John Sinnott Martin was a commanding figure. Well over six feet tall, he wore in cooler weather a long black cape. The schoolchildren called him "the Batman." He could by turns be friendly or formidable. Man of many talents that he was, he himself recruited and directed the mixed choir that sang for the high mass on Sunday and special occasions. As a man of letters, his talents ranged from poetry to humor. The latter found an outlet in the "St. Vincent's Notebook."

"ST. VINCENT'S NOTEBOOK"

Soon after his arrival Father Martin began to publish a four-page (then eight pages) folder, six by three inches a page, called "St. Vincent's Notebook." A potpourri of entertaining and instructional matter, it appeared usually at Lent, Easter, Spring, Summer, Fall, and Christmas. It had also a very practical purpose, to spread the word on the times for masses and other services in order to obviate the frequent calls to the rectory.

The "Notebook" allowed the pastor to give occasional instructions on church etiquette. In one of his lists of do's and don't's, he told the reader: "Don't leave your purse behind you. There were two thieves at Calvary. One of them stole heaven. Pious pinchers of prayer books and purses ply their profession in prayerful pose where people pile in pews."[40] Attire was a constant irritant to the pastor, the "dippy sub-deb addiction to dungarees" in the 1940s warranting one of his barbs. Others were directed at latecomers and their tendency to squeeze into the back of the church. "Why crowd the bleachers at Mass when you like the 1st base line for the Orioles?" The author's humor was displayed on matters other than etiquette. In reporting the closing of the parish school, he would admit: "We miss the Sisters and the children. Their happy voices and ear-splitting yells (the children's, that is) leave us in an atmosphere of almost frightening peace."[41]

The readers often found themselves awash in religious esoterica. The earliest known use of Christmas (*Cristes Maesse*), they discovered, was in

1038 and the first recorded mention of a Christmas tree in 1605. Altars were a combination of table and tomb; the steps leading up to them must always be an odd number. Voltaire had predicted that in 100 years the Bible would be found only in museums; 100 years later his home was the property of the Geneva Bible Society.

The readers were also regaled by verses chosen from a range of poets—Prudentius, Shakespeare, Poe, Ezra Pound, Phyllis McGinley, and a host of contemporary poets with less claim to fame. Father Martin's own poems were easily spotted because the poet was never identified. On the occasion of the centennial celebration he was moved to write:

> A century has passed. Once more
> God's praise from organ, voice and pipe
> Goes heavenward through the smoke
> Of crowded commerce. Once again the poor
> Are taught the Gospel in both word and deed.
> Sacrifice is offered, sinners shriven,
> The Bread brought down from Heaven
> To dwell amongst us.[42]

Many of his offerings were doggerel but some almost mystical, as the one that appeared three years before his death entitled "The Kiln."

> Within the vaulting gloom
> Of Heaven's anteroom,
> Faith and hope afire
> Surge heavenward in vain aspire
> To pierce the tomb.
>
> Gone now their power to breach
> The prison whence to reach
> Beatitude above;
> Only Light and Love
> Can bring desired release—
> Love infinitely fierce
> A path for perfect Light to pierce
> By which purged spirits move
> To boundless peace.[43]

The "Notebook" was distributed after each mass. In time it had a mailing list of about 500 scattered over thirty-six states and fourteen foreign countries.[44]

THE EDITOR AND THE ARCHBISHOP

It was undoubtedly Father Martin's literary talents that caused the new archbishop, Francis Patrick Keough, installed in February 1948, to name him editor-in-chief of the diocesan weekly, the *Catholic Review,* a year later. Martin wrote most of the editorials, whose content demonstrated his politics to a greater degree than his theology. In this first decade of the Cold War his editorials reflected the Catholic preoccupation with communism. Under his direction the *Catholic Review* became also one of the most outspoken of Catholic weeklies in its criticism of the Truman presidency.

Certainly outspoken was a page 1 editorial of December 8, 1950, by "J.S.M." that depicted the Korean War as the consequence of "our pinks or punks" trying to appease the Kremlin by the "timid, tepid temporizers agree[ing] to the dividing line." Plans for the United Nations Building in New York, in the editor's view, might be better changed to a parking garage.[45] A month later he charged the Fair Deal with "trying to put across socialization of medicine and federal control of the school system—measures which are clearly on the way to socialism." Truman he viewed as putting his "pet" deal ahead of "the first need of the nation—adequate defense."[46]

In all such views he was totally in agreement with his archbishop, who in his own quiet way was a true Cold Warrior.[47] In 1952, however, the *Catholic Review* underwent an editorial shift, away from international affairs toward support of state censorship of "dirty" movies, a crusade apparently imposed from above to which Martin seemed reluctant to lend his pen. A "larger social concern," his obituary would read some twelve years later, "led him, during his three years as editor-in-chief of the *Catholic Review,* to criticize areas as various as gambling in Ocean City, Md., and what he called 'the foolish fiction' of Santa Claus."[48] Martin was particularly blunt about the commercialization of Christmas.

In 1953 Archbishop Keough dismissed Father Martin as editor-in-chief for reasons none have been able to explain except to say that Martin believed "his talents had been sacrificed to political ends."[49] The rejection left him embittered and a bit cynical. There can also be little doubt that, like Father Didier, Martin believed himself deserving of "honors and favors" that were not forthcoming. In 1942 he had been named by Curley to the tribunal for marriage cases, a position renewed by Keough. He had also been appointed chaplain to the Carroll Club at Johns Hopkins University. Eventually he accepted the fact that the pastorate at St. Vincent's was as great an honor as any.

A PASTOR SANS PAREIL

All who knew him, and the pastor of St. Vincent's was perhaps the best known in the city, would agree that Father Martin was not your ordinary pastor. A maverick, some said. All could quote his "A penny for the poor—no more, no less." It was an effective appeal; there was always more paper money than pennies in the poorbox. Everyone had his favorite story about Father Martin. A parishioner, one of them went, met him on the infamous "Block" on Baltimore Street. "Father, what are you doing here?" he asked. "This is my parish," the pastor responded. "The question is, what are you doing here?"[50]

Father Martin, all agreed, had class. He lived in well-appointed quarters and set the best table of any pastor in the city. On special occasions his brother, a manager of the dining cars of the B&O, sent over a steward and waiters. Table conversation was always memorable; Martin was an excellent raconteur. In the rectory he was never stinting. In 1944 Archbishop Curley called his attention to his household expenses: "$6,253 to my mind is a pretty high figure, particularly when I think in terms of living for four dollars a week [actually five] for twenty-one meals and for the better part of three years [as a pastor in Florida] paying two dollars a week for a room over a grocery store."[51] Household expenses were reduced by about $1,000 in the annual reports until after Curley's death. Then in three years they went up to $10,000 and more.

ASSISTANT PASTORS

St. Vincent's rectory saw more than its share of men of the cloth. The Franciscan Conventuals who had come to help Father McGuire on weekends continued until 1955. They were replaced by Redemptorists from Annapolis and then Sulpicians from St. Charles College. In 1959 priests of the Society of the Divine Word came over from the Catholic University and would continue their weekend trek for several years.

Associate pastors came and went. Father Romeo was transferred to St. Joseph's, Baltimore, in 1943. There were seven more before 1957. Most were part-time: one traveled to Mount St. Mary's Seminary to teach music, one conducted the first "Catholic Hour" on television, one was studying for a doctorate in education at Johns Hopkins University, and one was director of the CYO (Catholic Youth Organization). At Martin's request for a young, energetic, full-time assistant the newly ordained Donald P. Croghan was sent in 1957. A musician, he relieved the pastor of his direction of the choir. When the newly ordained Thomas J. Penn was sent to join him in 1959, St. Vincent's had its first two full-time assistants in half a century.[52]

Father Martin, as one could guess, was not on the best of terms with them all. In 1961 he asked for Father Penn's removal while, unknown to him, Father Croghan asked for a change. They were replaced by two priests of several years experience: Maurice J. Wolfe and Edmond J. Stroup. In 1964 Martin asked that Father Wolfe be replaced but that Father Stroup stay. The latter was active with the blacks in the parish, Martin explained, and was not so temperamental.[53]

The rectory had also another resident. Mrs. Ida Brandenburg, an excellent cook, came in the 1940s to help out for a few months. "Mrs. B," as she came to be called, would become a permanent fixture. Luigi Romeo, a relative of Father Romeo, stayed around the rectory as full-time carpenter and handyman until replaced by Elmore Washington in the 1960s. There was also a full-time sexton and other part-time help. Salaries for the help, Father Martin boasted, "were raised somewhat nearer to the living wage teaching of the church."[54]

A CHANGING NEIGHBORHOOD AGAIN

Gradually at first but accelerating after World War II the neighborhood about St. Vincent's underwent a transformation as drastic as that of the turn of the century. From a parish population of 1,930 when he arrived in 1940, Father Martin recorded 900 parishioners in 1945, 375 in 1950, and 200 in 1955. Some of the abandoned homes were converted into machine shops and warehouses, but most were razed to make way for public housing projects. The school population was not allowed to decline so drastically. Students were sent over by surrounding parishes that had no schools. Of the 184 enrolled in 1955, only 52 were from the parish itself. Eighty came from Queen of Peace in Essex.

Federal and city plans for urban renewal determined the character of the change. The Lafayette Courts, Douglass Homes, and Flag House Courts, public housing projects to the east and southeast of St. Vincent's, were completed in 1956. Initially integrated, the residents in time became almost all African Americans. The city's Area 4 (or Shot Tower) Rehabilitation Program at the end of the 1950s claimed not only the school and convent but the last of the private residences on Front, High, Exeter, and Colvin streets. In their place would go up a regional post office. Parks planned at both ends of St. Vincent's would take all but church and rectory on the west side of Front Street.

St. Leo's Orphanage closed its doors in 1956, St. Vincent's Free School in June 1960. At the beginning of 1962 the pastor reported: "Demolition closes in slowly on our old school, convent, orphanage. Already there are signs of the rehabilitation we await." At the end of 1962 he complained, "We're like Job sitting on a rubble pile."[55]

The year 1962 brought another threat of extinction. One of the alternate routes for the extension of the Jones Falls Expressway (Interstate 83) ran straight through the church and rectory. Architects and preservationists, however, came to the rescue. "It [the church] is unique in Baltimore," said the *Architect's Report* in barely concealed outrage, "for its excellent proportions and its elegant and graceful tower." It was "the principal esthetic feature of a neighborhood otherwise sadly lacking in points of local identity."[56] Largely in response to the reaction of the architects, the city created the Commission for Historical and Architectural Preservation.

The archdiocese would also come to the rescue. In April 1963 Francis X. Gallagher, its lawyer, informed the new archbishop, Lawrence J. Shehan, that the city might consider it necessary to take St. Vincent's, "but if it is advised that the Archdiocese will oppose the taking, it will abandon any such idea. [The city's representative] tells me that Father Martin has not indicated any great opposition to the proposal." In the light of the reaction of the local chapter of the American Institute of Architects, Gallagher told the archbishop, he had advised the city's representative that the archdiocese would not willingly acquiesce to the sale.[57] On the attitude of Father Martin, the representative was ill informed. In 1962 the pastor thanked those "who came so readily to our defense" and in 1963 expressed the wish that not only the church but all the historic monuments of Old Town be preserved.[58]

THE PARISH'S RESPONSE TO CHANGE

In 1956 the parish population jumped from 200 to "c. 1200." The Notitiae explained: "A new census, to be completed Feb. 10 by the St. Camillus Society of St. Mary's Seminary, Roland Park, shows new housing project population of c. 1000 Catholics added to the parish in the past 6 to 8 months, ⁴⁄₅ of them in need of attention. We have already [taken] steps to meet the most urgent needs." Another census, however, taken in 1959 at the suggestion of Fr. Tom Penn revealed that about 200 of the 1,000 Catholics in the Lafayette and Flag House Courts attended St. Francis Xavier, the black parish on Caroline Street. In an attempt to attract the others to St. Vincent's, Father Penn began a Sunday school. With the lure of candy suckers he enrolled about 100.[59] Their numbers grew, as did the number of blacks who came to mass at St. Vincent's.

A few of the children of the projects also enrolled in the parish school in its last years, this before the Catholic schools of Baltimore were integrated. Father Stroup, who replaced Father Penn, visited the projects frequently. In 1961 there were twenty conversions, in 1962 eleven. In 1963 the associate pastor organized a Tuesday discussion club for teenagers and in 1964 accompanied the Sunday school pupils who were bused to Ilchester for instruction, a project of the seniors of Trinity Prep.

A census taken 1962 showed a parish population of 784 or 258 families, of whom 112 lived in the Lafayette Courts, 94 in the Flag House Courts, 37 in the Douglass Homes, and only 15 in other parts of the parish.[60] St. Vincent's welcomed its new members in a tentative way. Father Martin was concerned that the black altar boys Tom Penn was training would discourage attendance at the income-producing masses. Whenever the rectory's bell rang, Mrs. B's tone of voice was an unfailing clue as to the color of the caller.[61]

Physically, St. Vincent's adjusted to its new surroundings. In 1962–63 it put up a three-story addition at the rear of the rectory to provide a garage, housekeeper's apartment, meeting room, workroom, and storage room. From the city it acquired the lot north of the rectory and paved and fenced it for a parking lot.[62] The parish moved faster on its plans than the city. As the new additions neared completion in the spring of 1963, "St. Vincent's Notebook" (read: Father Martin) complained that for some years the parish would "be eating the dust of political procrastination and official inefficiency that is the essence of rehabilitation in our Shot Tower area."[63]

THE FINANCIAL PICTURE

For the school property the city paid the archdiocese in 1962 $242,000 but deducted $30,000 for the parking lot, leaving a reserve of $212,000 in the hands of the archdiocese for the future use of the parish.[64] Under Martin this reserve was never touched. Except for $34,000 borrowed from the archdiocese in 1961 for air conditioning, the parish was able to

Rev. John Sinnott Martin (1894–1965), eleventh pastor, with the graduating class of 1958. The twenty-five-year pastorate of this man of many talents witnessed a transformation of the parish greater than that at the turn of the century. ST. VINCENT DE PAUL PARISH

pay for the extensive alterations and renovations from its ordinary parish revenue. As the parish population again contracted, the midnight and printers' masses brought in more than ever, 3,000 to 4,000 on weekends, producing a triple overflow in the summer months. The year 1963, with an income of $95,454, set a record, an impressive gain over the $53,833 of Martin's first full year as pastor.[65] Of the $95,454, offertory collections (seat offerings stopped in 1946) accounted for $63,690 and the poorbox $9,669. Other sources above $1,000 were $5,504 from investments and rents, $4,419 from votive lights, and $2,260 from donations and bequests.

Sweeping changes in mass attendance, revenues, and even attitudes at St. Vincent de Paul, however, were in the offing.

VATICAN COUNCIL II

The Fall 1961 "Notebook" carried the first mention of the council that was to meet in Rome in 1962 in a piece entitled "Church Unity." Less than a year later it carried a quote on church unity from the president of the Vatican Secretariat for Christian Unity. Even more was Father Martin ready for the coming council in the matter of the liturgical reform it would promote. "The so-called 'new' liturgy," he told the readers of the "Notebook" at the beginning of 1965, "is not new. It is the *restoration* of older and simpler forms and a purging of things that have crept into the Mass thru the centuries." Proper English translations and good music, he believed, would take time and patience. "Certainly, most people like the changes that have been made and are convinced these will bring the Liturgy nearer to the faithful." The new altar facing the people, "solid, simple, and dignified," was ready for the first Sunday of Lent in 1965. Under Father Martin's tutelage most of St. Vincent's accepted the changes readily, although the head usher was quoted as saying that the new way of saying mass kept him "guessing a bit. He's waiting to see what it will do to the collections."[66]

A week before the conclusion of the Vatican Council the pastor of St. Vincent's had a heart attack that on December 19, 1965, proved fatal. Although on questions of church unity and the liturgy John Sinnott Martin was ready, even eager, to guide his flock onto an altered landscape, in such areas as the lay participation in parish affairs mandated by the council he would have proved, perhaps, as resistant as any pastor. Under his control, St. Vincent's was a one-man operation in matters of policy.

"Like the patron saint of the church of which he was pastor for 25 years," ran his obituary in the *Catholic Review*, "Father John Sinnott Martin had a particular solicitude for the poor."[67] This was the trait that made this original man so like most of the pastors of St. Vincent's. In a small biography of the patron of the parish entitled *Vincent de Paul: Saint of Circumstance,* which he published in 1943, Martin characterized the Frenchman: "Vincent de Paul was none of your cut-and-dried, dyed-in-the-wool, born-to-holiness kind of saint." In this respect Martin resembled the patron. At the same time his atypical traits defied analysis. This was perhaps the reason he insisted that at his funeral there be no eulogy.

REVOLUTION

1966–1973

Soon after Father Martin's death, his assistant Father Stroup was appointed administrator, a position he would hold for two years before being officially named pastor of St. Vincent's. Edmond J. Stroup was not quite 40 when he took over. Born July 25, 1925, in Essington, Pennsylvania, where his father, a convert, had a job with Westinghouse, he received the usual Catholic education. Upon the advice of his pastor he went to Mount St. Mary's College and Seminary, where in his first year of theology he was accepted for the archdiocese of Baltimore. He was ordained at Mount St. Mary's in 1949 by the then-auxiliary bishop, Bishop Lawrence J. Shehan, and sent to St. Charles in Pikesville. In 1955 he was assigned to St. John's in Westminster and in 1961 to St. Vincent's on Front Street.[1]

The acting pastor did not immediately reach for a new broom. "St. Vincent's Notebook" came out with its accustomed regularity and with little change in appearance and content. The mass schedule remained the same except for a 4:30 mass on holy days. Mrs. B and the caretakers stayed on. Lt. Col. John G. Volz refurbished the four flags in the sanctuary.[2]

It was not long, however, before the march of events overtook the little flock on Front Street. Cardinal Shehan returned from Vatican II rich in plans. St. Vincent's was as ready as any parish to respond to his efforts at reform and renewal, but it was not chosen as one of the pacesetters. It stumbled into the role on its own.

THE FOLK MASS

The seminarians at Paca Street were eager to be "involved," to be out where the action was—the inner city. Father Stroup readily accepted the

A folk mass at St. Vincent's, c. 1968, conducted by seminarians from Paca Street. SUNPAPERS

proposal of a group of seminarians to teach hymns to the black children in the Bible school. Then on the last Sunday of July, Philip Esserwein, guitar in hand, led the singing at the first communion mass. The response was so encouraging that he and the talented Askew "Skip" Sanders, a black seminarian, continued to come over for the 9:30 mass for the rest of the summer. Skip was the cantor. Word spread and mass attendance zoomed. There were other innovations: the first few pews were removed and the altar pushed closer to the people. The worshipers were told that it was all right to chew the whole-wheat wafers now used for communion.[3]

The next summer Skip organized a group of seminarians and laypeople in a "lively and lyrical rendition to this new liturgical expression," the folk mass, "pleasing most, but not all," the "Notebook" confided. "It was particularly interesting to see the number of young married couples with their small children who came to the Mass. We were 'overrun' with Sisters who obviously were taking advantage of the fact that they did not have to be present at the 'Children's Mass' in their home parishes."[4]

In the beginning the liturgy was geared to the children, but they were soon crowded out by the adults. By 1968, the folk mass, under George Quickly, another talented black seminarian, had grown to six guitars, a bass fiddle, a tambourine, and a set of bongo drums. Following his injunction to "just get some soul," most of the massgoers were soon clapping and swaying to such hymns as "Shout from the Highest Mountain" and "Sing to the Lord a New Song."[5] It was a far cry from the days of "Oh, Lord, I Am Not Worthy" and "Mother Dear, Oh Pray for Me."

Other features of the folk mass at St. Vincent's were the totally uninhibited handshake (or hug) of peace, dialogue homilies, and the congregational participation in baptisms that often followed the homily. The organ remained a part of the liturgy at St. Vincent's, even the folk mass. When Bruce Miller, the organist, left in 1968, the appropriately named Joseph Organ took his place. The author of "Abba, Father" lent his considerable skills to the orchestration of the folk mass. In the spring of 1967 the Mothers Club began to serve coffee and buns after the 9:30 mass, a custom that would continue to the present. Worshipers came from as far away as Harford and Anne Arundel counties.

SEMINARIANS, SISTERS, AND SOCIAL CONCERN

In addition to the folk masses, the seminarians from Paca Street involved themselves in such parish activities as census taking, tutoring, counseling, and the organization of social and political events. Sisters also came to St. Vincent's in large numbers. Not only were they attracted by the liturgy but also by the opportunities the parish afforded to try new programs in catechetics. The sisters from the Martin de Porres Center, an inner-city project begun by the Sisters of Notre Dame de Namur in 1965, were particularly active, assuming charge of a Sunday school program conducted in the homes of black parishioners after the 9:30 mass. They also took many of the children to participate in the activities of the Martin de Porres Center at St. John's some ten blocks north.

The liturgy was the door through which many at St. Vincent's entered the world of social concern. The growing awareness that St. Vincent's was positioned to play a special role in this work was reflected in the slogans that appeared occasionally in the "Notebook": "Helping 'to serve' the Inner City"; "'Old Town' looking to the 'New City'"; "The Inner

Harbor Renewal." The "Notebook" also carried such timely items as excerpts from Michael Harrington's *The Other America* and Archbishop Paul Hallinan's pastoral letter on war and peace. The Notitiae recorded collections for Biafra and Latin America in 1968. Informal but intensely serious discussions on matters of justice and peace kept many long after the coffee and buns were gone. "I found Saint Vincent de Paul Parish to be an important gathering place during the 1960's for the activism and fellowship through social ministry," Sen. Barbara Mikulski later recalled. "It was to me, as to many others, a wonderful place to come to worship."[6]

The heightened awareness of social problems at St. Vincent's was due in no small way to its pastor, who continued a close association with Fathers Joseph Connolly and Henry Offer, the originators of an archdiocesan inner-city board. It was due even more, perhaps, to the associate pastor who appeared at St. Vincent's in June 1966, Rev. Joseph R. Wenderoth, age 31. Joe, as he preferred to be called by the parishioners, was not cut of the same cloth as the former assistants, being one of the disciples of Fr. Eugene Walsh, the "guru" of Paca Street.[7] Baltimore-born, a product of St. Ambrose Parish School and the Sulpician seminaries of Baltimore, he had served in middle-class parishes before Cardinal Shehan, guessing correctly, asked if he would like to work in the inner city at St. Vincent's. As associate pastor, his relationship with the pastor differed markedly from such relationships in the past, resembling more the team or shared ministry that was being tried in some of the parishes of the archdiocese.

THE AFRICAN-AMERICAN COMMUNITY

Both priests were eager to bring the black families in the parish into the parish community. Within its boundary were some 7,000 souls or about 1,700 families, some 70 percent of whom were African American. Of these, 84 percent lived in the "projects," as the Lafayette-Douglass Homes and Flag House Courts were called. Not even 5 percent, however, were Catholic, and most of these still attended St. Francis Xavier, the closest black parish.

Catholic and non-Catholic alike were invited to most of the parish activities. Senior and junior branches of the Catholic Youth Organization (CYO) were organized largely for the teenagers of the projects. Ball games in the parking lot, outings at Fort Smallwood, "cabarets" in the church basement, and other events attracted enough to make the effort worthwhile. "Does anyone know where steel drums (musically speaking) can be rented or purchased?" the "Notebook" inquired. "We would like to form a musical band."[8] The same issue asked if anyone needed high school students for the summer. "We would be glad to act as employment agency for you." The Bible school under Darnel Burfoot, a dedicated young black student who lived in the rectory, flourished. "Mr. Don," as he was known, recruited a number of parents to assist him.

"While stationed at St. Vincent's," a memorandum to the urban vicar in 1970 would read, "Father Joe Wenderoth made many attempts to provide religious education for children of the area. He and the laity and Sisters who worked with him did have programs established. Their efforts evidently met with some success." It was not a large-scale operation, the memo conceded, but "seemed to be a creative attempt to answer needs. Such visions deserve praise and encouragement."[9] Joe also roamed the projects making friends, offering advice and help.

Both priests had an easy rapport with the black community. Among the contributions of the pastor was the integration of the restaurants of Little Italy, where he frequently took black youngsters to eat. Before the riots of 1968 they were cordially received. On a warm evening Ed Stroup enjoyed listening to the clearly audible hum from the projects; pastor and assistant felt at home in the neighborhood.[10]

THE INNER CITY

The inner city became increasingly the focus of social justice programs in the archdiocese. In 1966 the inner-city board was transformed into the more formal and hard-working Urban Commission. Ed Stroup was named a member. The tens of thousands of dollars allocated to inner-city programs grew to hundreds of thousands. Many of the inner-city parishes had to be subsidized. St. Vincent's never did. The demographic changes of the 1950s and 1960s emptied the parishes of the inner city. In 1962, St. Joseph's on Lee Street in South Baltimore, older than St. Vincent's, was abandoned. In 1966 St. John's, the daughter parish, also closed its doors. And there were others. "If we don't save the city," the cardinal was quoted in a special study of urban parishes, "we can forget about the Church in the Archdiocese."[11]

Cardinal Shehan had in 1965 invited specialists in urban planning to do a study of the city's parishes and to make recommendations. The *Baltimore Urban Parish Study* was released at the end of 1967. It revealed, among other things, an apparent inability of such major components of the archdiocesan bureaucracy as Catholic Charities, Education, and the inner-city board to communicate effectively and urged a more fruitful co-operation. The heart of the study, however, was a critical analysis of the fifty-one urban parishes, whose outlook the study characterized as ranging from "embattled inertia" to "outright heroism." There was no doubt that St. Vincent's fell into the latter category.

St. Vincent de Paul, the study observed, played an important role in the special services it offered parishioners who lived throughout the metropolitan area as well as downtown. "As a result, this parish is one of the few in the Inner City to have escaped the disastrous financial consequences of decline." Encompassing much of the public housing that was a part of urban renewal, it was in a position "to extend its apostolate to the service of these projects." The study envisioned an experiment that involved a team of priests living at the rectory who would run both the church and a storefront chapel in the projects. The chapel, operating around the clock, could provide religious counseling and an extensive referral service for the public-housing tenants. Adolescents should be especially targeted. The center could provide the kind of creative activity that recognized "the hostility and antipathy which is part of their inheritance." Opportunities for the release of aggression, the study insisted, should be provided in a physical way, through sports and the development of tool-using skills.[12] That these proposals were never implemented was due largely to the riots of 1968.

THE RIOTS

On April 4, 1968, Dr. Martin Luther King Jr. was murdered in Memphis and Baltimore suffered what a group of clergymen, including the priests at St. Vincent's, had managed to avert in the long hot summer of 1966—a three-day explosion of violence, arson, and looting. The riots began on April 6, the day before Palm Sunday, at 5:30 P.M. on Gay Street within the boundaries of St. Vincent's and spread to other sections of the city. Not long after their eruption Ed Stroup returned from Atlanta, where the cardinal and several priests had gone to attend the funeral of Dr. King. For three days pastor and associate went into the black areas in an effort to dampen the fever. Tenants of Flag House Courts, nevertheless, taunted and even fired upon police and firemen battling a blaze in a dairy on East Lombard. A group of black youths shouted obscenities at Father Stroup as he stood on the rectory steps. Only a few cars arrived for mass on Palm

Sunday, some with bricks on their roofs. But St. Vincent's was not touched. Catholic institutions in black areas, like the seminary on Paca Street, seemed pointedly immune.[13]

Eleven thousand soldiers were finally able to quell the fury that had taken only six lives but had produced 600 injuries, 1,150 fires, 1,500 lootings, and nearly 5,000 arrests, most for curfew violations.[14] Refugee centers were set up at most of the black Catholic parishes, but the expected number of homeless did not materialize. St. Vincent's served as a distribution center for food and clothing, greater needs in an area that had lost many of its stores. For weeks thereafter the city was tense. Joe Wenderoth was told one day to go back to the rectory; it wasn't safe in the projects.

AFTERMATH

The Holy Week riots were but the beginning of a series of shocks of different sorts. In May Catholic activists destroyed draft records in Catonsville. In July the papal encyclical *Humanae Vitae* forbidding artificial birth control provoked the dissent of seventy-two priests of the archdiocese, including the pastor and associate of St. Vincent's. A growing polarization within the Catholic community was reflected in the spate of letters provoked by the picture of a dancing nun in the *Catholic Review*. A "nut," "undisguised exhibitionism," fumed the critics, who were in turn reproved for their inability to appreciate ballet at mass and for their fascination with "The Flying Nun" on television.[15]

The pitiful few who appeared at the Easter masses at St. Vincent's following the riots gradually increased but never to the point they had reached before. Decline in attendance was particularly marked at the midnight mass. The Sulpicians who had begun in 1966 to assist on weekends were no longer needed. In the fall of 1968, however, Rev. Casimir Pugevicius, the archdiocesan director of radio and television, took up residence at 120 Front Street and helped out on weekends.

Conditions in the projects deteriorated; the Flag House Courts soon led all others in the city in maintenance problems, drugs, and guns. Even St. Vincent's fell victim to vandalism. Sometime after the Saturday evening mass on October 10, 1970, a chalice valued at $5,400 was stolen from the altar. "The new church is leaning toward simplicity," Father Stroup mused philosophically. The chalice did seem a bit "ostentatious." It was a sentiment shared by a number of parishioners, the *Sun* reported,

but Mrs. B who had contributed her jewels to its crafting in 1959, complained, "It's awful."[16] Not long after, Ida Brandenburg left the employ of
St. Vincent's. Father Stroup moved into her quarters in the rear of the
rectory.

The old cemetery out in Clifton Park provided a more serious cause
for concern. White gangs along Belair Road began in 1967 to break open
the vaults at night, remove the skeletons, and place them on the surrounding golf course. Father Stroup and a relative of some of the interred
went regularly to the cemetery to return the skeletons and seal the vaults,
with no help from the police or the archdiocese. Maintenance of the
cemetery, which had no provision for perpetual care, would remain a
problem for the parish.[17]

CHANGES PHYSICAL AND PSYCHIC

Physical changes accompanied those of the spirit. In 1967 the old orphanage was finally demolished. Where a door in the vestibule had connected the church and orphanage a stained glass window depicting saints
of the Americas was installed in memory of Father Martin. In 1969 pile
drivers began to prepare the empty, level land between the church and the
Lafayette Courts for the post office. With its completion, barriers to contact with the parish residents were effectually raised on all sides. In front
was the post office, in back the Fallsway, to the north a police garage, and
to the south a park that stretched to Fayette Street.

At the same time, a psychic separation from the African-American
community also developed. Not long after the riots Rev. George H.
Clements, a noted black activist from Chicago, told pastor and people of
St. Vincent's that they were not doing enough for the black community
within the parish borders, that they should, in fact, devote their principal
energies to it.[18] The pastor was discomfited. In June 1969 he wrote the
cardinal that St. Vincent's was faced with a "particular problem" regarding the relevance of the Sunday liturgy to its black parishioners, especially
the young. "The one mass that was considered 'theirs,' the community
liturgy, has proved popular with whites. But now it seems no matter how
we try to relate it to our own parish community, they have become more
alienated from it." The pastor requested permission for a special Sunday
afternoon mass in the lower church "more attuned to our parish
needs."[19] The permission was granted, but the mass never materialized.
Not even the pastor, in retrospect, is certain why. But increasingly an am-

Church and rectory, c. 1980, isolated by expressway at the back, post office in the front, city park to the south, and parking lot to the north.   st. vincent de paul parish

biguity in the pastor's mind was resolved in favor of St. Vincent's being what it had been in fact for half a century and more: a metropolitan parish.

THE PARISH COUNCIL

The recognition of this metropolitan character arose from the parish's attempt to respond to another of the mandates of Vatican II, one for which it had been unable to play a pacesetting role because of its disparate membership: the formation of a parish council with active and responsible lay involvement. In 1968 the guidelines came from the chancery for the creation of parish councils and five subsidiary committees: finance, maintenance, education, liturgy, and parish and community relations. Conscientiously Ed Stroup set the wheels in motion. "We are now in the process of trying to organize such a council," the "Notebook" revealed in the fall of 1968, "hoping to realize the unique opportunity of utilizing the capabilities of our own parishioners as well as the friends of St. Vincent's."[20] A questionnaire was passed out to each adult and teenager at the weekend masses for them to sign up for a committee. For that on parish and community relations a committee on social action was substituted. Describing the purpose of the latter, the questionnaire explained: "We are an Inner-City parish that includes members of not only the immediate geographical area, but also members throughout the entire Metropolitan area. This committee helps all of our parishioners to gain an understanding of the problems of our day."[21] This concept of parish had been broadened without recourse to the chancery. And for the first time, perhaps, the "friends" of the parish who came in regularly were told they were full-fledged members of the parochial congregation.

By the summer of 1969 all but the committee on education had been formed. "There is still room for additional membership if you are interested," the "Notebook" announced.[22] Laypeople of talent and expertise came forward. Barbara Mikulski was elected to the council. Albert "Pete" Puliafico, vice-president of the Mercantile Safe Deposit and Trust Company, headed the finance committee. Most of the members of the council and its subsidiary committees came from outside the parish.

Still looking to the pastor and assistant for leadership, however, the council was unable to define itself or its goals. And the long distances many were required to cover for largely fruitless discussions reduced attendance to the point where the parish council and its subsidiaries died of inanition. "Describe briefly the composition of your Parish Lay Council," the annual report of 1971 requested. The pastor put simply "N/A" (not applicable).[23]

THE PEACE MOVEMENT

There may have been another reason that the council and committees at St. Vincent's were allowed to fall into desuetude. In 1970 the parish suffered a second shattering blow. The Holy Week riots of 1968 had affected

Ed Stroup more, perhaps, than he was prepared to admit. The same was true of the abrupt removal of his assistant in February 1970 for illegal trespass and the destruction of government property.

While Joe Wenderoth had a strong commitment to civil rights and racial justice when he came to St. Vincent's, he had not the same intense interest in the peace movement occasioned by the war in Vietnam as had some of the sisters with whom he worked closely or his friend Fr. Neil McLaughlin. His involvement stemmed from his work with the young blacks whom he had accompanied to court for probation hearings so that they could be drafted into the army. When challenged on this role, he consulted Neil. The two, Cardinal Shehan explained later, "became particularly concerned about poor youths, on whom the provisions of the Selective Service Act weighed far more heavily than on their more fortunate brothers." In short order Joe was drawn into the antiwar network that would earn for Baltimore the epithet of "Christian Guerrilla Capital" of the United States.[24]

Neil McLaughlin had worked with Philip Berrigan at St. Peter Claver, where the Josephite had first conceived his tactic of disrupting the war effort by the destruction of draft files. In 1967 the "Baltimore Four" had poured blood on the files at the Custom House. In 1968 the "Catonsville Nine" burned files at the draft board housed in the Knights of Columbus building in that Baltimore suburb. The trial of the latter in 1969 had activated a heterogeneous body of Catholics not only in Baltimore but throughout the nation. They called themselves the Catholic Resistance.[25]

The civil rights and peace movements had merged as early as 1968 in Baltimore when the lines around City Hall protesting the failure to appoint Walter Carter, a black leader, to office mingled with those around the federal court house supporting the action of the Baltimore Four. The waning of black involvement at St. Vincent's coincided with the waxing of the peace movement in Baltimore, in which few blacks played an active role.[26] Neil McLaughlin, whom the cardinal had appointed in March to the staff of the Urban Commission, was spokesperson for those who raided offices in New York in September. Anthony Scoblick, a Josephite at St. Francis Xavier, was part of a group of raiders in Boston.

Occasionally the plans were laid at St. Vincent's itself. Father Stroup remembered Phil Berrigan as one of the group that met behind closed doors. The parishioners at St. Vincent's were aware of their associate pastor's involvement in the antiwar movement but not of the particulars until February 1970. Rarely did he mention the movement from the pulpit. The parish was split between support and disapproval of his views until they read in the paper of two raids carried out by the East Coast Conspiracy to Save Lives.

The East Coast Conspiracy, like the Catholic Resistance generally, was an amorphous group. The eleven who plotted and participated in its raids in February consisted of a diocesan priest, Wenderoth himself, two Jesuits, a black Josephite, two sisters, three laymen, and two laywomen, ranging in age from 18 to 39. Five were Baltimore residents. On February 6 they destroyed draft files in Philadelphia and the next day records of the Washington, D.C., offices of General Electric, the second largest war contractor in the nation. "We have done so," they said in a statement released to the press, "because of the need for serious and continuing resistance to the racist and militarist institutions operating in the United States. And we have done so because through our acting we have found a new life style which offers opportunities and hope, for ourselves and others."[27]

The cardinal relieved Father Wenderoth of his duties at St. Vincent's. On the first Sunday in March the congregation at the 9:30 mass was startled by an episode, the details of which Father Stroup himself called in to the chancery. He was "anxious that the Cardinal get the right story and not act hastily," a memo of the assistant chancellor read. Fathers Wenderoth, McLaughlin, a Josephite, and "a number of 'peaceniks,' 'hippies,' etc." came to the mass. After the homily Father McLaughlin informed the congregation of Father Wenderoth's dismissal and invited the auditors to stay after the mass to hear him. "Most did stay, and Father Wenderoth spoke about 20 minutes."[28] The incident was calculated to stir the congregation to demand the assistant's reinstatement, but the parishioners were either too distraught or too timorous to respond.

As long as Wenderoth and McLaughlin insisted upon remaining in the peace movement, they remained unassigned. The FBI maintained a close surveillance over them and their friends. The East Coast Conspiracy, director J. Edgar Hoover claimed, were plotting to blow up power lines under the nation's capital and kidnap a high official, Henry Kissinger it turned out. Acting as spokesperson for the "conspirators" at a press conference, Wenderoth called the charges a "fabrication," another demonstration of "the inability of the FBI to deal with reality." The Berrigans were not, as Hoover had claimed, the leaders of the East Coast Conspiracy, he insisted. Congress called upon Hoover to turn over whatever evidence he had on the East Coast Conspiracy to a federal attorney.[29]

On January 12, 1971, Fathers Wenderoth and McLaughlin and Tony

Scoblick were arrested in Baltimore. "I couldn't believe it," Father Stroup was quoted as saying. "It sounded like a vendetta of Hoover's. But I don't know."[30] Cardinal Shehan visited the three that same evening in jail and the next day had them remanded to his custody. The cardinal's visit proved the most controversial act of his career. Father Wenderoth called it "a beautiful experience." One supporter expressed regret that there "are not more leaders in the church like you." A letter to the *Sunday Sun*, however, signed by "A family of disgruntled Catholics," recommended an end to contributions to the church until "every radical un-American priest in this archdiocese" had one-way tickets to Red China or North Korea.[31]

Father Stroup, and two parishioners of St. Vincent's, Pete Puliafico and Clinton Bamberger, went up to testify as character witnesses for Father Wenderoth at the trial of the "Harrisburg Seven," as the "conspirators" were called. The government failed to prove its case. Joe returned to Baltimore to continue to minister to the disinherited of the inner city.[32]

BISHOP GOSSMAN'S VISIT

Upon his return from Vatican Council II Cardinal Shehan had inaugurated pastoral visits to every parish in the archdiocese either by himself or one of his two auxiliary bishops. St. Vincent's was one of the last to be visited. The visit was entrusted to Bishop Joseph Gossman, who had been created an auxiliary bishop in 1968 and the first urban vicar in 1970. In the fall of the same year he came to Front Street. The report he composed for the perusal of the cardinal offered a detailed analysis of the problems and prospects of St. Vincent's at another critical point in its history.

> I arrived at St. Vincent's about 6 PM on Saturday evening, October 24. After dinner, I preached at the 7:15 PM Mass attended by about 40 persons. Fr. Stroup told me they were trying to change the Mass schedule in order to make it realistic. About 9 PM we talked about St. Vincent's, his being there, etc. The parish is slowly losing both in the members attending Mass and in the overall amount contributed—not drastically, but gradually, and to such an extent that something eventually will have to be done.
>
> Basically Father Stroup is faced with the keen awareness that if St. Vincent's as a parish is to "do" anything, he will have to "engineer" it, and he feels inadequate to the needs he sees. He knows that programs and outreach need more staff and he hasn't any staff besides himself, and very scant hope that finances will allow him additional Staff person(s). Ed is

very happy at St. Vincent—happier and more content than he has been for a long time. He is not interested in moving. He desires very much to be community and neighborhood oriented, and feels totally inadequate personally to this direction. Hence the rather undisputed fact that right now, at least, nothing is really "happening" at St. Vincent's. He does not relate very well to the only people in the immediate neighborhood—the public housing poor who live in the "project," who are entirely black. Most of the "project dwellers" consider their stay in the housing facilities as temporary and most are so anxious to get out they have little patience or desire to get involved in any kind of on-going parish programs or plans.

Traditionally, St. Vincent's has been attended and supported by whites who literally came to it from all over Baltimore. This is still true today—even many suburban people come, though not nearly as many as in the past because of the Saturday evening Masses available almost everywhere. But this dependence on a very transient group of people, who have no interest or relationship to the immediate area or neighborhood, only makes the parish more unable to really become a parish community church in the usual sense. Still, the largest part of this impasse derives from the problems of the poor of the housing, who do not identify with St. Vincent's, its location (not really near anybody) and the fact that Father Stroup is entirely alone (except for Fr. Casimir Pugevicius who is in residence). It deserves to be mentioned that Joe Wenderoth did relate to the neighborhood and community (especially the "projects") and that he did do very effective work there.

Church and rectory seem in good repair. Much of the rectory is furnished most elegantly—from the time of Fr. John S. Martin, no doubt. Some effort has been made to accommodate the upper church for the new liturgy and the basement church has been transformed into a daily chapel with some space for meeting. The new post office building, now being built, will remove the rectory and church from any northerly [easterly] visibility. The planned new police headquarters [garage] and planned expressways seem only to aim at cutting off almost all visibility and access to a parish already very isolated from its few surroundings. It is unfortunate, not just esthetically but also practically, since the new building and roads will merely give a rendition in concrete to a situation already existing for other reasons.

I did not preach at the midnight (Saturday) or the 2:30 AM Mass (Sunday). Attendance has been declining and the 2:30 Mass will be discontinued. The main Mass is at 9:30 AM; it is a folk Mass attended by the CCD [Confraternity of Christian Doctrine] kids (mostly black) and many of those who come from almost everywhere. It was pretty well attended, although I felt the singing and music was not nearly as well done as it was several years ago when this 9:30 AM Mass had the reputation of being the "best" folk Mass in Baltimore. Undoubtedly the steady increase in the number of folk Masses in so many parishes has also had much to do with the development at St. Vincent's. There were still many people, even whole families, who come to St. Vincent's because, for some reason, they felt alienated or unhappy in their own parish. There is a fairly large number who come from Sacred Heart (Glyndon) for this reason, if I can quote some of these who made themselves known to me. I also preached at the noon Mass and met with some of those who attended 9:30 Mass at the customary "coffee klatch" after the service. There is a catechetic program run by "outsiders" for the children, mostly indigenous to the community. There is still a segment of people (outsiders) who attend with some regularity and who consider St. Vincent's "their parish."

At 3 PM on Sunday afternoon we had a "meeting" attended by about 6 ladies who live (and have lived for 10–15 years) in the "projects." They express fear about the violence and crime, and expressed a feeling of almost complete helplessness about doing anything about the awful conditions, especially in the high-rise apartments. A few other people who lived or worked in the area came to the meeting. Very little was discussed and the meeting was, in my opinion, pretty much a waste of time for every one. I personally am of the opinion that if we desire to see anything begin to happen at St. Vincent's, Father Stroup has to be given at least another man. As it is, St. Vincent's cannot be more than a "holding operation." I also think that Ed has a pretty contemporary pastoral sense which is not being called into much use in this assignment. I say this because it is clear that many of our men in places where such a sense is desperately needed (by the people) seem to be totally lacking it and any understanding of its need in ministering to today's people. We really should be asking ourselves—in conjunction with Father Stroup—some very important questions about the future of St. Vincent's and where he fits in that future.

Some additional information: Donald [sic] Burfoot, a black student, lives in the rectory and is in charge of the educational program for the children. Parish income has dipped to $700–$800 per week total since the Saturday evening Masses have become a fact. Previously they got $1,100–$1,200 weekly. Present Saturday-Sunday attendance is 800. $7,000 a year is given to the poor.

The report was dated December 29, 1970.[33] Five days before, Bishop Gossman had written Father Stroup personally. He thanked him for his hospitality and the "excellent" meals. "I must say I think you are doing a

Rev. Edmond J. Stroup (b. 1925), twelfth pastor, on the occasion of the suspension of the printers' mass in 1971.   SUNPAPERS

good job at St. Vincent's under the circumstances. . . . I also must say that I think that your pastoral sense is not being used to the extent it deserves because of the limited possibilities open to you at St. Vincent's." It could be put to better use in a larger, more modern parish, the bishop suggested, although he did not wish to imply an impending move.

"I think that some decisions really should be initiated," he continued, "about the kind of future St. Vincent's has—either how it can continue as it has been in the past, or whether to become a part of something new. We have seen only recently how St. Joseph's (Lee Street) would have been an excellent spot for our involvement in the 'inner harbor project.' Maybe St. Vincent's could play such a role in some other plan. It would be a shame if we missed that kind of opportunity again."[34]

Finally there was the bishop's letter to the people of the parish itself. "I am sure you will agree with me when I say that Father Stroup, your pastor, is doing a good job," he wrote. "I think Father Stroup has tried to provide leadership and understanding of the issues facing people in today's world and today's Church. Still he feels very inadequate to the many needs simply because he is attempting to manage the parish entirely alone. And I would like to tell him, and you, that he will get another man soon, but honesty prevents me from making that kind of promise."

"I do think," the bishop continued, "that St. Vincent's may be coming to a crossroads in its venerable history—whether to continue as it has been these last 40–50 years, or whether to become something different in a changing neighborhood and community." Was it possible, he asked, for the parish to stay the same? "As you already know, I think the answer is 'no'—that the parish must change and make adjustments." The city's plans for the area could spell revitalization for the parish. "But none of us has the crystal ball needed to know about the future." The archdiocese would have to make "hard decisions" about five parishes in downtown Baltimore, the bishop warned.[35] He did not have to say that St. Vincent's was one of them.

THE END OF ANOTHER ERA

Bishop Gossman's assessment of physical and fiscal decline was fairly accurate, and the trend continued in Father Stroup's remaining years at St. Vincent's. A parish count of 875 in 1966 would fall to 330 in 1972, and the total income from $102,491 to $59,532. Ed Stroup was quite prepared to recognize his inability to devise and launch the new and exciting programs the bishop thought the parish needed. He had tried to revive the St. Vincent de Paul Society in 1967. It did not last a year. Instead he saw himself phasing out services of long standing. With the Christmas edition of "St. Vincent's Notebook" of 1969 a twenty-seven-year tradition ended but not before it had carried Father Martin's history of the parish in ten installments. The seminarians stopped coming for the folk mass and other activities soon after their removal from Paca Street in 1969, and the Sisters from the Martin de Porres Center for the catechetics classes in 1970.

Even more was the end of an era marked at the opening of 1971. "In the midst of general revelry," the *Sun* reported, "a somewhat poignant trio gathered at 2:30 A.M. New Year's Day in the sanctuary of St. Vincent de Paul Church." The three were the pastor and the night foremen of the composing rooms of the *Sunpapers* and *News American*. They had come together to record the demise of the printers' mass. After 1968 attendance had dwindled to an average of thirty to fifty at most. There was no mass this New Year's. Instead the three reminisced. "It was a right touching thing," said the foreman of the *Sun*. "I feel that something has really gone out of my life," added the foreman of the *News American*.[36]

No longer able to launch ambitious programs but reluctant to leave St.

Vincent's, Ed Stroup continued to conduct the "holding operation" for two years and more after the episcopal visitation. In 1973 a member of the personnel board of the archdiocese came to St. Vincent's to ask if he would accept the pastorship of a larger and more modern parish, St. Rita's in Dundalk. He accepted. Three years later he would enroll at the Catholic University for an "educational update" on the postconciliar church. After pastorates in two growing parishes in Anne Arundel County, he would in 1981 accept a chaplaincy at Greater Baltimore Medical Center while acting as liaison between the archdiocese and its retired priests. In the summer of 1990 he himself would retire.[37]

The triumphs and tribulations of Edmond Stroup in the years after Vatican II were typical of many priests who devoted themselves to the problems of the inner city. "They fought racism in themselves and others, worked for adequate housing and employment for minorities and the underprivileged, and carried the Catholic social gospel to the slums." They "picketed, rallied, and applauded radical prophets such as the Berrigan brothers."[38]

This was certainly true of Ed Stroup before the riots. Then came the concomitants of the burnout that afflicted many of the inner-city priests of the early 1970s, problems that had before "escaped serious analysis, including alcoholism and loneliness."[39] In retrospect both Ed Stroup and Joe Wenderoth were prepared to admit that they had imbibed too freely in these turbulent years, and Ed, who had always considered himself something of "a loner," felt even more the emptiness of the rectory with the departure of his associate and suspension of a number of activities.

There was also a degree of that disenchantment that troubled many of the active priests. Ed felt deeply the apparent lack of appreciation for what he was trying to do, especially for the blacks. He was hurt by the implications of Father Clements that he was not doing enough. He was hurt by the obscenities hurled at him by the black teenagers. He was disheartened by the chancery's silence at critical moments when advice and support were sorely needed, especially at the time of the riots, the arrest of his associate, and the acts of vandalism at the cemetery.

Edmond Stroup, however, was in many ways the ideal pastor for a parish in transition in a revolutionary age. He was a man devoted to healthy traditions, yet open to, even eager, in the first half of his pastorate, to seize upon new ideas. Somehow he was able to blend them well. Soft-spoken, gentlemanly, he was attentive to white and black, rich and poor. He was just enough of an organizer to get things done but equally disposed to give associate, seminarians, sisters, and lay volunteers a long leash. He did most of the "dirty work" himself. And he could usually be found in the rectory when the doorbell or telephone rang.

Yet he admits to having stayed longer than he should have at St. Vincent's. The archdiocese was anxious to place the parish under a younger man, one with the energy and imagination needed to give sail once more to the unsinkable parish on Front Street.

CHURCH
1973–

R ev. Richard Thomas Lawrence arrived at St. Vincent's the third week of June in 1973 with a directive from the archdiocese to study the possibility of closing the parish. This option he never seriously entertained. When asked if he would accept the parish, according to his own reckoning he took twelve seconds to decide. Well acquainted with its history from his work on the Urban Commission, he thought to himself, "They are my kind of folks. It would be fun." He has never regretted the decision.[1]

THE THIRTEENTH PASTOR

At age 30 and only five years ordained, however, Dick Lawrence was thought by the personnel board to be too young to assume the full burdens of canonical pastor, even administrator. So he arrived at Front Street with the less-than-impressive title of temporary administrator. Two years later the parish council would conclude that he had grown sufficiently in office to be voted in as pastor. The archbishop would confirm the council's decision.

The sixth of thirteen pastors to have been born in Baltimore grew up in the suburbs, in St. Charles Parish, Pikesville. After four years at Loyola High School and two at Loyola College, he entered the seminary at Paca Street, where Fr. Gene Walsh was still the "major guru." As a seminarian he participated in the inner-city programs. Ordained in 1968, he spent five years at Blessed Sacrament Parish on Old York Road while working his way up the chain of command at the Urban Commission.

SETTING GOALS

The first task the latest incumbent set for himself at St. Vincent's was a study of the parish demographics.[2] It lay in the second poorest census tract of Baltimore. It was also the youngest, two-thirds of its population being under 16. It contained over half of the high-rise public housing in the city; 85 percent of its residents subsisted on "transfer dependency" benefits; 85 percent lived in households headed by women. The post office, covering an area two blocks by three, had gobbled up all but two of the remaining single-owner homes of the parish, one of them the rectory. On work days a fair amount of bustle enlivened "Corned Beef Row" on Lombard, and there was some commercial activity on Baltimore, Fayette, and Gay streets, but the rest, aside from public housing, was pocked by silent warehouses and vacant buildings. The parish could boast, nevertheless, 20 percent of the historic sites the city would place on the National Register. Redevelopment had not yet touched it. It was waiting for something to happen.

As important as were the needs of the neighborhood, however, those of the parish came first. With his two corporators, positions mandated by the archdiocese for legal reasons, the new administrator proposed three goals to the parishioners: (1) to employ a coordinator of religious education, (2) to create a parish council, and (3) to establish a historic trust fund.[3] The approval was unanimous.

THE PARISH COUNCIL

Convinced that declericalization was the paramount challenge to the postconciliar church, Dick Lawrence saw as the most important of the three goals the creation of the parish council. "I came here," he admits, "trying to see how many wanted to seize how much power and how little work I could get away with." In his covering letter for the first annual report of the parish, issued September 1974, he could boast, "Our Council has been elected, our Constitution ratified, our Committees established, and the work has begun in earnest: we have stepped into collegial government."[4] Rosemarie Malinowski, an English teacher who played a key role in drafting the constitution, was elected the first president of the council.

All parish committees and organizations were created by and made responsible to the parish council. Each "liturgical community" elected members proportionate to its number for a two-year term. Attendance at the different masses was fairly constant. The parish council met every month except July and August. All parishioners were invited to attend. A member of the council would later tell the pastor that she knew it had come of age when it voted him down.

In the first annual report the administrator announced that two and a half of the original three goals had been realized. In addition to the creation of a parish council, the coordinator of religious education, Sr. Nancy Jean Class, SFCC, had already developed a successful catechetics program, and lawyers had completed the initial draft for the historic trust. Also appended were the reports of the original committees created by the council: those on the liturgy, community service, education, and administration. Other committees would be added as the need arose.

The parishioners themselves reported on their administrator:

> At the parish, we've found a man who delivers well-rounded sermons and has a gigantic capacity for remembering details. Among his attitudes that have had the strongest impact are: every meeting of people is a celebration; the Church can be an inspiration and a center for artistic and cultural development; and every Christian has a ministry to define and perform.
>
> Being an administrator can be rather mechanical. We're delighted Dick's decided on a pastoral role.

THE HISTORIC TRUST

By 1973 the cost of repairs and improvements had begun to nibble away at the reserve on deposit at the archdiocesan chancery. The historic trust was created to provide a substantial endowment for the maintenance of the church, but it was also a stratagem to assure its survival. On February 12, 1974, St. Vincent's was placed on the National Register of Historic Places, rendering it next to impossible for civil authorities to bulldoze it out of existence in the name of redevelopment. On August 12, 1974, the Historic Trust Fund itself was officially created. Survival was doubly assured because church authorities were seldom known to surrender endowments.

A campaign for an initial $50,000 was launched to match a $50,000 grant by the Jacob and Annita France and Robert G. and Anne Merrick Grant foundations. In 1983 there was a campaign for $100,000, the result of matching grants from the France and Merrick foundations and Henry Knott, to which the A. S. Abell Foundation added $25,000 for the maintenance of the exterior of the church. A third campaign for $220,000 was

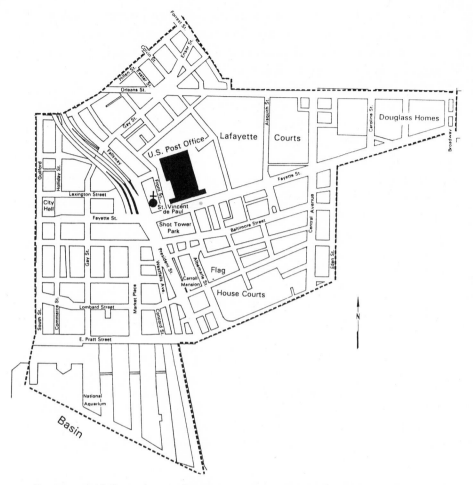

Present parish boundaries of St. Vincent de Paul with a configuration of city streets quite different from that of a century before. JAMES DILISIO

conducted in anticipation of a thoroughgoing renovation of the church building, the gift of the people of St. Vincent's to its home on its 150th birthday. By that time the trust fund itself could boast over half a million dollars.

REVENUES AND EXPENDITURES

Occasionally finances bordered on the precarious but the parishioners kept the budget from slipping into bankruptcy. "Stewardship [financial support] is high here," the parish's 1985 directory boasted, "partially because we don't talk a lot about it. The [Administration] Committee makes an annual report and appeal, and the offertory is reported along with the attendance in the bulletin every week. That's all. No envelopes. No visits. No sermons. No hassle." There were never, in fact, any envelopes at St. Vincent's.

In the 1970s there had been worrisome deficits. For 1974–75, for example, parish income totaled $61,884 and parish expenses $65,136.[5] A pep talk on the part of the president of the parish council and chairperson of the administration committee was enough to do the trick. By 1990 parish revenues at $158,188 were well ahead of parish expenses at $144,135. Even with inflation taken into account it was an impressive increase.

Old parishes, the parishioners discovered, demanded an inordinate number of extraordinary expenditures for maintenance and repair. Such expenditures at St. Vincent's would not only deplete the $105,000 on deposit with the archdiocese in 1973 but also would necessitate drives, borrowings, and eventually drawing upon the historic trust. To pay the $102,000 cost of a new roof and renovation of the tower in 1978–80, $60,000 was borrowed from the deposit, $30,000 obtained from a grant by the National Park Service, and the rest acquired from a "Raise the Roof" campaign. In 1980 the archdiocese added a $9,000 subsidy to the $14,000 taken from the deposit to clean up the cemetery, which remained a problem.[6] From various sources came needed funding for furnace conversion, repair of the bridge between the church and rectory, and termite control. In 1987 the parish purchased the ground at its northern edge from the city for $70,380 in order to expand the parking lot, $60,000 of it borrowed from the archdiocese. And so it went.

The most ambitious undertaking of the little community on Front Street was the renovation of its church building for the sesquicentennial celebration in 1991 at a cost of $388,000. As early as 1983 the Committee on Art and Architecture, inspired by a parish task force on the liturgy mandated by the Catholic bishops, was created to do long-range planning. Its work will be detailed in part 2.

LITURGICAL CRAFTSMANSHIP

Much of the work done under the thirteenth pastor represented an advancement of the legacies of his predecessors, especially in the liturgy, religious education, and community service. Its liturgy was the feature for which the parish remained best known. While the parish council, the

1985 directory explained, "is the brain of our community, Liturgy is its heart." The vivacity of Father Stroup's earlier years was revived. In 1974 the parish's music director, cantor, and choir were all invited to lead the archdiocesan celebration of welcome for the new archbishop, William D. Borders. In 1981 St. Vincent's was one of the parishes chosen by the American bishops to give input on the liturgy.

The liturgical committee was perhaps the hardest working of the committees. The 9:30 mass continued to be the main event of the liturgical week. It never succumbed to standardization. The remarkably creative Sunday liturgies of the mid-1970s, based on a series of themes, proved as attractive as the folk masses of the 1960s. The energy demanded, however, took its toll upon the designers, who by the late 1970s sought inspiration more often from the Lectionary, the official cycle of readings. The thematic approach was never entirely abandoned. In the 1980s the parish was visited by such "saints" as Thomas More, Thomas à Becket, Oscar Romero, Dorothy Day, and Catherine of Siena, who engaged pastor and congregation in dialogue.

There were movies, slides, sometimes liturgical drama, such as the inquisitor's interrogation of Christ from *The Brothers Karamazov* or a scene from Graham Greene's *The Potting Shed*. For its liturgical music and drama the parish was never wanting for genuine talent and enthusiastic volunteers. George Quickly left to join the Jesuits and Joe Organ retired as choir director in 1980, but Skip Sanders returned to direct the folk mass. Brahms and Mozart, however, continued to vie with *Jesus Christ Superstar* or *Godspell*. The music commanded an array of talent: organist, pianist, flautist, drummer, guitarist, and so on. A fine set of bells was unwrapped for special events. An attempt to introduce a gospel choir will be considered later. Several times a year there was a children's mass in which the younger members of the parish acted out the readings. For most Sundays, however, the children had their separate liturgy of the word.

The Holy Week liturgies and events remained the most exciting of the year. A true seder meal was introduced in 1972. In 1990 the pastor overcame some skepticism among his parishioners to re-create an ancient tradition, the all-night Easter vigil—from 10:30 P.M. until the 9:30 A.M. mass.

RELIGIOUS EDUCATION

A low-key intellectual, Dick Lawrence encouraged the development of programs that provided firm foundations in scripture, theology, and spirituality. "Ongoing Christian formation" found expression in seminars and workshops on topics ranging from biblical criticism to child-rearing to the impact of personality types on spirituality. Two of the best attended were those on Edward Schillebeeckx's *Jesus* and Richard McBrien's *Catholicism.* The parish itself assumed the cost of the books for as many as enrolled.

The CCD program that Sister Nancy Jean designed to attract neighborhood children was never a great success. Almost three-fourths were from outside the parish. In 1980 the CCD was replaced with a catechetical program called "Faith, Fun, Fellowship" that brought the children together one Saturday a month and a full week in the summer. In 1980 Linda Houck succeeded Sister Nancy Jean. Bursting with ideas, she introduced *Together Sharing Christ,* a packet issued monthly the first year and every other month thereafter. It contained articles on adult growth, texts for home liturgies, tips for the religious education of younger members of the family, and parish news. Linda also organized a retreat program. In the fall was a one-day retreat for adults only. Better attended, drawing eighty to a hundred, or a quarter of the parish, was the weekend retreat in the late spring. An extended-family campout with singing, praying, playing, and sharing, it was one of the high points of the year for the people of St. Vincent's.

When Linda married and retired as director in 1984, Sr. Joy Milos took her place. When she left a year later, it proved increasingly difficult to find a full-time director. The position was split. While Anne Gibson, director of religious education for children, would work effectively with the growing number of parish youngsters until the present, the position of director of religious education for adults would be filled in succession by Sandra Mize, Nancy Cavadini, Shannon Little, Br. John Bardo, CFX, and Helen Scimeca.

COMMUNITY SERVICE

The committee on community service, later community planning, was formed to address the needs of the permanent residents of the parish. Direct aid, or emergency relief, continued as in the days of Fathers Stroup and Wenderoth with vouchers for food, or food itself, now purchased from the Maryland Food Bank, and clothing distribution once a week, three items per customer. One of the first projects the committee devised was a program of instruction to prepare people living within the parish to take the Civil Service exam for employment at the new post office that loomed like a fortress in front of the church. Of the 150 who took the course, 52 passed. All 52 eventually moved from the projects.

In 1976 the parish council approved the withdrawal of $25,000 from the archdiocesan deposit to purchase three adjoining row houses on Exeter Street as part of the East End Hotel, Inc., a detoxification center, in order to keep it afloat. In 1985, however, when the center moved to another part of the city, the property was sold for a tidy profit.[7]

JONESTOWN PLANNING COUNCIL

From the start the committee on community service, and the parish as a whole, found itself increasingly involved in neighborhood planning and institution building. The parish environs were, as the pastor expressed it, like "a hole in the doughnut," an area that ran from the Falls-way to Central Avenue and from Orleans to Pratt Street, surrounded by neighborhood associations but with none of its own. To fill this need the Jonestown Planning Council was incorporated on March 4, 1975.[8] Head-quartered at St. Vincent's, its chairman of the board was president of the parish council and its executive director and later president, Rev. Richard Lawrence, but representatives of the residential and business communities were also on the board and actively involved.

The first order of business was a survey to determine the needs of the neighborhood. Gallup of Princeton was hired to design a questionnaire. In the summer of 1975 trained interviewers, all residents of the projects, visited over 500 randomly chosen households. The data was programmed by the Johns Hopkins University Center for Metropolitan Planning and Research, and the "Jonestown Needs Survey" was ready for an intensive planning session in the spring of 1976. A mix of about thirty professionals and ordinary residents focused on the three principal goals: (1) residential development, (2) commercial development, and (3) historic preservation. It was obvious that the most immediate need was in the area of residential development, a day-care center.

Incorporated November 12, 1981, the Jonestown Day Care Center was a private, nonprofit corporation with both members of the parish and community leaders on the board.[9] Federal Community Block Grants of over three-quarters of a million dollars financed the construction of a building and "tot lot" on South High Street in 1982 that were leased to the Center by the city for $1.00 a year. By 1991 it accommodated 107 chil-

dren, most under 6. That year a new addition provided one more class-
room for preschool day care and another for "latch-key kids" after school.
An adult education program was also begun.

The most important and successful activity dictated by the second of
the three goals of the Jonestown Planning Council, that of commercial
development, was the pioneering shopsteading program it launched. Approved by the mayor's office in 1977, it had within a few years endowed a
dozen vacant buildings with small-scale businesses.

In the matter of historic preservation, the third goal, the Jonestown
Planning Council was recognized as the official voice of the neighborhood at public hearings. One of the most important of these concerned
the extension of Interstate 83, at which the council's voice weighed heavily in the matter of preserving not only the neighborhood's architectural
treasures but the neighborhood itself. This will be considered later.

PEACE AND JUSTICE

Although the Peace and Justice Committee was not created until 1984,
issues of war and peace and of social justice continued to surface as in the
days of Father Stroup. Early in Father Lawrence's pastorate, Cardinal Shehan urged the priests of the archdiocese to attend an address delivered
from the pulpit of St. Vincent's by Cesar Chavez and to support his call
for a boycott of farm produce that was the result of exploitation. Later, at
the time of a referendum on gun control, three local TV stations descended on St. Vincent's to cover a homily on the subject.

Seminars, lectures, special liturgies, and many pages of *Together Sharing
Christ* were devoted to particular issues in such parts of the world as
Lithuania, South Africa, and Central America. The situation in El Sal-
vador and Nicaragua brought about the creation of the Peace and Justice
Committee, but it also evoked the most serious cleavage within the
parish community.

The possibility of adopting a sister parish in El Salvador was raised in
the spring of 1985. One of the most outspoken proponents of the Sandi-
nistas, however, brought about the adoption of a parish in Nicaragua in
1986, San Juan de Limay. Some parishioners asked if this decision was au-
thorized by the parish council. Some expressed annoyance at the use of
announcement time for what seemed to many political statements. A
"town meeting" was called by the parish council president, Diego
Merida, a fortunate choice at the time, to clear the air and a liturgy of rec-

onciliation was held. San Juan de Limay remained the sister parish of St. Vincent de Paul, and the parish funded an exchange of visits, whose effectiveness was somewhat tempered by mild to moderate cases of culture shock on both sides.

THE CHURCH AT LARGE

Few parishes could probably match St. Vincent's in its extraparochial involvement with the church at large. Its members devoted nearly as much time to archdiocesan and world concerns as to those of the parish and the neighborhood. At the archdiocesan level St. Vincent's was the parish that played the most visible and vocal role in area councils created by the archdiocese. St. Vincent's contributed more than its share to archdiocesan posts. No other parish could match its response to requests for input for archdiocesan, national, or Vatican statements.

Having drafted a mission statement of its own (see appendix C), it submitted a draft for an archdiocesan statement. St. Vincent's contributions to the constitution of the Archdiocesan Pastoral Council won commendation for its "continued leadership and vision for the collegial structures of our Archdiocese."[10] Archbishop Borders was particularly pleased with the input of St. Vincent's in 1987 for an important pastoral letter on ministry. For this letter a questionnaire had been devised at St. Vincent's and answered by all parishioners. Among other things, it revealed that 69 percent of the parish favored the ordination of women.

Multipage commentaries were mailed from St. Vincent's in response to the American bishops' requests for input on their pastoral letters on war, the domestic economy, and women. The last mentioned was in part responsible for the creation of the last (to date) of its parish committees, that on women in ministry. The parish did not, of course, sit and wait for invitations. Quite frequently, it volunteered its opinions to the proper bodies—the archbishop, the apostolic delegate, the pope—on such matters as appropriate wording in the liturgy and women as eucharistic ministers. Sometimes it was thanked for the gratuitous advice, more often not.

FUN AND GAMES

In striking contrast to the more serious concerns and activities at St. Vincent's were its antic moments. "But, boy," ended the introduction to

Rev. Richard T. Lawrence (b. 1942), thirteenth and present pastor, in the tradition of a long line of gifted, imaginative, and energetic pastors, presides over an evolving parish.   SUNPAPERS

its 1991 directory, "do we have fun trying to be disciples." The social events committee was almost as active as the liturgy committee, planning a variety of parish events, among them the annual picnic, flea market, crab feast, oyster roast, spaghetti dinner, raffle, Halloween dance, and Christmas dance. Even the socializing after the 9:30 mass, with children darting back and forth in the undercroft, took on a festive air each Sunday. In 1977 the parish also introduced a "Street People's Party" for the homeless at Christmas.

In September 1977, for the Feast of St. Vincent, the committee designed a three-day homecoming festival with dance, special liturgy, and street fair.[11] One of the attractions, called "Dunk the Monk," gave parishioners their chance "to get even with the pastor for a year of bad jokes."

After eight years the planners and volunteers decided that it had become more work than fun, and the festival was voted into the parish memory book.

THE PASTOR'S OTHER LIFE

In addition to the indispensable liturgical, sacramental, and administrative functions he performed, Dick Lawrence filled admirably such other roles of pastor as catalyst, counselor, crisis manager, and public relations man. But he has worn many hats other than that of pastor, all of which have carried him well beyond the geographic and ministerial boundaries of St. Vincent's. When assigned to the parish in 1973, he continued as assistant director of the Urban Commission. In 1976 he agreed to be fiscal director of the archdiocese. At the same time, he signed up for a master's degree in business administration at Loyola College. Then in 1982 he moved over to the office of director of computer services, all the while accommodating a duodenal ulcer.

Undoubtedly the most signal service that St. Vincent's thirteenth pastor rendered the archdiocese of Baltimore was to save it from virtual bankruptcy, the reason he was asked to assume the thankless task of fiscal director. In its recounting of this role the *Baltimore Magazine* dubbed him "God's fiscal fireman," describing at the outset an incident in which he had beat out a fire in his own church.[12] The year that he accepted the position of fiscal director the deficit was, as it had been for the preceding eight years, over a million dollars. Within four years the archdiocese was $1.2 million in the black. The unassailable budget ceilings he imposed won him few friends but a number of grudging admirers. Having done the job expected of him, he resigned as fiscal director.

When Archbishop Borders, a man he came to admire, asked him to be fiscal director, he also asked him to suggest a successor for St. Vincent's. The parish, Lawrence expostulated, was the only source of emotional satisfaction he got out of life, "and I ain't giving it up." The other life has always had to play second fiddle to that of pastor.

In 1983 Father Lawrence decided to leave as full-time employee of the archdiocese to pursue a doctorate at the Catholic University of America. He continued, however, to serve on five archdiocesan bodies, for example, the archdiocesan investment committee. A seat on the board of Bishop Walsh High School in Cumberland demanded a 260-mile round trip every other month. National organizations also tapped his expertise.

Since 1978 he has been on the task force of the Financial Accounting Standards Board for nonprofit organizations. As the parliamentarian for the National Federation of Priests Councils, he coauthored a model constitution for such councils.

In 1991 he finally won his Ph.D. at the Catholic University by taking an in-house sabbatical to complete the dissertation. It was entitled "The God Image Inventory: The Development, Validation, and Standardization of a Psychometric Instrument for Research, Pastoral, and Clinical Use in Measuring the Image of God." Off and on its author has also taught courses in practical theology at St. Mary's Seminary.

OTHER RESIDENTS AT THE RECTORY

For nine years the pastor had an assistant. Charles "Chuck" Canterna had come as a deacon in 1974. He had studied for the diocese of Pittsburgh but wished to serve the poor. When told that the diocese could not afford "any more radical priests coming out of the inner city," he applied to Cardinal Shehan.[13] On November 6, 1976, he was ordained for St. Vincent's at the request of its parishioners.

Most of Chuck's waking hours in his first years at St. Vincent's were devoted to a street ministry not unlike that of Joe Wenderoth. After celebrating for a time the 11:45 A.M. mass on Sunday (the old 11:15 and 12:15 masses combined) he was allowed to introduce a 4:30 P.M. liturgy on Saturday in order to create a gospel mass to attract the African Americans living in the parish. It soon, however, became identified as a charismatic mass, attracting more whites than blacks. As the street ministry waned, the prayer community waxed. In 1980 Chuck volunteered to hold prayer services at the city jail. From this his prison ministry developed. In 1983 he resigned as assistant at St. Vincent's to serve full-time as Catholic chaplain for both the city jail and state prison.[14] The charismatic community scattered.

Chuck Canterna was not the only other resident at St. Vincent's rectory. Father Pugevicius stayed on for a time. In the spring of 1976 Bishop J. Francis Stafford, the urban vicar, took up residence at the invitation of the congregation. In a few years, however, the pastor's "tolerance for dirt," as the pastor regretfully explained, persuaded the bishop to move to tidier quarters. (And from there he would move on to Memphis as its second bishop and to Denver as its third archbishop.)

Then there were those who in daytime could be found in the rectory almost as much as the pastor. Elmore Washington, who since the days of Father Martin had made a valiant effort to keep the dirt of the parish buildings to a minimum, would in 1991, for reasons of age and ill health, all but terminate his long career as one of those unsung heroes of parochial history. Helen Jacobson and Gloria Wiedorfer, parish administrators in turn, spent long hours at the rectory. There was, and is, in fact, a constant stream of volunteers and visitors. Until a recent series of burglaries, a quarter of the city, according to the pastor's reckoning, had keys to the rectory.

PARISH PROFILE

St. Vincent de Paul of Baltimore continued its accustomed role of metropolitan parish, seeking to fill the psychic and spiritual needs of a heterogeneous and geographically dispersed community. The majority have remained middle class, but the poor find a home. It is an educated community, 16.1 being the average number of years of schooling. Perhaps 12 to 15 percent are African Americans, about half of these from within the parish boundaries, some of them middle class and some poor. (In the "Jonestown Needs Survey" it was found that of the nine churches most frequently attended by the residents of the housing projects in the parish 3.3 percent went to St. Francis Xavier, the oldest black Catholic parish in the city, and 1.3 percent went to St. Vincent's.) There is a scattering of worshipers of Hispanic and Asian origin. The community counts probably a larger number of former priests, seminarians, and religious than would the ordinary parish. In 1977 there were 233 families on the parish rolls, 49 from within the parish bounds, 184 from outside. By the year 1991 there were 321 families for a parish total of 683 souls.

The heterogeneous character of St. Vincent's is best shown by the constituency of the four weekend masses, which have remained fairly constant in the number and type of people they draw. The masses range from the innovative 9:30 A.M. liturgy that still attracts as many as the other three combined, to the more traditional 12:15 A.M. mass, where the pastor does just about everything but pass the collection basket. It draws forty to fifty, more in the summer.

Changing literary and artistic tastes have been evidenced by the liturgies, the reading fare of *Together Sharing Christ* and other parish publications, and the artwork it is willing to fund. The parish has, in fact, taken seriously the traditional role of the church as patron of the arts by com-

The sesquicentennial celebration, 1991, with Archbishop William H. Keeler and the pastor at the altar. Mayor Kurt Schmoke also attended.   CATHOLIC REVIEW

missioning a number of works of local artists and composers, all related to the liturgy. The most notable of these is the flame sculpture designed for the Easter vigil by Laura Oliphant, which occupies a prominent place in the parking lot.[15]

PARISH DYNAMICS

The people of St. Vincent de Paul during the thirteenth pastorate have taken seriously the need to develop effective working relationships. The coordinating body is, of course, the parish council. It counts elected members from the different masses; chairpersons of the standing committees, who are themselves elected to these positions; certain members of the staff, who are hired by the council; and the pastor ex officio. The parish council at St. Vincent's is, perhaps, more representative than most. The terms are short and staggered. The parish council has numbered from about fifteen to twenty—a good working number, the members have found.

The parish has been blessed with people of leadership caliber to fill the different positions. They have learned, without undue stress and strain, to

work as a team. A concept they have come to accept as a working principle is that of consensus. Talking things out, they found quite early, was
more effective than resorting to majority vote. Decisions made by consensus tended to stay made.

One of the first prickly questions the parish council had to decide was
whether to allow the gay Catholic support group called Dignity to use
the undercroft for its meetings. Sentiment for and against was fairly
evenly divided at the end of a lengthy exchange, producing an uncomfort-
able impasse, until one of the members quoted that part of the parish
mission statement characterizing St. Vincent's as a community that welcomed, among others, "the disaffected, and the exiled." Increasingly
thereafter the mission statement was invoked to create consensual agreement. A two-thirds vote, after all had had their say, came to be accepted as
a working consensus.

Sometimes when there was no clear consensus, a "town meeting" of
the entire parish was called. The first and only time to date the pastor exercised the veto allowed him by the parish constitution was when, on a
close vote, the council was ready to proceed on a matter of the renovation of the church. It was too important an action to be taken without the
support of most, he explained. A "town meeting" would also be called to
resolve a serious division of sentiment in the community, as was that occasioned by the sister parish in Nicaragua.

In 1985, at the invitation of the archdiocesan Division of Collegial Services, the parish drew upon its talented members to produce the videotape on the theory of parish councils mentioned in the introduction. This
was followed by another in 1990 entitled *Ministry of the Parish Council. Part
II: Putting It into Practice.* The second, based upon sixteen years of experience, included recommendations on size, composition, and operation.
Among the principal lessons learned and helpful hints provided were
those on how to avoid "spinning wheels around procedural maypoles,"
"how to keep from getting mired in such trivia as how many slices to cut
from a pizza," and "how to face down the tyranny of the minority." The
council, it insisted, was the policymaking body, which must learn to leave
all details to the standing and ad hoc committees. The second videotape
sold as well as the first.

THE CHANGING NEIGHBORHOOD

The parishioners of St. Vincent's had come to accept the inevitability
of change. The neighborhood itself had been the focus of civic debate

even before the word "renewal" was heard. It began in the late 1940s with plans for what came to be called the Jones Falls Expressway (Interstate 83) and was intensified by the designs of the 1960s to link the interstates that claimed Baltimore as their terminus (I-70 and I-83) or as one of its principal way stations (I-95). In 1968 the bright vision of an "urban design concept team" provoked more than mild disapproval. Plans to carry I-83 through southeast Baltimore came to a halt with the decision in 1983 to end the Jones Falls Expressway at the rear of St. Vincent's. At the interminable hearings, one of which he described as "the seventh annual final hearing," Rev. Richard Lawrence, as spokesman for the Jonestown Planning Council, recommended a boulevard-type facility with a pedestrian mall that would link the historic sites through lower Jonestown in place of the extension of I-83. The council had to settle for half a loaf.*

The area in question nevertheless became a part of the Baltimore renaissance that began with Harborplace and radiated east, west, and south, in the process giving such neighborhoods as Little Italy a new lease on life. The impact on Jonestown was less dramatic, but the drama is still being played out. The Shot Tower, 9 Front Street, and the Caton-Carroll Mansion have all been placed in attractive settings for an increasing number of visitors. A subway station just down the block from the church is under construction. Scarlett Place, a combination of high-rise condominiums and offices four blocks farther down, suggests the kind of redevelopment that may perhaps claim the projects in the parish, especially the Flag House Courts. The Jonestown Planning Committee has gone on record, however, as being opposed to displacement of their occupants without providing appropriate housing.[16] The parish, it is clear, is on the threshold of still another era.

THE EVOLVING PARISH

Every major demographic and ecological change that St. Vincent de Paul Parish had experienced had caused its people to redefine themselves as a community. In the past the process had been an unconscious one, revealed only in such actions as the renovations of their home. But in the postconciliar years it had become increasingly a self-conscious analysis. In 1983 the parish conducted an exercise in self-identity called "Reflections on Parish Life." The liturgy was placed by all at the center of parish life and a sense of community was cited almost as often as a clearly identifying characteristic. "There is a reaching out—and friendliness—involvement—closeness in the celebration of the Mass," one of the parishioners summed it up. One, however, wrote:

> St. V's is a church that never dies. There is always thinking and rethinking going on about the meaning of life in all its aspects, about how God relates to life and to my life in particular. It's a church that's not afraid to change or try something new, or to challenge *me* to change or try something new. Conversely, it's a church where I feel my contribution will help to change and renew not only St. V's, but also the Church as a whole. . . .

The process of rethinking what it meant to be a church was most palpable in the renovation of the church building, the home, that will be described in part 2, when the parishioners themselves were required to assume the role of architect.

By the time of the celebration of their sesquicentennial the parishioners had come to see themselves as church. No longer a second parish, no longer even a metropolitan parish with special attractions, St. Vincent's was a community that people joined to experience a genuine sense of being church. They were truly the "People of God," sharing in the most vital way at the lowest institutional level the life of what had for so long been called parish.

PART TWO

THEIR HOME

Panoramic view of St. Vincent's and the downtown skyline with City Hall to
the right, 1963.   SUNPAPERS

A rchitecture combines the functional requirements of building with the aesthetic requirements of art. Building designers manipulate scale, mass, proportion, plan, materials, and ornamentation to enclose and direct the use of space and to achieve an architectural image. The architectural image of a building reflects its use through building type and aesthetics through architectural style. Influenced by the philosophies and tastes of the culture that produces them, building designs evolve over time in response to changes in fashion, technology, and use. The architectural image of a building allows us to quickly classify it by functional type. Type distinguishes the design of dwellings from those of churches, or schools, or city halls. A building's style reflects its associations with a specific architectural fashion, historical periods, economic status, and the public image desired by the users.

The examination of the changes to St. Vincent de Paul Church over time offers a unique opportunity to examine the spatial priorities, the design preferences, and the public image that this parish has sought to project. This analysis is made more meaningful because St. Vincent's has retained its original use and institutional association. This stability has limited the number of variables that could affect the building's architectural program. St. Vincent de Paul Church, therefore, offers a potential model to which other churches erected by the archdiocese of Baltimore may be compared.

Three tasks were involved in completing this architectural study. First, empirical data pertaining to the building were amassed. The building itself served as the primary document in this effort; ongoing renovation revealed physical evidence of past work. This phase of the study was supplemented with archival research in order to develop a building chronology for the structure, and to create a framework for addressing such questions as who built what, for whom, and when. The second task involved placing the building within its historical and architectural context. Research conducted during this stage sought to identify general historical trends that had influenced the design and construction of the building. Particular emphasis was placed on relating the design of St. Vincent's to the broader patterns of ecclesiastical architecture in Baltimore. The third task involved the analysis of the design of the church in order to identify and to understand the significance of the design choices made by the parish during each of the four episodes of construction and renovation. The results of the research and data analyses are presented in part 2.

THE NEOCLASSICAL
AESTHETIC

1840–1841

A Baltimore landmark for over 150 years, St. Vincent de Paul Church was constructed in 1840–41. St. Vincent de Paul was the seventh Roman Catholic parish established in the city of Baltimore.[1] The design of the church integrates the architectural style characteristic of Federal period church design with the Greek Revival style that became popular during the second quarter of the nineteenth century. The church's historical pattern of construction, renovation, and rehabilitation reflects the evolution of Baltimore's urban landscape, and also documents the changing demographics, priorities, and architectural tastes of St. Vincent's Parish.

The significance of St. Vincent de Paul Church to the architectural and historical development of Baltimore City and to the state of Maryland was recognized in February 1974 when the building was listed on the National Register of Historic Places. This designation by the U.S. Department of the Interior documented the architectural significance of the building and officially recognized the structure as worthy of preservation.[2]

Architecture is a dynamic process whose end product represents the tangible expression of functional and aesthetic objectives through the choice and arrangement of materials, structure, and ornamentation.[3] Intended use, architectural tastes and fashion, construction budgets, building technology, and ecclesiastical and social values all influenced the original appearance of St. Vincent's. Moreover, buildings with a long history of active service, such as St. Vincent de Paul, frequently were modified to accommodate changes over time. Thus, the history of a building's modifi-

St. Vincent de Paul Church has been a Baltimore landmark since its construction in 1840–41.   HARRIET WISE, 1994

cations often is as historically and architecturally significant as the structure's original design. These changes provide insights into the practical and aesthetic concerns of the building's occupants over time.

Churches like St. Vincent de Paul were symbols of prestige and status for their congregations. The site was located immediately adjoining the east side of Jones Falls, and the first parishioners represented the affluent residents in the area. The census of 1840 for Baltimore's Ward 5, which included the urban community in the vicinity of the church, suggests that most residents of the neighborhood were of English and Irish extraction. A random sample of 80 of the 1,350 households recorded in the ward revealed that the average household had six members. Of the 469 persons represented in the sample, 418 (89 percent) were recorded as "free white persons," 27 (6 percent) were identified as "free colored persons," and 24 (5 percent) persons were recorded as "slaves." Three households, containing a total of 13 individuals, were recorded as "free colored persons," while the remaining African-American residents were identified as part of "free white" households. The majority of the employed individuals represented in the approximate 6 percent sample of the ward worked in commerce, manufacturing, and trades. In the neighborhood, the majority of male residents over the age of 15 were between 20 and 30 years of age.[4]

Nineteenth-century maps suggest that the site on which St. Vincent's was constructed was located in an area of mixed residential and commercial development. Low-scale residential dwellings lined North Front Street, while commercial establishments were concentrated at the intersection of East Fayette Street. Most of the 2½- to 3-story dwellings adopted the attenuated ground plans required to accommodate Baltimore's long, narrow urban lots. Dwellings fronted immediately on the street, as was characteristic of Baltimore residential development of the period. Most of the structures shared common party walls. The combination of these characteristics produced an architecturally unified streetscape.

The church originally was conceived as part of an urban complex by the St. Vincent of Paul Benevolent Association, a group organized in 1840. Plans for the complex initially included a church, an orphanage, and a school.

The cornerstone for the new church was laid on May 21, 1840, by Archbishop Samuel Eccleston. The new church could accommodate 2,000 parishioners; the original cost of construction was $61,502.91.[5] Applying commodity price index numbers for the years 1840 and 1991, the cost of building an equivalent church today would be at least $963,135.57. More-over, even that figure probably is low. While commodity price indices re-flect general prices and provide an approximate conversion factor to de-termine the contemporary money values for historical buildings, they do not reflect increases in specific building costs that exceeded the average level of prices between those years.[6] In addition, this conversion does not account for such contemporary requirements as heating, cooling, plumb-ing, electricity, and life-safety considerations.

ARCHITECTURAL CONTEXT: TRADITIONS IN CHURCH DESIGN

The classical design developed for St. Vincent de Paul integrated ele-ments from the Georgian or Federal (1700–1780) and Greek Revival (1825–60) architectural styles. The original building incorporated a plan and a tower associated with the forms popular during the Federal period, but utilized the structural massing, proportion, and ornamentation fre-quently associated with the Greek Revival architectural style. Stylistic designations in architectural history, such as Georgian and Greek Revival, are used to classify buildings constructed during the same historical pe-riod that possess similar character-defining features, including scale, proportion, massing, materials, and ornamentation (see the glossary). A collection of buildings with common design features represents an archi-tectural style or fashion.

Both the Federal and Greek Revival styles were manifestations of a larger Neoclassical movement that extended from the mid-eighteenth to the mid-nineteenth century. Neoclassicism, an international architectural reform movement that developed in reaction to the earlier highly orna-mented Baroque and Rococo styles, emphasized principles found in Greek and Roman art and architecture, and adopted a design philosophy based on the laws of nature and reason. Baltimore City was noted for the quality of its Neoclassical design, and provides numerous examples of Neoclassical buildings executed by nationally influential practitioners in the movement, including Maximilien Godefroy (c. 1765–c. 1845), Ben-jamin Henry Latrobe (1764–1820), and Robert Mills (1781–1855).

Although the Roman basilica form was the ancestral prototype for the plan of St. Vincent de Paul, influences can be found in European and American traditions of ecclesiastical architecture. Eighteenth- and early nineteenth-century American church architecture continued the tradi-tion of Georgian design that dominated English building throughout the

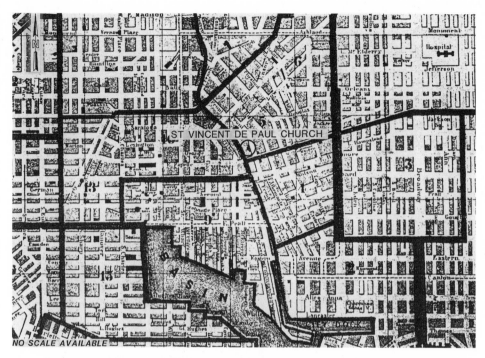

NO SCALE AVAILABLE

William Sides's map of Baltimore, published by Richard Matchett in 1852, depicts church location in Ward 5.

eighteenth century and was transmitted to North America through travelers, craftsmen, and a series of architectural pattern books that proliferated throughout the eighteenth and nineteenth centuries. European designs were adapted and modified by carpenters and avocational architects to meet the demands of their particular building programs. As a result, regional variations and adaptations in design and ornamentation developed in North America.

The combination of Georgian and Greek Revival styles integrated in St. Vincent de Paul produced a design rooted firmly in Baltimore's past. The building illustrated an architectural aesthetic that contrasted with the Gothic or pure Greek Revival styles that were gaining popularity during the second quarter of the nineteenth century. These later styles can be found in other Baltimore Roman Catholic churches of the period.

The original design of St. Vincent de Paul Church is conservative and consistent with Baltimore's architectural tradition. Fr. John B. Gildea, often credited as the architect of St. Vincent de Paul, and the church's first pastor, was a Baltimore native who undoubtedly was familiar with the pattern of Baltimore building as well as the design of its prominent edifices.

Baltimore's nineteenth-century architecture, as a whole, was characterized by its classical and conservative integration of plan and geometry and by its minimal ornamentation. The city's building stock, dominated by low-scale brick buildings, was skillfully designed, well crafted, and mannerist in design approach. Baltimore's unique architectural character was defined by an economic classical interplay of scale, mass, and proportion; the interior spaces of these buildings were complex geometric volumes enlivened by subtle and delicate detail.

Baltimore's tradition of ecclesiastical architecture can be traced to the second quarter of the eighteenth century. New England and mid-Atlantic ecclesiastical designs, as well as regional Tidewater examples, exerted an influence on early Baltimore church building design. The earliest examples, such as St. Paul's Episcopal Church (1730), were simple structures that adopted domestic scales and functional designs. St. Paul's Church, attributed to Thomas Hartwell, was a modest rectangular brick building that measured 23 feet by 50 feet and terminated in a gable roof. The building included entrances on both its lateral and longitudinal elevations and was similar to early churches surviving throughout Maryland.[7] A design of similar domestic scale and proportions was used in St. Peter's Pro-Cathedral (c. 1770).

The influence of the meetinghouse form on eighteenth-century Baltimore church architecture has been noted in discussions of the First Presbyterian Church (1789–1853).[8] The meetinghouse form is characterized by its longitudinal plan, gable-end portico, and gable-end entry. Simple interiors are accented by galleries. Ground plans are defined by aisles formed by box pews; pulpits are located at the end of the building opposite the main entrance.

The vehicle by which the meetinghouse form was introduced to Baltimore probably combined architectural traditions and ideas transmitted through architectural pattern books. Architectural pattern books were contained in the collections of such eighteenth-century Baltimore institutions as the Baltimore Library Company, founded by Archbishop John Carroll; they also were present in many private libraries throughout the Chesapeake and Tidewater regions. However, investigation of surviving librarian ledgers in the collection of the Maryland Historical Society have failed to connect Father Gildea with specific titles.

Architectural pattern books were employed widely for designs during the first quarter of the nineteenth century. As a profession, architecture was in its infancy in the United States at that time; local craftsmen or avocational designers frequently developed the plans for all but the most ambitious structures. The geometry and theory underlying architectural design were studied widely, and were applied by interested laymen prior to the development of architecture as a specialized field. The architectural pattern books of the period provided both sample building plans and the geometric formulas and specifications for executing elaborate ornamentation. The text accompanying these richly illustrated manuals encouraged readers to adapt designs to meet their own specific architectural requirements. The books provided scenarios for adjusting the size and proportion of various building plans while retaining their overall design balance.

Two period pattern books in circulation at the time of the construction of St. Vincent de Paul contain designs bearing similarities to the church. Both pattern books were written by Asher Benjamin (1773–1845), a New England carpenter-architect and a prolific writer. *The American Builder's Companion* (1806) was published in six editions, the last of which appeared in 1827. Plates K and L of this book depict designs for the construction of a church utilizing a Greek Revival core and incorporating many elements similar to those found in St. Vincent de Paul. A courthouse design illustrated in the volume includes a single-stage domed spire similar in plan to that for the lower stages of the St. Vincent's spire. The second book, *The Builder's Guide* (1839), includes designs for interior fixtures, such as pews.

Previous studies of St. Vincent de Paul Church have noted the similarity between its ornamentation and the work of John Hall.[9] Hall, a draftsman and cabinetmaker-turned-architect, was listed in Baltimore City directories from 1835 to 1850. The U.S. census for 1850 identifies Hall as a 41-year-old architect who was born in England and who resided in Ward 3.[10] Hall also authored an architectural pattern book published in Baltimore in 1840. Two editions of this work, *A Series of Select and Original Modern Designs for Dwelling Houses for the Use of Carpenters and Builders,* were published at John Murphy's Baltimore printing shop, and copies were available at the time of the church construction. Murphy had established his business in Baltimore in 1835, and he later was noted as the leading Catholic publisher in the country. At least one connection between Father Gildea, pastor and possible architect of St. Vincent's, and John Murphy has been established during the early 1840s. Gildea was active in the Catholic Tract Society, an organization responsible for the monthly literary magazine *Religious Cabinet* (later *United States Catholic Magazine*); John Murphy published the *Religious Cabinet*.[11]

Examination of Hall's 1840 pattern book suggests that the designer was a proponent of that school of Neoclassical architecture that integrated elements from both the Federal and the Greek Revival styles. Hall emphasized the geometric relationships of interior spaces in his publication. However, his study was confined to the design of low-scale domestic and commercial structures; no examples of church designs or interior finishes were included.

The designer and builders of St. Vincent de Paul undoubtedly were aware of the architectural designs utilized in existing Baltimore churches. The design of the First Presbyterian Church (1789–95), the third building to house that Baltimore congregation, is credited to builder-architects James Mosher and John Dalrymple; that building was similar in core volume to St. Vincent de Paul. Mosher, a native of Roxbury, Massachusetts, started his career as a bricklayer and engineer. Whether Mosher was responsible for the design or construction of the First Presbyterian Church has not been established. Interior watercolor sketches by contemporary architect E. G. Lind depict a simple design that incorporated galleries and a pulpit similar to those found in the New England meetinghouse plan.[12]

Many exterior design devices found in St. Vincent de Paul Church are reminiscent of those employed in the core structure of the First Presbyterian Church. In addition to its gable-front orientation and its podium, a comparable eave treatment is found in the design of the two structures. The influence of the meetinghouse also is reflected in the church plan.

Two other early nineteenth-century churches contributed important elements to Baltimore's ecclesiastical design tradition. The first, one of the most architecturally significant and nationally influential buildings erected in Baltimore, was the Roman Catholic Cathedral of the Assumption, designed by the renowned architect Benjamin Henry Latrobe in 1805. The second was St. Paul's Episcopal Church, designed by the locally important architect Robert Cary Long Sr. in 1814.

The Cathedral of the Assumption, commissioned by Bishop John Carroll, was the first Roman Catholic cathedral constructed in the United States. Latrobe submitted two designs for the structure, one Gothic, the other a Neoclassical design in the Roman mode. The Gothic style had a history of use for the designs of major public buildings in England and was adopted widely for ecclesiastical designs in the United States after 1839. However, in 1805, no major building in the United States had been erected using the Gothic style; consequently, this design was rejected in favor of Latrobe's more familiar Neoclassical concept. The cornerstone of the cathedral was laid by Archbishop Carroll on July 7, 1806. The roof was on the building in 1808, but the War of 1812 interrupted construction between 1812 and 1817. Although the edifice was dedicated on May 31, 1821, work on the building's portico and corner domes continued into the 1870s.[13]

Latrobe's original design depicted a Roman portico rather than the Greek portico that eventually was constructed. The design of the building's corner towers, originally envisioned as shallow domes, was altered to onion domes in the completed building.[14] While the architectural programs and construction budgets for the Basilica and St. Vincent de Paul Church differed dramatically, the selection of a Neoclassical design for the cathedral is significant in that it established a conservative, classical image for Roman Catholic ecclesiastical architecture in Baltimore.

St. Paul's Episcopal Church, built in 1814 and burned in 1854, was a building comparable in scale to St. Vincent de Paul. This church occupied a rectangular ground plan that measured 84 feet by 126 feet. The senior Long's refined Neoclassical plan for the Charles Street church combined architectural references to Christopher Wren's St. Paul's Cathedral, London (1668–1710), with references to the work of Scottish architect James Gibbs. The scale and proportion of the St. Paul's tower is of particular interest in comparison with that of St. Vincent de Paul.

Neoclassical design interpretations of the period, similar to those employed by Latrobe in the Basilica, emphasized strong horizontal geometry. This horizontal emphasis generally was extended to elements such as church towers, as seen in the corner towers of the cathedral. In contrast, the west tower of St. Paul's Church rose to a height of 126 feet and equaled the depth of the structure. The extreme height of the spire, documented in Georgian-style churches but more common during the medieval period, has been interpreted as a device intended to symbolize Episcopalian preeminence in Baltimore. Tall towers and monumental porticoes had been integrated into the designs of several prominent Episcopalian churches during the eighteenth century. St. Michael's (1756–62) in Charleston, for example, included both elements.[15]

JOHN BAPTIST GILDEA, POSSIBLE ARCHITECT

Neither the architect nor the builder of St. Vincent de Paul church has been documented definitively. Tradition credits the church's first pastor, Fr. John Baptist Gildea (1804–45), with the design. There is evidence to support this tradition. From his first years as pastor in western Virginia, Gildea was active in church construction. In September 1830 he wrote Archbishop James Whitfield that the church at Martinsburg was nearly finished, and that he had acquired a lot for one at Harper's Ferry, which, he wrote, "will be sixty feet by forty—Gothic."[16]

Gildea's selection of the Gothic style for the Harper's Ferry church was an unusual choice for the period. The style was not adopted widely in the United States prior to the 1840s, when literal interpretations of medieval European prototypes became popular. Early buildings designed in this style were less academic in their interpretations; they include the 1806 Baltimore example, St. Mary's Chapel, which has been credited to architect Maximilien Godefroy (c. 1765–c. 1845). The Gothic Revival style was more common in English ecclesiastical architecture constructed prior to 1840, where the style was related to theories of architectural determinism. In these theories Revival architecture styles were thought to embody the character of the period and were thought to influence building users through their physical design.[17] No evidence has been uncovered to suggest that Gildea credited architecture with the ability to influence its users to the degree that some of his English contemporaries did. However, his application of the Gothic style to the Harper's Ferry church suggests that Gildea was aware of current trends in architectural design. After he supervised the construction of the Martinsburg church, Gildea reported the following summer that the church there was finished, and that it was "worthy of the Lord to whom it was erected." With high mass, benediction, and vespers the congregation in Martinsburg was more regular and pious, he added, and so it would be in Harper's Ferry when the church was completed.[18] There is no doubt that, in the mind of Father Gildea, the church played a central role in the life of the parish.

Gildea was not long at his second pastorate, at St. James Church in Baltimore, before he began improvements to that structure, which had been built only a few years before. The steeple, erected in 1837, was a substantial addition. Although smaller in scale, it bore a striking resemblance to the future steeple at St. Vincent de Paul. The St. James steeple had two stages, while St. Vincent's would rise to three. The builder and year of construction are documented by a receipt included in the papers of the estate of Father Gildea: "Received of John B. Gildea twelve hundred dollars on account due for erecting and furnishing materials for the Steeple of St. James Church." The receipt was dated January 3, 1838, and signed by Henry Staylor.[19]

Staylor, who also may have been associated with the construction of St.

Vincent de Paul, was a parishioner of St. James and later of St. Vincent de Paul's. *Matchett's Baltimore City Directory* for 1845 identified Staylor as a carpenter who maintained a business at 191 N. High Street. Staylor therefore came into contact with Father Gildea frequently, and may well have influenced Gildea's concepts about architecture and building. For work done on St. James Church and its cemetery in late 1835 or early 1836, Father Gildea deducted from Staylor's bill of $229.50 the sums of $26.25 for his pew rent, $10.00 for a subscription to the church, and $12.00 for "Schooling." Staylor (1792–1862) was a respected man in his community; in 1843 and again in 1845, he was elected to the city council from the Sixth Ward. He also was a respected builder who executed frequent ecclesiastical commissions. In 1840, the year St. Vincent de Paul was begun, Staylor also completed the sexton's house at the Cathedral of the Assumption according to designs by Robert Cary Long Jr.[20]

Robert Cary Long Jr. (1810–49), like his father, was one of Baltimore's

The two-stage steeple of the original St. James Church, Baltimore, is illustrated in this undated photograph. The steeple was constructed under the pastorate of Fr. John Baptist Gildea and is similar, although simpler in design, to that constructed for St. Vincent de Paul Church.

outstanding architects.[21] Among the younger Long's work was his 1844 design for the Presbyterian Church at Franklin and Cathedral streets. However, between 1840 and 1843, he also served as the architect for most, if not all, of the Catholic Church's construction projects in Baltimore. In 1840 he designed a railing for the cathedral grounds, as well as the sexton's house and a steeple for the Gothic chapel at St. Mary's Seminary. In 1842 he developed plans for the Calvert Hall school and the Gothic church of St. Alphonsus on Saratoga Street. In 1843 he designed the Greek Revival style church of St. Peter the Apostle on Poppleton Street.[22] These previous commissions make Long a potential candidate for the architect of St. Vincent de Paul Church in 1840.

Gildea may well have consulted Long. He also may have perused the pattern books of John Hall and other architects who were discussed earlier. The future pastor of St. Vincent's obviously was familiar enough with the fundamentals of architectural design to be his own draftsman. At the bottom of a scrap of paper on which he had noted the baptisms performed in December 1836, Father Gildea executed schematic designs for Doric and Ionic order columns or pilasters.[23] These sketches may have been done with St. James in mind. However, it is more likely that they were intended as features for the Carmelite Chapel then under construction. As director and chaplain of the Carmelites, Gildea made many important decisions for these cloistered nuns. No representation of the

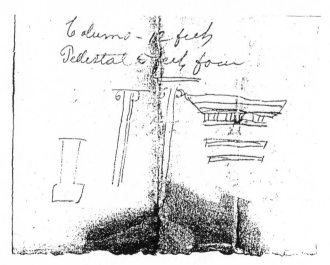

Among Rev. John B. Gildea's papers is this sketch for a column or pilaster.
SULPICIAN ARCHIVES OF BALTIMORE

Carmelite Chapel on Aisquith Street, or of the original interior of St. James, has survived.

Obscure documents found in the course of this research often contained clues that suggested Father Gildea's fundamental role in the design and construction of St. Vincent de Paul. For example, in a letter to one of the nuns in 1841, Bishop Benedict Fenwick of Boston wrote, "Rev. Mr. Williamson speaks in raptures of Rev. Mr. Gildea's chapel. He says it is far superior to the cathedral."[24] Although the date of the letter suggests that the "chapel" may have been St. Vincent de Paul Church, the letter itself concerned the affairs of the Mount Carmel Monastery. Gildea's possible role as architect for St. Vincent de Paul also was suggested by the following notice that appeared in the *Baltimore American* of May 22, 1840: "The Church of St. Vincent de Paul is to be erected, we learn, under the supervision of the Rev. Mr. Gildea, who is to have spiritual charge of the congregation when the edifice is finished." A final piece of evidence that indicates Father Gildea's active role in the construction of St. Vincent de Paul was a receipt addressed to him from the firm of Pouer & Donald. Dated June 22, 1841, this document listed items of millwork, including 173 feet of window sills, 150 feet of coping, 64 feet of chimney capping, and 32 feet of marble facings.[25]

Although a body of trustees had been incorporated to handle the financial and organizational affairs of both St. Vincent de Paul Church and St. Vincent de Paul Orphan Asylum, there is no evidence that these trustees took an active role in the planning and construction of the church itself. This situation contrasts sharply with the active role played by the trustees, or vestry, of the cathedral. To them Archbishop John Carroll had entrusted not only the choice of the architect and clerk of the works for the new cathedral, but also the supervision of its progress. The chairman of the cathedral's building committee was John Hillen, father of Solomon Hillen, who later became mayor of Baltimore and a member of the St. Vincent de Paul Parish. A running battle developed between Hillen and Benjamin Henry Latrobe, architect of the Cathedral of the Assumption.[26] The precedent of this conflict may have encouraged Gildea to serve not only as his own architect, but also as clerk of the works.

Whatever his role, Father Gildea succeeded in designing, or commissioning, a church that accorded well with the tastes and expectations of trustees who represented the stratum of society that the church was intended primarily to serve. It was expected that the majority of pewholders would be men of substance—merchants, professionals, property holders—or the widows of such notables. In its demographic composition, the original membership of St. Vincent's Parish more closely resembled that of the cathedral, rather than those of St. Patrick's or St. John's, which claimed a large Irish or German membership. However, the predilections of each parish's wealthier trustees determined the character of the church buildings, even within these more heavily ethnic parishes.

The design of old St. Peter's Cathedral, which stood next to the rectory of St. Paul's Episcopal Church, demonstrates the degree to which the Catholic Church in Maryland conformed to the architectural precedents set by the Episcopal Church. With little tradition of church building in a colony that for three-quarters of a century had denied Roman Catholics the right to erect churches of their own, it was only natural that the architects and builders of Baltimore's archdiocese looked to the denomination that had dominated Maryland as a model of church organization and architecture. Existing churches commonly were used as models for new buildings.[27] By the time Gildea was planning for Baltimore's sixth Catholic parish, the designs of the Presbyterian churches of Baltimore also were architecturally notable.

Thus, the first Roman Catholic churches of the Baltimore archdiocese were perfectly integrated in their design with earlier Maryland traditions. They differed little in their outward appearance from their Protestant counterparts. The architect and builder of St. Vincent de Paul, whoever he was, had an exceptionally rich tradition of ecclesiastical architecture in the city of Baltimore from which to draw his own design inspirations.

THE PARISH COMPLEX

The building complex associated with the new parish expanded rapidly during the parish's first two decades. Three buildings were encompassed in the initial core parish complex that lined North Front Street: St. Vincent de Paul Orphan Asylum, St. Vincent de Paul Church, and the church rectory. A fourth structure, the St. Vincent's Male School, was added to the core complex in 1860 on a site adjoining the rear of the orphanage. Other buildings were added to, or subtracted from, the parish holdings over the years. The three core buildings lining North Front Street, which ultimately were connected physically, established the parish's public architectural image from its early decades through the 1960s. While the orphanage has been removed, both the church and its rectory have survived intact, although the latter has been modified over the years.

The architectural hierarchy adopted in the design of the original complex reflected building use and served to distinguish the complex as a whole from the surrounding area. Site, scale, and proportion were used to their best advantage in creating this hierarchy. The church, recessed and elevated from the street, was the centerpiece of the complex; it was flanked by the secondary orphanage to the south and the subordinate rectory to the north. The scale, the gable-front orientation, and soaring tower of the church clearly signified the separation of the church from the surrounding residential development.

In contrast, the brick orphanage was elevated on a raised basement and rose four stories to a shallow gable roof ornamented by a simple cornice. The four-story scale of the orphanage exceeded the wall height of the church. This factor was mitigated through site location and design. The structure was situated closer to the street than the church, and it adopted a simple symmetrical design created by slightly recessed six-light-over-six-light windows and domestic proportions. The subdued exterior ornamentation of the orphanage building focused on the recessed central entrance, which was defined by a surround incorporating a full entablature supported by pilasters. The Greek Revival stylistic references of the entry surround provided a design link between church and orphanage.

The brick rectory flanked the church to the south. Originally a 2½-story private dwelling, the house was acquired as a rectory by Father Gildea in 1842. The structure's location (immediately adjoining the street), its scale, and its residential use no doubt provided a physical transition between the religious complex and the surrounding residential neighborhood. The asymmetrical design of the dwelling reflects its side hall plan, a common plan type for townhouses in Baltimore. In this plan, the side hall characteristically corresponds to the location of the entrance, and extends the depth of the first floor of the principal block. The remainder of the first floor principal block is occupied by double parlors. The building has been modified using a common pattern of domestic addition and alteration. The scale of the building was raised to three full stories, and additions at the rear of the building accommodated a dining room and kitchen.

THE CHURCH

St. Vincent de Paul Church is a monumental scale, load-bearing brick structure with a rectangular ground plan that measures approximately 69 feet by 124 feet. The 2½-story building is supported by a raised foundation of coursed granite and terminates in a gable roof. The selection of masonry for the construction of the church undoubtedly was influenced by a 1799 Baltimore City ordinance that banned wood buildings in the central area of the city. Moreover, the Baltimore area historically contained large deposits of marine and alluvial clays due to its proximity to the Patapsco River and to the Chesapeake Bay. The availability of these materials fostered the development of brickmaking as a major Baltimore industry from the eighteenth through the twentieth centuries. The 1799 ordinance, combined with the noteworthy quality and availability of Baltimore brick, not only reduced the instance of fires, but also promoted a cohesive use of building materials in the city that continues to contribute to Baltimore's distinctive architectural character.

The walls of St. Vincent's are load-bearing brick; the exterior is laid in five-course common bond, the most common brick pattern of the period. The building's exterior walls measure approximately 40 inches in depth at the building's water table and decrease in proportion to the height of the building. The church's exterior walls were laid in regular "face brick," while its interior walls were composed of softer and more irregular "salmon brick." The average dimensions of the bricks used in St. Vincent's construction measured 8¼ inches in length, 4¼ inches in width, and 2¼ inches in thickness; no maker's marks were identified. Practical limitations in manufacturing and building construction dictated overall brick size. The width of the brick could not exceed the average man's grasp, thus enabling masons to lay the units with one hand. The length of a brick generally was twice its width to insure an adequate bond within the wall.[28]

St. Vincent de Paul adopts a symmetrical temple form that is created by its gable-front elevation. Oriented along a northeast-southwest longitudinal axis facing North Front Street, the building is recessed slightly and is elevated from the street plane. Access to the structure is by means of an open flight of nine steps, which terminates in an open porch that spans the building's façade. The level of the landing is marked on the remaining elevations by a water table. The building's slight elevation, combined with the open stairs, serves to distinguish it visually from the surrounding streetscape, thus making the structure a visual focus in the area. The surrounding streetscape originally was dominated by low-scale rows of buildings that rose directly from the public right-of-way. This development is documented in historical maps of the area. The façades of these structures created a flush plane that was marked by a regular sequence of doors and windows, and frequently was punctuated by projecting marble stoops ornamented by delicate wrought-iron balustrades.

The church's setback, its elevation, and its ceremonial entrance create a physical separation of public and religious space that has been maintained to the present. The transition is reinforced by the church's open porch spanning the full façade. Period illustrations also indicate that access to the church was defined further by a cast-iron railing located parallel to the street.

The principal elevation of St. Vincent de Paul includes a pedimented gable with full entablature composed of a cornice, frieze, and architrave. Inspection suggests that the front frieze originally included metopes and triglyphs, the ghosts of which survive. A dentil tenia separates the frieze from the architrave. Vertical emphasis in the exterior design is created on all elevations through the use of paired pilasters that lack bases and that terminate in simplified Roman capitals. The pilasters and entablature are a design device that visually reinforces the suggestion of a temple design, and eliminates the need for the construction of a full portico to convey the temple effect.

The building's pedimented gable (tympanum) includes a round arch window on the principal elevation; an eight-light oculus highlights the gable-end of the rear elevation. The principal elevation is divided into three vertical divisions or building bays, while side elevations include six bay divisions. Side bays are defined by shallow arches that are achieved by raising the spring line of the arch above the true impost level. The arch articulation of the wall plane frames the building's windows. Although the original window sashes later were replaced, there is no structural evidence to suggest that alterations were ever made to the bay openings. Twentieth-century accounts indicate that the original windows were multipane units with painted and etched window lights. It is likely that the side galleries, which originally lined the longitudinal interior walls, were visible through the windows. The existing windows are slightly recessed from the wall plane. Window openings are supported by projecting sills and terminate in shallow arches.

The principal entrance to the building is located on the northeast elevation. All three bays house monumental scale entries of robust Greek Revival design; the middle pedimented unit is the primary entrance. This central focus is reinforced through the location of an arched statuary niche above the pediment. The statuary niche above the principal entrance may have been incorporated to reinforce the symmetrical design of the elevation. However, if the niche was intended to house a statue of St. Vincent de Paul, its integration was an unusual and uncommon architectural feature for the period.[29]

The entrance to the church is framed by a complex surround incorporating a shouldered architrave. This distinctive molding is derived from classical Greek prototypes and is found on such monuments as the north portico of the Erechthum in Athens. The architrave houses a two-light transom, beneath which is found a Gothic arch. The double leaf doors of the building are recessed and incorporate raised panels; door reveals are similarly paneled. Secondary front entrances include a similar door design; however, the surrounds for these units incorporate a shouldered architrave and entablature with three-part corbeling.

The three-stage tower of St. Vincent de Paul Church dominates the design of the building.   *CATHOLIC REVIEW*

A central, three-stage brick tower rises approximately 150 feet from the roof of the narthex. A complex geometry is employed in the plan of the spire, incorporating a rectangular base, an octagonal first stage, and circular second and third stages. The scale of each stage diminishes with the height of the tower. The base of the first stage incorporates rectangular recessed panels. Paired corner pilasters, similar in design to those found on the main body of the building, rise from the base to a full entablature similar in design to that found on the front elevation. One-light-over-one-light sash windows are housed in round arch openings that occupy the wall plane between the pilasters. Recessed rectangular panels are located beneath the window units. This overall design is repeated, on a smaller scale, in the design of the second stage of the tower. The spire's design is simplified at the lantern. Paired pilasters are replaced by recessed rectangular panels and an austere cornice. The tower terminates in a dome surmounted by a cross. The dome is sheathed in metal that has been painted green to simulate oxidized copper and to complement the roof of the building's principal block.

The design of the church tower is derived from classical prototypes reminiscent of eighteenth-century Georgian architecture, and its scale is a unique and character-defining element of the building. Classical tower designs were used widely in combination with temple-front porticoes in church architecture beginning in the second quarter of the eighteenth century. The Scottish architect James Gibbs is credited with introducing the form through a series of London churches, the most notable of which is St. Martin's-in-the-Fields (1722–76). Gibbs's designs were disseminated in North America through his architectural pattern book, entitled *Book of Architecture,* first published in 1728. American interpretations of Gibbs's design range from the literal, as illustrated by Joseph Brown's First Baptist Meeting House in Providence, Rhode Island (1775), or by the 196-foot spire of Christ Church, Philadelphia, that was added to the existing building (1751–54), to the liberal interpretation of classical form found in St. Michael's Church in Charleston, South Carolina, erected between 1751 and 1762.[30] Numerous examples of Gibbs-inspired church spires are found throughout Maryland, but few rise to the impressive height of St. Vincent de Paul.

Period illustrations suggest that the exterior of St. Vincent de Paul, including the tower, originally was painted a light color. Painted brick was a common exterior finish found in both Georgian and Greek Revival styles; it created consistent expanses of wall that emulated the condition of

Greek and Roman monuments. Exterior wall planes frequently were enhanced through stucco or the addition of sand to paint films.

The original interior of St. Vincent de Paul adopted a modified basilica plan with narthex, nave, and apse spatial divisions. The basilica plan was first introduced in ancient Rome, where structures of this type served as public meeting halls. The building type is characterized by rectangular plans that incorporate aisles, clerestories, galleries, and an apse located opposite the entrance. The building form was adopted widely by the early Christian church; by the fourth century A.D., this building type had assumed the identifying characteristics of an oblong plan, longitudinal axis, and either a rectangular or an apse termination.

The narthex of St. Vincent de Paul survives with minor modification to the original plan. It is divided into three interconnecting cells. Those adjoining the exterior walls are occupied by circular staircases that rise to the second-story level. The balustrade, similar to those seen in Baltimore's domestic architecture of the early nineteenth century, forms a delicately proportioned continuous curve. The turned stair newel is massive by comparison. The tread ends of the open stair are decorated with applied scrolls of thin cut-out wood, a feature common to Baltimore houses of the period. The stringer faces of the staircases are sheathed in fluted paneling struck with cavetto moldings. The massive walls of the central cell of the narthex serve as the entry hall to the nave and support the church spire.

The plan of the nave has undergone several alterations since the construction of the church. The original design included a semicircular apse framed by a rectangular terminus. The apse was referred to as a "circle" in architectural documents of the period, and it commonly was used in both eighteenth- and nineteenth-century ecclesiastical designs.[31] Its appearance in the original plan of St. Vincent de Paul was suspected and confirmed by structural evidence uncovered during the 1990 building rehabilitation. Intact floor framing suggests that the floor level of the apse originally was raised approximately eight inches above the main floor.

Three sides of the nave were surrounded by galleries supported by freestanding cast-iron columns, ornamented with palmetto capitals enriched by acanthus leaves. The original location of these columns corresponded to the cast-iron supports found in the basement level of the building, so that a point-on-point loading system was achieved. The use of cast-iron columns, as opposed to load-bearing walls, made the desired open plan assembly area possible. Evidence of the location of the original

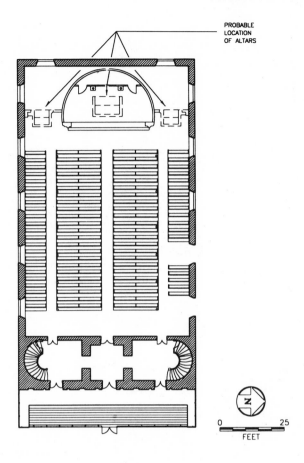

PROBABLE
LOCATION
OF ALTARS

This 1840 plan of St. Vincent de Paul Church was reconstructed from physical evidence uncovered during the 1990 renovation of the church.
R. CHRISTOPHER GOODWIN & ASSOCIATES, INC.

gallery supports can be seen in the nave floor, where the weight transferred through the columns compressed the wood in the pattern of the column base.

Historical references to double galleries in the original church plan survive, but detailed descriptions of the exact gallery design do not. Physical evidence supplemented by the designs of surviving galleries found in churches of the period suggest a probable design for those at St. Vincent's. It is likely that the first gallery was divided into three spaces and included a central choir area flanked by side galleries that extended the length of the nave. Evidence of this possible plan is provided by the dou-

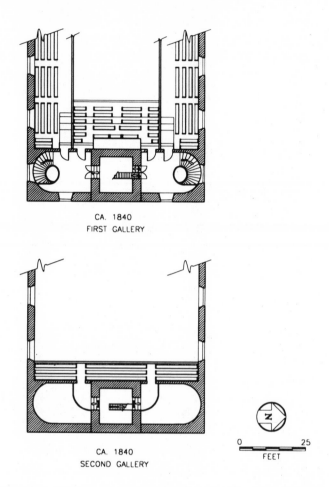

CA. 1840
FIRST GALLERY

CA. 1840
SECOND GALLERY

0 ———— 25
FEET

The above plans depict the likely original configuration of the first- and second-tier galleries.   R. CHRISTOPHER GOODWIN & ASSOCIATES, INC.

ble entrances found in the second floor north and south stair halls. This spatial division of the first gallery also is supported by the surviving seating plan, which retains low partitions between the choir and congregational seating areas.

A separate space devoted to the choir and to the church's organ demonstrates the historical emphasis on music at St. Vincent's. An account in the *United States Catholic Miscellany* of October 1, 1842, included a report originally published in the *Boston Pilot* of September 12, 1842: "The immense organ in the Church of St. Vincent de Paul is completed and we may safely say it stands without a superior in the United States. It literally shakes the strong building to its foundation, and rolls forth like thunder, the very atmosphere of the building seems to tremble under the burden of sound and yet it is in harmony with the most delicate pipe." References to the size of the organ and the location of the later replacement instrument argue for a central location on the rear nave wall.

The choir and side galleries were defined by railings. Precedents exist for both a solid panel partition similar in design to the raised panels featured in the main floor pew doors, as well as an open balustrade similar to that defining the circular side stairs. While no evidence of the seating plan for the side galleries has been uncovered, it is likely that seating was arranged in stepped tiers, with the gallery pews oriented perpendicular to the arrangement of the main floor.

A second gallery spanned the rear of the nave. This second gallery provided seating for African-American members of the parish. Evidence of this gallery survives on the rear wall, where a slight framing ghost is visible in a raking light. Physical evidence suggesting the location of original second gallery entrances also survives in the first stage of the church tower.

Access to the first stage of the tower from the church interior is provided by a narrow straight boxed stair located behind the first gallery choir. The size and central location of the organ in the first gallery choir probably made access between the first and second galleries impractical. Brick arches on the north and south walls of the first stage of the tower, which descend three steps and lead to recent lath and plaster walls, suggest a possible solution. In this scenario, access to the second gallery was by way of the tower whose first stage was connected to the rear of the nave. While evidence of the connection between the arched entries and the rear wall of the nave has been lost, it is possible that the design that was adopted was similar to the circular design used for the main stairs.

The segregation of slaves and free black members of the congregation in upper galleries was a common feature in both Northern and Southern churches constructed during this period. Double galleries survive in the Old South Meeting House in Boston (built 1730, restored 1783, 1857). In Maryland, acceptance of the practice was documented through an act authorizing the construction of St. Anne's (Episcopal) Parish Church in Annapolis (1774); the act provided for a gallery for servants and another for slaves who wished to attend services. Segregated second galleries also have been documented in antebellum Baltimore churches, including St. Paul's Church, which was constructed in 1814.[32]

Judging from wear patterns in the nave floor, it is likely that the original pew plan of the main floor of St. Vincent's was similar to that found in the church prior to the 1990 renovation. The main floor of St. Vincent de Paul's has been patched selectively over the years. However, there is no evidence to indicate a total replacement of the random-width, tongue-and-groove heart pine flooring during the life of the building. The original pew plan included double rows of pews on the center aisle flanked by side aisles. The doors of the original box pews were removed in subsequent alterations to the building. A scrolled arm and panel design was utilized for the pews; variations on this scroll design were used in American churches throughout the nineteenth century.

Architectural pattern books of the period, which circulated widely, presented building details as well as building plans. Asher Benjamin's *The Builder's Guide* contains two illustrations comparable to features found in the original design of St. Vincent de Paul. The first, "Plan for a Church" (Plate LIX), presents a similar spatial division to the church's exterior. The second, "Detail of a Pew" (Plate LXI), depicts a box pew with a scrolled-arm design. The open scroll pattern used in St. Vincent de Paul Church

The scrolled arm and panel design of the pews at St. Vincent de Paul are similar to designs used in American churches throughout the nineteenth century.

was in character with the city's tradition of simple refined interior ornamentation and consistent with the original finishes found throughout the church.

The plan of the church established a ceremonial presence focused on the apse. While the basic form of the church's circle termination has been established, its original ornamentation has been lost. However, the most elaborate interior decoration typically was focused in this section of the building. St. Vincent's original marble altar survives and is incorporated in the current design, although it was reconfigured over the years, including during the most recent rehabilitation of the church. The pencil signatures of "Samuel Ruborg" and "Jacob S. Rogers" were revealed on the interior face of the right side panel during the course of the rehabilitation. These signatures, dated 1841, document the date of the installation of the original altar. The similarity in the marble of the main altar and that used in the side altars, which were removed in the 1990 rehabilitation, suggest that these elements also were installed as part of the original church furnishings. No evidence survives to document the exact location of the original side altars.

Little written documentation exists to suggest the original interior finishes of the church, but physical evidence provides several clues to its probable appearance. Interior moldings and woodwork are robust Greek Revival–style elements. Plaster was applied directly to interior brick walls. As was common during the period, interior plaster contained a binder of animal hair and was applied to the walls in several coats.

There are no records of other ornamentation or aids to piety in the church, perhaps because there were none. The devotional habits of early Maryland Catholics were simple.[33] The parishioners of St. Vincent de Paul would not have felt out of place in a "meetinghouse" church. Catholic houses of worship of the Federal period, in general, may have included paintings, but they rarely had statues or stained glass representations of saints or sacred symbols.

A small sample of an early paint scheme was uncovered on the rear nave wall during the 1990 building rehabilitation. This sample suggested that a waterbased paint was applied to the plaster in a stylized panel design. Although it is probable that the intensity of the pigment had faded over the years, the sample depicted rose tones graduating in intensity from a light panel field to a darker ground. If so, the overall effect of the church's interior was light and well articulated.

It is likely that the surviving paint sample dates to 1855. The financial

View of one of the two semicircular staircases that rise from the east end of the church.

reports for the parish, dated January 1, 1856, record: "Within the past year the Church has been fresco-painted inside, and oil-painted outside at an expense of about $500.00, improving much its general appearance." While the financial report referenced frescoes, physical evidence does not support this technique of painting in wet plaster. It is more likely that murals were added to the existing smooth plaster finishes.

Some structural evidence and period accounts document the later addition of the existing coved ceiling. However, the original ceiling undoubtedly was flat. The integration of the second-tier gallery in the original building design suggests that a flat ceiling that maximized usable space between the gallery and ceiling would be desirable.

Additional features of note were uncovered during the 1990 rehabilitation of the structure. These features, including a massive brick flue con-necting the first floor to the basement level, suggest that a heating system was incorporated in the church early in its history. Examination of the area between the first-floor joists and floor also revealed framed spaces large enough to accommodate ducts from the brick flue. By the mid-nineteenth century, the integration of technologies for central heating of major edifices was relatively common.

The original design of St. Vincent de Paul Church reflects the influence of the Neoclassical movement that historically dominated Baltimore ar-chitecture. St. Vincent's related physically and symbolically with Balti-more's prevailing ecclesiastical tradition in its use of materials, its scale, its massing, its design prototypes, and the design of its tower. The overall ar-chitectural design aligned the church and its parish with the historical tra-dition and the established social fabric of old Baltimore. The selection of a traditional design for the church in a period marked nationally by design innovation and experimentation suggests that St. Vincent's trustees and congregation were theological moderates. The original membership was aligned socially and economically with established Baltimore, and the con-gregation was predisposed to emulate those Protestant Episcopal church organizational models favored by the church under Bishop John Carroll. The public image of St. Vincent de Paul established a clear association with traditional Baltimore. This image was one of conservative stability.

An additional factor accounted for the selection of an established and noncontroversial design for the core complex of the parish. The mission of the St. Vincent trustees was not limited to the erection of a church. Rather, it encompassed an ambitious program of church, orphanage, and school. These philanthropic priorities required the broad support of the economically advantaged members of the parish, archdiocese, and secu-lar community. The subdued image of the parish may have been adopted intentionally to align St. Vincent's with established Baltimore to engen-der support for its ventures. The success of the parish in achieving these ends is evidenced by the number of benevolent institutions added to parish activities during the second half of the nineteenth century. The church's original design and disposition of space remained intact until the last quarter of the nineteenth century.

THE AESTHETIC
OF PRESENCE

1876–1895

ARCHITECTURE AND THE NATIONAL PARISH

The membership of St. Vincent de Paul Church originally was drawn from Baltimore's economically and socially secure professional and merchant class, which was identified with established Baltimore. However, the church was built during a period that witnessed a wave of immigration and the rise of national parishes in the Roman Catholic Church. Immigrant groups, most notably the Irish, transformed American Roman Catholicism. The Irish brought an orientation toward parochial life in which church construction had played an important role since the Emancipation Act of 1829. To a strong Tridentine Catholicism, the immigrant faithful added a devotion to organizations, institutions, and a militant press; all were designed to sustain the faith in a new and frequently hostile world.[1]

By 1850, an estimated 21 percent of Baltimore's 170,000 residents were foreign born. Baltimore's immigrant population during this period was predominantly young (aged 20–30 years) and male (by a ratio of 3:2). German immigrants accounted for one-half of the immigrant population, while Irish immigrants accounted for one-third of the total number of foreign born. Competition for jobs, housing, and social status generated friction between Baltimore's German and Irish communities. The plight of the immigrant in Baltimore during this period is illustrated by the city's almshouse statistics. An estimated 30 percent of those committed were foreign born; of those, one-tenth had resided in the city for less than a week, and one-quarter had lived there less than six months.[2]

In response to this influx, Baltimore archbishop Samuel Eccleston supported the construction of national churches to serve Baltimore's growing immigrant population. The new emphasis on parish organization also gave rise to the "brick and mortar priest"; throughout the antebellum period, the most successful priests were those who built the largest churches and organized the most societies.[3]

St. James Parish, founded in 1833 to serve the Old Town area of Baltimore, included long-time Baltimore families, German immigrants, and Irish immigrants. St. Vincent de Paul Parish was subdivided from St. James at the end of the decade to serve a predominantly affluent congregation of established merchants, property owners, and professionals. By the second half of the nineteenth century, St. Vincent de Paul had become the leading Irish parish in Baltimore.[4]

An examination of census data for 1880 suggests that the area in the vicinity of St. Vincent de Paul Church was a neighborhood in economic and demographic transition. A sample of 100 households in Ward 5, Precinct 5, and Ward 4, Precinct 2, reflects a predominately white, native-born population with an average age of 35. However, the area's immigrant population was increasing steadily. Census data record Ireland (19 percent) and Germany (8 percent) as the birthplace of the majority of the sample's immigrant population; Russia, Holland, Canada, Poland, England, and France also were represented. These first-generation immigrants worked primarily as laborers and skilled craftsmen. The numbers of residents recorded at individual addresses suggest that the neighborhood contained a mixture of multiple-family residences and single-family dwellings. Twelve households in the area had servants; the occupants of these households were primarily professionals such as judges, physicians, and merchants.[5]

Parish divisions were neither unusual nor unexpected in urban areas with high immigrant populations. Because the church served as the religious and social focus of the immigrant community, it was a tangible center rather than an abstract entity. Religion was a stabilizing constant in lives disrupted by relocation. In addition, the national churches and their membership organizations encouraged ethnic cultural cohesion and provided a psychological buffer against an unfamiliar native-born society.[6] Changes in neighborhood ethnicity underscored the differences in language and culture between native-born and various immigrant groups. These factors, together with the social and economic competition between immigrant factions, made the creation of greater numbers of ethnically identified parishes desirable, if not inevitable.

The newly created churches that served these immigrant parishes in-

TABLE 10.1. Selected Baltimore City Churches Listed on the Maryland Inventory of Historic Properties

Church	Style	Architect	Year
St. Vincent de Paul	Georgian/ Greek Revival	Not identified	1840–41
St. Peter the Apostle	Greek Revival	Robert Cary Long Jr.	1843–44
St. Alphonsus	Gothic Revival	Robert Cary Long Jr.	1842–45
St. Ignatius	Baroque Influence	Louis L. Long and Henry Hamilton	1853–56
St. John the Evangelist	Italianate/ Romanesque	John Rudolph Niernsee and John Crawford Neilson	1855–56
St. Michael's	Romanesque Revival	Louis L. Long	1857–59
Holy Cross	Gothic Revival	Not identified	1858–60
St. James the Less	High Victorian Gothic	George A. Frederick	1865–67
St. Leo's	Italianate/ Romanesque Revival	E. Francis Baldwin	1880–81

Source: Data generated from architectural survey forms for Roman Catholic churches constructed in Baltimore City between 1840 and 1890 in the collection of the Maryland Historical Trust, Crownsville, Md. Construction dates are revised.

cluded architect-designed buildings that reflected current trends in American architecture and buildings inspired by European prototypes familiar to the parishioners, rather than historic Baltimore prototypes. Professional architects have been identified as the designers of seven of nine Roman Catholic churches constructed in Baltimore between 1840 and 1890; all nine are documented in the Maryland State Inventory of Historic Properties maintained by the Maryland Historical Trust. The designs of these churches reflected nationally popular Revival styles, including the Italianate, Greek Revival, and Gothic Revival, the style most commonly associated with period immigrant churches. Because of its "pagan" associations, the Greek Revival style was used least frequently for the design of Roman Catholic churches, despite its wide secular application and its popular identification with democratic ideals (see Table 10.1).

Two notable Baltimore churches constructed during this period illustrate this transition in church design. St. Alphonsus, built in 1842–45, utilized the Gothic Revival style; St. Peter the Apostle, erected 1843–44, was pure Greek Revival in its imitation of the Greek temple, the Theseus.

Both St. Alphonsus and St. Peter the Apostle were designed by Baltimore architect Robert Cary Long Jr. The quality of the buildings reflects the talent of their architect; their styles document the preferences of their clients.

The stylistic vocabulary of nineteenth-century architecture was a symbolic language. The selection of an architectural style for a major building such as a church embodied associations beyond artistic composition. In the case of St. Alphonsus, a parish composed of German immigrants, the church symbolized "a beautiful monument of German art, because it is designed and is being executed after German models." St. Peter the Apostle, which eventually became known as an Irish immigrant parish, selected a fully developed Greek Revival style with associations with that "democratic" American style and its references to Greek civilization.[7]

NINETEENTH-CENTURY RENOVATIONS TO ST. VINCENT DE PAUL

While the original design for St. Vincent de Paul Church was derived from established Baltimore prototypes in church architecture, the additions and renovations to the building undertaken during the late nineteenth century conformed to nationally popular architectural styles that dominated church design in the archdiocese, as well as in the city of Baltimore at large. Minimal alterations to the church's original fabric, all considered general maintenance, were undertaken prior to a major renovation in 1876. These modifications involved only the addition of finishes to secondary spaces. The interior of the church was repainted in 1853 and 1855. An exception to this pattern of cosmetic improvement was the installation of a new organ in 1873. Built by the Pomplitz Company of Baltimore, it cost the parish $5,200.[8]

In 1876, the *Catholic Mirror* reported that the basement at St. Vincent's had been "considerably enlarged and beautified" by 1874. The physical constraints imposed by the masonry construction of the church render it unlikely that the basement was enlarged physically. It is more likely that the individual room configuration of the 1840 building footprint was improved.[9] As noted earlier, the Italian congregation of the future St. Leo's Parish originally utilized a chapel in the basement of St. Vincent's. It is probable that improvements to accommodate use of the basement as a chapel were completed during the early 1870s.

The parish undertook three major building campaigns during the closing decades of the nineteenth century. The first, in progress by 1876, re-

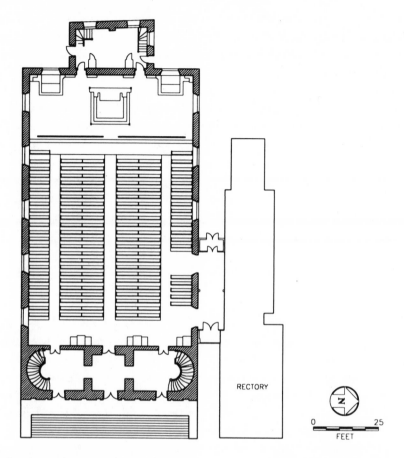

The above plans depict the late nineteenth-century configuration of the first-tier gallery and the removal of the second-tier gallery. Ŕ. CHRISTOPHER GOODWIN & ASSOCIATES, INC.

sulted in a reconfiguration of the church's plan, including the removal of the original circular apse. By 1876, the original interior plan and decoration of the church was decidedly out of fashion, even by the most conservative architectural standards. This extensive and ambitious renovation program was launched under the pastorate of Rev. Edmund Didier, who commissioned Baltimore architect George Aloysius Frederick to complete the church renovation.[10]

The renovation process continued into the next decade, as Father Didier, in anticipation of the parish's golden jubilee, undertook a second major building campaign. The c. 1887–91 work proceeded under Father

Didier's architectural guidance, and was directed by Baltimore architect George Frederick. The church's interior ornamentation was supplemented. The 1887–91 improvements reflected the elaboration associated with designs of the late Victorian period and the gilded age. The renovations also echoed the design aesthetic adopted for churches in many of the national parishes. These designs established an architectural presence through monumental scale, rich finishes, and robust ornamentation.

The third major episode of renovation that marked the nineteenth century was completed under the pastorate of Rev. John Daniel Boland. These modifications, focused on redecorating St. Vincent's, were done in 1895.

GEORGE ALOYSIUS FREDERICK

When Father Didier commissioned Frederick to complete the church renovation in 1876, the pastor hired a recognized Baltimore architect. Frederick (1842–1924) was born in Baltimore to German Catholic parents and attended local parochial schools. He received his architectural training through the atelier system, a common practice of professional apprenticeship in architectural offices. Prior to establishing his own office in 1862, Frederick was associated with two of the most prominent architectural firms in Baltimore. He served four years with the firm of Lind and Murdoch, and he also was employed in the offices of Niernsee and Neilson, the firm responsible for the design of the extant Camden Street Station (1851) and the Calvert Street Station (b. 1855, d. 1950).[11]

Frederick was a prolific architect who designed numerous domestic, religious, public, and commercial buildings. Moreover, he also was responsible for the design of major portions of Baltimore's public park system, including architectural components in Druid Hill and Patterson Park. During his forty-one-year practice, Frederick undertook the design and renovation of several Baltimore Roman Catholic churches, including St. James (1865–67), Fourteen Holy Martyrs (c. 1870), and St. Pius (1872). His commercial work included the Rennert Hotel and the Abell block of commercial structures.[12]

However, Frederick's reputation was established when he was still a young man by his execution of one of his first major commissions: the design and construction supervision of Baltimore City Hall (1867–75). The commission for the structure was awarded through an open design competition, a process frequently used to select architects for major public buildings. Frederick received a commission of $10,000 for the design and $10 for each day of on-site supervision of the project.[13]

Baltimore City Hall is recognized for its quality and innovation. The building is an early example of Second Empire–style architecture in the United States. Pioneered by architect James A. Renwick in the design of the Corcoran Gallery, Washington, D.C. (1859), this style was later adopted by Supervising Architect of the Treasury Alfred B. Mullett for such structures as the State Department Building (Old Executive Office Building), Washington, D.C. (1871–75). The Baltimore City Hall predated not only the Mullett designs, but also municipal examples such as John McArthur's Philadelphia City Hall (1874) and the now-demolished J. J. Egan's Cook County buildings (1872–75). The Second Empire style, characterized by irregular massing, robust ornamentation, elaborate cornices, and distinctive mansard roof treatments, was well suited to the demanding spatial requirements of a major office building. The scale and elaborate ornamental treatments found in the style enabled the integration of formal and impressive public spaces.

By 1876, Frederick was recognized as an established Baltimore architect with a proven track record of successful design and construction supervision. His professional reputation was firmly established by the city hall commission, and references of the period often cited Frederick as "the architect of City Hall."[14]

THE 1876 REDESIGN

The late nineteenth century was a period of increased specialization in the fields of architectural design and construction. Architects frequently viewed their primary role as providing designs for exterior and interior ornamentation and decoration. Construction fell to specialized craftsmen. While Frederick's earlier work had illustrated that the architect was well versed in construction as well as spatial design, his program for St. Vincent's demonstrated his ability to revise existing structures in accordance with popular architectural fashions. Frederick's design for the St. Vincent renovation was executed by William Murphy (contractor), Emmart & Quartiey (frescoers), Thomas Sheehan (painter), and John Bilson (stucco and plaster). The work, finished at a cost of $13,000, included the complete redesign of the church nave as well as the construction of a two-story rear addition. The building was "thoroughly modeled and enlarged"; the interior was subject to a "complete change."[15] The cost of

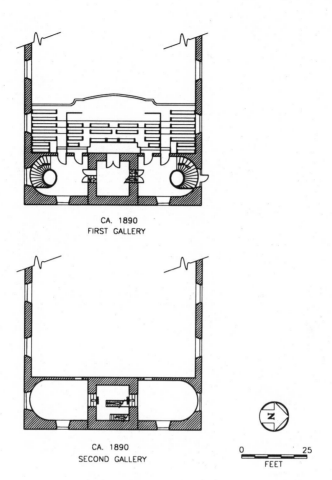

CA. 1890
FIRST GALLERY

CA. 1890
SECOND GALLERY

0   25
FEET

The above plan depicts the configuration of the church following a renovation completed between 1887 and 1891.   R. CHRISTOPHER GOODWIN & ASSOCIATES, INC.

the redesign work undertaken in 1876 is roughly equivalent to $160,420 in 1991 dollars.

Perhaps the most dramatic alteration to the building was the removal of the original church termination. The original "circle" was deleted from the plan, thus providing a larger sanctuary and expanded space for side altars. Demolition extended to the removal of the second gallery, an alteration viewed as improving "considerably the appearance of the organ gallery."[16] Frederick's rear extension of the building, which housed the sacristy on the first floor and storerooms on the upper floor, was a

The rear addition to St. Vincent de Paul Church as designed by noted Baltimore architect George Aloysius Frederick in 1876.   HARRIET WISE, 1994

sympathetic addition to the church. The addition was centered symmetrically on the original rear elevation, and it continued the design precedent established for the original church in its scale, proportion, materials, and restrained ornamentation. Double entrances to the addition were placed symmetrically behind the main altar; stairs adjoining the exterior walls of the addition provided access to the church's full basement. The footprint of the rear sacristy addition is roughly rectangular. The slightly irregular angles of the rear wall were necessitated by the boundaries of the church site, overlooking Jones Falls.

The walls of the church were accented by new stained glass windows.

While complete depictions of the exact designs of these windows have not been found, the subjects and dedications of the windows were summarized in the October 10, 1876, issue of the *Catholic Mirror.*

> The handsome stained glass windows add much to the beauty of the building. The window to the right of the sanctuary represents the sacred heart, and was presented by Father Didier in memory of Father Gildea. The window to the left represents the Immaculate Conception, and was presented by Mrs. M. J. L. Lourham. The remaining windows are as follows: St. Vincent in memory of Father Myers, presented by the Father Myers Benevolent Society; Prayer in the Garden, by B. McKenna; St. Joseph and the infant Jesus, in memory of William Clagett, from his widow now in New York; Mater Dolorosa, in memory of Jno. E. Benzinger, by his family; in memory of Bridget and Kate Byrne; in memory of John Copper; in memory of John McDonald and Philip McKittrick; in memory of Ann Shrill. Another window was presented by the Cadet Temperance Society.[17]

The interior ornamentation of the church, which originally emphasized restrained Federal-period styles, was replaced by robust ornamentation. The new decorative elements included a nonstructural coved ceiling supported by a heavy plaster cornice and frieze. This cornice can be inspected behind the present organ face at the choir level. The new ceiling reportedly was frescoed, according to period accounts. Fresco is a process in which a mural is painted with waterbased color on fresh lime plaster; the pigment bonds directly with the plaster as the finish dries. Inspection of St. Vincent's does not indicate that this textured technique was applied to the church's interior. It is more likely that murals were applied to smooth plaster finishes. Murals as decorative devices for church interiors were introduced as part of the original design in Trinity Church, Boston, which was designed by H. H. Richardson in 1872. The use of murals in the St. Vincent renovation would illustrate an awareness of the most current trends in American church decoration.

The new sanctuary wall was defined by eight engaged scagliola columns. Scagliola, a plaster and marble composite molded to imitate marble, was used for ornamentation throughout the seventeenth and eighteenth centuries.

The renovation resulted in an imposing interior that visually increased the height of the nave. The expansion of the sanctuary increased the visibility of the altar area to the congregation, thus providing greater access to the celebration of the Mass. The newly redesigned St. Vincent's was re-opened on October 1, 1876.

THE BELLS OF ST. VINCENT'S

Fr. Edmund Didier was responsible for providing an additional legacy to the church of St. Vincent de Paul. On February 1, 1883, Didier placed order no. 1846 with the Baltimore-area McShane Bell Foundry. This foundry remains in operation and continues to service St. Vincent's bells.

The company forged fourteen inscribed bells for St. Vincent de Paul ranging in weight from 113 to 2,863 pounds (see tables 10.2 and 10.3). The bells, composed of copper and tin, were delivered to the church by wagon on April 21, 1883. The addition of an excess of 13,000 pounds to the church tower required the timber reinforcement of the already substantial brick tower structure. In addition, alterations were made to the interior plan of the tower to provide easier access to the ringing console. The joists of the second-stage floor framing were cut to accommodate a straight stair that connects the bell room to the first stage of the tower. It is likely that access to the new bell room was provided previously by a simple ladder. The bells were hoisted in place by horse-drawn rope and tackle anchored to the trees that then lined Front Street.

A number of parishioners were disappointed that the chimes were not louder. At the suggestion of Prof. James Mallon, "who has the ringing in charge," four more windows were opened. As a result, the *Catholic Mirror* reported, "the volume of sound that so musically wells upon the palpitating air, both at Matin and Vesper time, is calculated to rouse fervor of the most indifferent Christian."[18]

THE GOLDEN JUBILEE RENOVATION

The interior elaboration of St. Vincent de Paul Church continued under the pastorate of Fr. Edmund Didier. Records are unclear as to when this second major nineteenth-century program was begun. Period accounts contained in the *Catholic Mirror* suggest that work was underway by 1887. The annual financial statement for the parish indicated that payment for at least portions of the project was expended in 1890.[19]

Improvements to the edifice completed during the renovation included the installation of the skylight, the erection of a baldachino (canopy), the repainting of the exterior of the church, and the gilding of the dome. The

TABLE 10.2. Bell Weights, St. Vincent de Paul

Pattern Weight	Bell Weight	Iron Parts	Total Weight
3,000	2,863	245	3,108
2,100	1,924	149	2,073
1,600	1,443	127	1,570
1,300	1,240	105	1,345
1,100	985	100	1,085
900	840	73	913
650	645	57	702
600	558	55	613
500	459	54	523
400	349	39	388
300	342	26	368
250	244	29	273
200	213	27	240
150	113	13	126

Note: All weights are in pounds.

TABLE 10.3. Bell Tones and Inscription

Tone	Inscription
C	Rev. Edmund Didier, Pastor
D	Most Rev. James Gibbons, Archbishop of Baltimore
E	St. Vincent de Paul, Pray for Us
F	Sacred Heart of Jesus, Have Mercy on Us
F sharp	Immaculate Virgin, Pray for Us
G	St. Joseph, Pray for Us
A	William Pinkney, Mayor of Baltimore
B flat	Guardian Angels, Protect Us
B	Mother of Jesus, Pray for Us
C	St. Vincent de Paul Church
D	Rev. John B. Gildea, Founder of This Church
E	In Memory of Rev. H. Myers
F	No inscription
G	The Orphans of Our Asylum

inclusion of the skylight in the redesigned ceiling of the nave was, no doubt, undertaken for practical as well as aesthetic reasons. This element was installed in 1887.[20]

Industrial development in the vicinity of the church gradually changed the once-residential neighborhood. The larger height of surrounding buildings, combined with the smoke, ash, and congestion that characterized late nineteenth-century urban centers, decreased the amount of light available to the church. Natural light was limited further by the introduction of stained glass windows during the 1876 redesign. The addition enhanced the vertical emphasis established in the 1876 redesign. The skylight served a role similar to a dome in visually establishing a monumental scale for the church's interior. This monumental scale is juxtaposed to the church's original intimate spatial geometry defined by the circular sanctuary and horizontally divided upper spaces.

The erection of a baldachino over the main altar can be viewed as a restatement of the church's original structural separation of altar and congregation created by the "circle." The element installed at St. Vincent's was a gilded wood structure of classical proportions designed by architect George Frederick. The baldachino has a long history of use in the Roman Catholic Church. Perhaps the most famous and influential example of such an element is Bernini's Baroque baldachino erected in 1624–33 in St. Peter's, Rome. Bernini's bronze design was supported by massive twisted columns terminating in a roof incorporating angels. While the design bears little or no similarity to the canopy erected at St. Vincent's, the rationale for the element was the same. Both examples were used to articulate an altar from a surrounding monumental interior. Frederick's baldachino was in place for the parish's three-day celebration of its golden jubilee. Mullian & Sons undertook the marble works. Cornelius Sheehan was responsible for the associated wood work, and Myers & Hedian completed the gilding.[21]

An isolated reference to a church fire was included in the November 7, 1891, issue of the *Catholic Mirror*. The previous spring, a fire had ignited the basement of the structure, which was decorated with palms. The article noted that "considerable damage had been done before the fire was extinguished." Physical evidence of fire damage in the vicinity of the basement apse was uncovered during the course of the 1990 rehabilitation. This evidence was confined to smoke-blackened framing. No physical evidence was uncovered to suggest that the flames extended to the upper reaches of the building.

THE 1895 BUILDING CAMPAIGN

The October 26, 1895, issue of the *Catholic Mirror* announced the reopening of St. Vincent de Paul following a "thorough renovation." Work undertaken during this project focused on redecorating the church interior in keeping with the Renaissance-influenced baldachino erected approximately five years previously. The architectural program included removal of a component dating from the church's original construction. The shallow gallery that surrounded three sides of the nave was removed. The side galleries were eliminated completely while the rear choir gallery was enlarged to approximately its present configuration.

The gilding and Baroque stylistic references first introduced in the design of the baldachino were repeated in wall, ceiling, and organ finishes. Frescoing and design were undertaken by the Baltimore firm of Forresti & Orlando. The firm's work included panels ornamented with gilded stucco in high relief, a gilded arch over the altar, partial gilding of the ceiling cornice, the addition of a radiating host ceiling motif, and the regilding of the organ front located in the choir. There were also frescoes of the four evangelists on the ceiling. On the walls were frescoes with emblems symbolizing the Old and New Testament, the episcopacy, and the papacy.

The interior fittings of the church also were renewed or replaced. A new oak pulpit was added, altar railings were finished in mahogany. It is probable that the majority of the original pews were retained. Interior photographs of the nave dating from 1939 indicate that the original boxed pews were still in place in that year. As a final addition to the church's interior, plaques depicting the Stations of the Cross were located along the outer walls in 1895. These plaques were crafted in Munich.[22]

The overall effect of the redecorating effort brought the interior of St. Vincent de Paul as close as physically possible to the appearance of a Baroque church. The liberal gilding, visual manipulation of scale, redesign of the sanctuary, addition of the rear sacristy, and removal of the original galleries brought the interior of the church into conformity with popular architectural taste. The contrast between the structure's austere classical exterior and interior was dramatic. The stylistic contrast was retained until the church's first twentieth-century renovation.

THE AESTHETIC
OF TRADITION

1940–1941

THE NEIGHBORHOOD

The migration of parishioners to the suburbs, increased industrialization in the neighborhood, and the physical decline of Baltimore's historic center all affected the fortunes of the St. Vincent's Parish in the early decades of the twentieth century. The state of the parish was reflected in the results of a Baltimore Area Catholic Census published in the March 7, 1941, issue of the *Catholic Review*. St. Vincent de Paul, one of the smaller parishes enumerated in District 1, claimed 1,500 members, including 770 adults and 730 children; the membership represented 200 families. In contrast, St. Elizabeth's Parish, also in District 1, reported a total of 9,012 members.[1]

The neighborhood surrounding St. Vincent's continued to change. Statistics compiled during the 1940 census for tracts 5-1 and 5-2 surrounding the church depicted a mixed residential-industrial neighborhood. Industries in the area included the Baltimore Poster Company (140 Front Street), the National Film Company (140 Front Street), Toland & Son, Inc. Saw Manufacturers (230–234 Front Street), Clement & Ball Shoe Manufacturing Company (324 Front Street), and Corman & Wasserman Pants Makers (12 Front Street). In addition, five wholesale meat and fish suppliers were located in the vicinity. Moreover, ten of the twenty-six buildings located within three blocks of Front Street around the church were vacant.[2]

There were 102 residential buildings containing 195 dwelling units within the blocks of Front Street between Gay and Baltimore streets. Ninety-eight of these residential buildings had been constructed before 1899; the remaining four were erected between 1900 and 1919. Attached houses accounted for the majority of the building stock. One hundred twenty dwelling units were found by census takers as "needing repair or having no private bath."[3]

The major native countries of the area's foreign-born residents, in ascending order, were Russia, Poland, and Italy. Thirteen percent of the 475 foreign-born adults in Tract 5-1 were born in Italy, as were 65 percent of the 505 adults recorded in the foreign-born category for Tract 5-2. Forty-nine percent of the total adult population in the two census tracts were naturalized American citizens.[4] In 1940, most of the residents of census tracts 5-1 and 5-2 were employed as domestic-service workers and laborers.

The national economic depression of the 1930s had imposed severe hardships on the city of Baltimore. By 1933, an estimated 10 percent of the city's total population was on relief.[5] The people of St. Vincent's suffered as much as any. The declining membership and eroding residential base of St. Vincent's Parish abated temporarily, however, as the United States mobilized for World War II. As was the case in most American industrial cities, Baltimore's role in the war effort created a demand for labor that outstripped the available workforce. The resulting influx of temporary residents into urban areas included many practicing Catholics; the number that adopted St. Vincent de Paul as their home parish taxed the physical capacity of the church.

THE PARISH CORE

An engineering report and assessment completed the same year as the census provides a profile of the St. Vincent's Parish church property in 1940. The *Engineering Report on the Property of St. Vincent de Paul R.C. Church and St. Leo Orphan Asylum, Baltimore, Maryland,* was prepared in June of that year by the firm of Tongue, Brooks, and Zimmerman of Baltimore.[6] This report identified eight buildings as owned by the church: the rectory, the church, a convent, two school buildings, two orphanage buildings, and a caretaker's house. These properties were concentrated in four areas. The original North Front Street core contained the orphanage buildings, the church, and the rectory; the brick school complex, including the convent and the school buildings, occupied opposing lots on North Front Street and North High Street; and a frame caretaker's house associated with the parish cemetery was located in Clifton Park.

The assessment portrays the original core complex of orphanage, church, and rectory as a maze of four buildings connected by wings (or

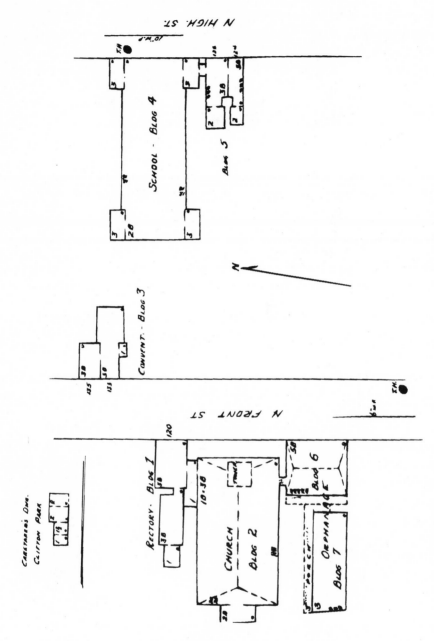

A map of parish property was prepared by the firm of Tongue, Brooks, and Zimmerman in 1940.

hyphens), porches, and brick walls. The orphanage, which was transferred from the jurisdiction of St. Vincent's Parish in the early twentieth
century and renamed St. Leo's Italian Orphan Asylum, occupied two
buildings south of the church. However, despite their operation as separate entities, St. Leo's Italian Orphan Asylum and St. Vincent's Church
and rectory maintained a close working relationship that was reinforced
by their proximity.

The principal orphanage building, which fronted on North Front
Street, was described as a brick structure supported by a stone foundation. Its shallow gable roof was clad in metal and composition shingles.
The main building occupied a ground area of 2,350 square feet and contained a total cubic volume of 145,700 cubic feet. The building's mechanical systems included electric lights and an oil-fired hot water furnace system. Interior spaces were finished with plaster walls and one-inch wood
board floors; upper-story ceilings were suspended pressed metal panels.

A three-story secondary brick building was located perpendicular to
the rear of the main structure. This annex was connected to the North
Front Street building by double-tiered porches, and it shared the main
building's heating plant. Interior finishes of the gable-roofed annex included plaster, wood sheathing, and suspended pressed metal panel
ceilings.

The report also suggested the interior plan of the buildings, and how
the rooms of the orphanage complex were used. The basement of the
four-story main building housed the boiler room and storage. A kitchen,
dining rooms, and storage rooms occupied the first floor; second-floor
rooms were devoted to offices, reception rooms, and a chapel. The third
floor served as the infirmary and contained living quarters for the Sisters;
the upper levels of the building were devoted to dormitories.

The first floor of the annex, originally constructed in 1860 as the Male
School, provided space for a gymnasium, a play room, a laundry, and
unidentified electrical machinery. The second story housed a study hall
and the third was devoted to dormitory space. The orphanage buildings
were valued at $51,000.

Photographs accompanying the engineering report show that only
minimal alterations had been made to the exterior of St. Vincent de Paul
Church. A glazed wooden vestibule with a box-like design had been appended to the central church entry. The black-and-white photographs
show that the building was painted in a contrasting color scheme with a
light body and dark trim.

Interior view looking toward the main altar of the church, 1939.   COLLEC-
TION OF CATHERINE YOUNG AND CATHERINE SINCLAS

Information in the report provided supplementary data on the
church's mechanical systems. The lighting system was described as "electric, wiring poorly installed." Insurance maps for 1890 and 1902 recorded
that the church was using a combination of gas and electricity for its lighting system.[7] Evidence of the early gas lighting system is found in the
stairways between the main floor and choir where fixtures from gas jets
survive. The church heating system relied upon hot air from two oil-fired
furnaces. The two items of concern identified in the report were the antique electrical wiring system and the potential fire hazard posed by a carpenter's shop in the church basement.

The church building was valued at approximately $140,000, based
upon a cubic-foot unit cost and square-foot floor area. The valuation
equals $1,358,000 in 1991 dollars, applying commodity price index num-
bers for the two years.[8]

Interior view looking toward choir, 1939. COLLECTION OF CATHERINE
YOUNG AND CATHERINE SINCLAS

The final building in the core complex, the rectory, was described as a
three-story brick dwelling to which two rear additions had been appended. The age of the dwelling was said to be "over 100 years old." The
rectory was the only building of the church complex that was dated in the
report. The total value of the church property, including the orphanage
complex, was assessed at $328,400, or $3,185,480 in 1991 dollars.[9]

A RETURN TO SIMPLICITY

By the 1940s, the late nineteenth-century interior of St. Vincent de Paul
again had become unfashionable. Photographs of the church taken in
1939 depict an ornate interior illuminated by electric lights supplemented
by pew candle sconces and altar candles. Wall and ceiling planes were enlivened with detailed murals, while the organ front and baldachino were

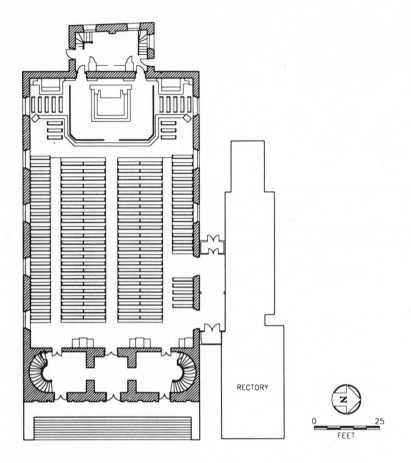

Plan depicting the c. 1940 design of the church.   R. CHRISTOPHER GOODWIN
& ASSOCIATES, INC.

gilded. Candles and statuary were found on the main and side altars, producing an overall late Victorian period interior.

Fr. John Sinnott Martin, who became pastor of St. Vincent de Paul in
May 1940, recognized the approaching parish centennial as an opportunity to redecorate the interior of the church. Among Martin's first projects was an elaborate rededication celebration that he scheduled to coincide with the church's centennial on October 19, 1941.

Father Martin's interests extended beyond liturgical and parish concerns. As noted earlier, he was an avocational poet and writer. He also offered architectural assistance to fellow priests in redesigning their
churches and rectories.[10] While his background does not suggest that

Martin was formally trained in design, he unquestionably had very defi-
nite tastes in art and architecture as well as more than casual knowledge
of their application within the church. As in the case of the original architect, the designer of the 1940 redecoration is not known for certain.
As with Father Gildea, however, credit can probably be assigned to the
pastor.

On Sunday, October 19, 1941, a day-long celebration was held to mark
the centennial of St. Vincent de Paul Church. The observance was intended to promote cohesion and a renewed sense of common dedication
within the parish, and to mark the physical renewal of the building. The
renovation was executed within the existing building fabric without
major structural changes or additions. Liturgy, fashion, and, no doubt,
economics all influenced Martin's renovation plans, just as had been the
case with the original design of the building. However, the redecoration
of St. Vincent de Paul also became the vehicle used by Father Martin to
integrate architecture, art, and liturgy. The redecoration provided the
dual opportunity to revitalize both the spirit of the parish and the church.

ART AND THE CHURCH

Martin outlined the relationship between architecture and the church
in two publications: the *Centenary Manual,* a program printed to commemorate the parish celebration; and a 1943 brochure entitled *St. Vincent
de Paul Church: Art and Architecture,* which was available in the church.
Martin used both publications to impart his understanding of theological
and aesthetic theories. For example, he recognized a clear distinction between secular art and church art; while secular art and architecture were
"expressive of human rather than divine aspirations," church art was
"governed by good taste developed through the ages and often fixed by
the positive laws of church authority." Martin held that art and architecture had been elevated to the level of "man's prayer offered to God or
God's truths taught to men."[11]

Martin's approach to ecclesiastical architecture was reminiscent of that
utilized by Father Gildea, St. Vincent's founder, in the construction of the
church in Martinsburg, West Virginia. However, Martin also recognized
that art and architecture are culturally bound and that styles can assume
historical connotations. His appreciation of the implied meaning in art
and architecture was reflected in his reservations about the appropriate-
ness of St. Vincent's original Neoclassical design with its ties to classical

Greek and Roman prototypes and associations with a secular interest in nature and reason. Although Neoclassicism had been a truly international movement, Martin traced the design inspiration for St. Vincent's through the eighteenth-century British architect Inigo Jones back to the Italian Renaissance architect Andrea Palladio. The British Palladian school influenced the development of the Neoclassical tradition in North America and frequently was cited as a dominant design source. Moreover, his interpretation gained added credibility by attributing the church's original design concepts to high-style Italian sources with connections to Rome, rather than to the more modest meetinghouse forms that influenced American ecclesiastical architecture until the mid-nineteenth century. It is interesting that both Father Martin and his late nineteenth-century predecessors wished to impose an Italian Renaissance image on the church. The difference lay in their interpretation of that image. Martin acknowledged the twentieth-century popularity of the "Palladian domestic styles" reflected in the pervasive Colonial Revival style. He sought to promote a design hierarchy in which architectural styles were selected according to the function of the building. Martin further refined the distinction between residential and ecclesiastical styles by focusing on art's symbolic and instructive value in his redecoration program. For example, the interior cornice of the church was inscribed with English excerpts from the Gospel, Epistles, and the Creed to relay the "oneness of the Catholic faith, practice and organization." Father Martin used the redecoration of St. Vincent de Paul as a tool to combine art and theology in the architectural program of the church. This architectural program also took into account the influence of the fashionable Colonial Revival style.

THE COLONIAL REVIVAL

The roots of the Colonial Revival style can be traced to the nineteenth century, when the Centennial Exposition held in Philadelphia in 1876 sparked popular interest in American colonial history. The Colonial Revival style was then refined during the early twentieth century through house designs that frequently were built in suburban contexts. Designs in this style commonly drew inspiration from local buildings that had been constructed during the Colonial and Federal periods. The revival of the colonial past evoked images of patriotism, agrarianism, security, and social stability that stood in stark contrast to the social and economic problems associated with the industrialization and urbanization of the Victorian period. The simplicity of Colonial period design became popular and replaced the ornate Victorian period styles.

The first examples of the Colonial Revival style rarely were historically correct reproductions; rather, they were interpretations heavily influenced by nineteenth-century eclectic styles. However, as scholarship increased, Colonial Revival architecture exhibited greater historical accuracy and resembled its period prototypes more closely.

The restoration and reconstruction of colonial Williamsburg during the 1930s marked the apex of popular interest in the Colonial Revival style—it became the dominant influence in domestic architecture and decorative arts. For those unable to visit Williamsburg, mass-circulation magazines, catalogues, and builders' guides provided access to the style. The influence of the Colonial Revival movement surpassed fashion in architecture and decorative arts: "Colonialism is not a surface phenomena, a thin veneer over the real body of American life, but a network of communications and linkages that reaches deep into American experience and behavior."[12]

The Colonial Revival style also was viewed as an educational tool. The cultural and economic differences between native-born American and "second wave" immigrant groups from southern and eastern Europe had become a source of social tension during the late nineteenth and early twentieth centuries. Assimilation of the nation's ethnically identified populations was encouraged during outbreaks of xenophobia, and by social reform movements. The role of art in the movement was reflected by Edwin Howland Blashfield, the noted muralist responsible for two historical works executed in 1903 at the Baltimore County Courthouse. Blashfield held that art in public buildings was "good . . . for the uneducated Irishman, German, Swede, Italian, who may stroll into some new city hall in our country." Such art served a public function by teaching "patriotism."[13]

Rev. John Sinnott Martin applied the concept of art as a public educator within an ecclesiastical context. For Martin, the art developed in the redecoration of St. Vincent de Paul became a medium for divinely inspired religious education.

THE CENTENNIAL REVIVAL

Father Martin capitalized upon the prevailing interest in earlier American architecture in choosing design sources for the church redecoration.

In addition, the simplicity in ornamentation and emphasis on hand-crafted materials found in examples of the popular Colonial Revival style also lent themselves to the integration of design references to early church history.

As noted by Fr. Richard Lawrence, St. Vincent's current pastor, many of Father Martin's devices, such as the use of English inscriptions, anticipated the later direction of Roman Catholicism. The centennial redecoration of St. Vincent de Paul adapted the historical approach found in the secular Colonial Revival style, which was rooted in American history, to an ecclesiastical program that drew upon the early church for inspiration.

Popular support for historic restoration projects and the association of such a project with St. Vincent's, no matter how modest, also may have appealed to a man of Martin's tastes and varied interests. The redecorating program supported Martin's more immediate goal of reviving interest in St. Vincent's and sprucing up the image of the parish.

Father Martin sought to reconcile the interior decoration with the exterior of the edifice. Architecture, art, and furnishings all were integrated in the redecoration scheme; all were instilled with ecclesiastical meaning.

The three principles that guided the redecorating project were, as Martin stated, simplicity, sincerity, and suitability. Compatibility with the original architectural style of the building was established as the primary objective under the principle of simplicity. By the 1940s, the elaborate late nineteenth-century finishes were no doubt frayed by fifty years of service and darkened by the city dirt. In contrast, the simplicity of the classically derived church exterior was once again fashionable. The Victorian period ornamentation was removed and the interior structure of the late nineteenth-century building was revealed. However, no attempt was made to restore the church's original plan or finishes; rather, a redecorating approach was applied to the interior.

An architecturally honest regard for building materials was implemented under the principle of sincerity. Under Martin's scheme, the artificial was considered to be "always bad art and as an offering to God, it is artistic insult."[14] Therefore, faux finishes, commonly used during both the Federal and Victorian periods to give inexpensive materials the appearance of more expensive ones, were rejected in principle. Martin's design theories implied sharp criticism of the late nineteenth-century church renovation with its painted marble and its elaborately gilded finishes. However, in practice, faux finishes were applied during the 1940 renovation in instances where they were appropriate to the program. For example, woodwork that combined various woods received a uniform mahogany finish rather than the more modest natural finishes of its components.

Martin's third principle, that of suitability, required that the altar dominate the overall design. Throughout the church's history, the altar had been the central focus of the building's interior, although the way in which this objective was achieved varied from period to period. In the original design, the congregation's attention was drawn to the rear wall circle through the plan, scale, and interior geometry of the building. The circle was the dominant element of the original design. The congregation, seated at floor level and in the tiered galleries, was an audience to the celebration of the Mass.

The physical segregation of the main altar in the circle was eliminated under the 1876 redesign of the church, but was restated with the addition of the baldachino in 1890. However, by 1895, the exuberant Victorian period ornamentation had overtaken the church. While the altar remained the visual center of the building, it competed for attention with elaborate secondary ornamentation.

ART AND ARCHITECTURE

Although no major structural changes were undertaken during the 1940s redecorating, Father Martin categorized changes to building finishes as architectural improvements. There is little doubt, based on Martin's writing of the period, that he approved all work directly.

The interior of the church was repainted by the Baltimore firm of Charles Fritz Company. The gilding and fresco work undertaken in 1895 were "softened" or eliminated. Ornamentation extraneous to structural elements was deleted, and emphasis was placed instead on the simple enhancement of existing building elements through the subtle use of color. In emphasizing the structural components of the building, Martin utilized the concept in modern architectural theory that relates form to function. Under this concept, the structure of a building serves both a practical and an aesthetic purpose, and it becomes the basis for ornamentation.

A blue color scheme was selected for the ceiling; the ceiling plane was painted pastel blue while the skylight was lacquered blue. In contrast, the robust bracketed cornice was emphasized in off-white pigment, and inspirational inscriptions were delineated on the frieze in red. As previously mentioned, these inscriptions were executed in English to maximize their

educational value. The inscription read: "ONE FOLD AND ONE SHEPHERD
∴ ONE GOD AND FATHER OF ALL ∴ ONE SACRIFICE ∴ ONE LAWGIVER AND
IVDGE ∴ ONE HOLY CATHOLIC AND APOSTOLIC CHVRCH ∴ ONE BODY AND
ONE SPIRIT ∴ ONE LORD ONE FAITH ONE BAPTISM." Martin explained the
significance of the frieze in his 1943 booklet:

> The heavy cornice and frieze seemed to invite the use of inscriptions.
> Texts were chosen from the Gospel, St. Paul's Epistles, the Creed and the
> Fathers to point [to] the oneness of Catholic faith, practice and organiza-
> tion. These are done in English so that anyone may read. The use of V for
> U and I for J is the Latin classical style. Red lettering, chosen for its carry-
> ing power, set the note for lower details like the consecration crosses,
> sanctuary floor coverings and confessional curtain designs. The zodiac
> signs among the texts on the frieze suggest the passing seasons thru which
> stands unchanging the teaching and character of the one true Church. At
> the altar end, these are replaced by the winged symbols of the four Evan-
> gelists: the Angel of St. Matthew who emphasizes Jesus' Messiahship; the
> Lion of St. Mark who stresses His kingship; the Ox of St. Luke who cen-
> ters attention on His atoning sacrifice; the Eagle of St. John whose keen vi-
> sion is fixed on His divine nature. The haloed Dove on the frieze behind
> the altar symbolizes the Holy Spirit.[15]

Off-white walls, white woodwork, and red accents were selected for
the remaining work. Mahogany finishes were chosen for wooden furnishings including railings, pews, and the pulpit, regardless of wood type.
Gilding was used to accentuate reliefs on the altar rails and on the shouldered surrounds of the doorways. These reliefs adopted grapevine motifs
that symbolized the "Holy Eucharist as well as the unity of Christ and the
Church."[16]

The plaques depicting the Stations of the Cross, which were installed
along the outside walls in 1895, were polychromed in the 1940s redecoration. Historically, multicolored paint treatment was applied to statuary in
Greek and Roman temples, but this historical design precedent was not,
understandably, cited by Martin in his descriptions of the project.

Mullan Harrison Company, the Baltimore firm involved in the construction of the baldachino designed by Frederick, was retained to rework
the sienna marble altar so that the tabernacle would comply with church
law. The existing narrow altar steps, intended to support candlesticks and
flowers, were replaced with single steps designed for the same purpose.
The gilding of the baldachino was "antiqued" to achieve a greater integration between the altar and the canopy.

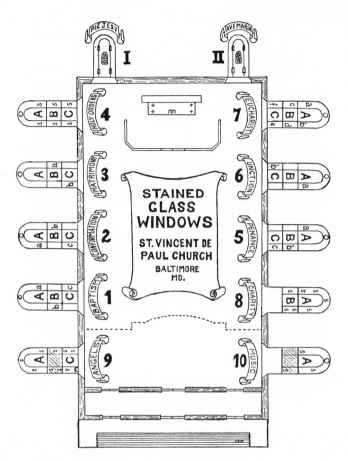

Diagram prepared in 1940 by Father Martin depicting the installation of stained glass windows.

The most ambitious change completed during the 1940s redecorating was the replacement of the church's stained glass windows. Stained glass windows first were installed in the church during the late nineteenth century. Black-and-white photographs of the church interior dating from the 1930s suggest these earlier windows adopted a traditional design depicting single scenes. Based on the time of installation and the tonal qualities of the photographs, it is probable that the earlier examples were richly colored in keeping with the elaborate interior decoration of the period.

The new windows installed under Father Martin's charge were purchased through donation and were fabricated by the Henry Lee Willet Studios of Philadelphia. Each triple panel unit was comprised of pastel lights inset with medallions of brilliant antique glass. Subjects depicted in

TABLE 11.1 Description of Windows, St. Vincent de Paul

Subject/ Sacrament	Panel 1	Panel 2	Panel 3
1. Baptism	A. Jesus baptized by John the Baptist a. The Lamb of God	B. The Disciples baptizing under the Lord's direction b. Stag symbol of baptism	C. Baptism in the early Church c. Light and vestment given at Baptism
2. Confirmation	A. Feed My Lambs, Feed a. Peter's denial	B. Pentecost b. Peter's sermon in tongues	C. Confirmation at Samaria c. Cornelius, first Gentile convert, receives the Holy Ghost
3. Matrimony	A. Creation of Adam and Eve	B. Marriage of Joseph and Mary a. Christ's teaching on marriage	C. Marriage Feast at Cana b. Thomas More and John Fisher, Martyrs in the cause of Matrimony
4. Holy Orders	A. Melchisdech's Sacrifice of bread and wine	B. Call of the Twelve to be "fishers of men"	C. Ordination in the early church
5. Penance	A. Cure of the paralyzed Man a. The cured man taking up his bed	B. The Woman Taken in Adultery b. Christ dismissed the woman: "Go and sin no more"	C. The Gift to Peter of Keys to bind and loose from sin c. A penitent at confession
6. Extreme Unction	A. Death of St. Joseph, patron of a happy death a. Priest bringing last sacraments to the sick	B. Mary Anoints Jesus beforehand for His burial	C. St. James the Less writing in his inspired Epistle the doctrine of Extreme Unction b. Sick call table prepared
7. Holy Eucharist	A. Multiplication of Loaves and Fishes a. Crossed fish symbol of Christ b. Seven baskets of fragments	B. The Last Supper c. & d. The Passover Lamb and the Pelican, symbols of sacrifice	C. Communion at Mass in the Catacombs e. & f. Rising and Setting Sun
I. Pie Jesu			
II. Ave Maria			
8. Charity	A. The Sermon on the Mount	B. St. Vincent and the Poor	
9. The Angels	A. The Archangels		C. Guardian Angels
10. Sacred Music			

the medallions included the seven sacraments, music, and angels. The windows were operational to insure adequate church ventilation. Each window was fabricated at a cost of $500 per unit, or $4,850 in 1991 dollars. An illustration is included that reproduces Martin's diagram for the windows; Table 11.1 provides a key for this illustration.

The basement of the church, which historically had been utilized by the parish schools, as a parish hall, as an overflow area for gatherings on the main floor, and to house mechanicals and services, also was modified during the 1940s renovation. The cast-iron columns were clad with Corinthian capital sleeves. The original circle was retained in the basement plan.

Improvements to the basement gathering space included the installation of pews from St. Edward's Church, and the addition of plaster models of the stylized Art Deco–style statuary used in St. Katharine's Church. The former parish was founded in 1880 and was building a second church during the early 1940s; the latter parish was founded in 1902. Exit doors also were installed to provide access through the side elevation facing the rectory.

Improvements to the exterior of the building were minimal, as was the case during earlier renovations. The church again was painted white; the dome was painted green to simulate oxidized copper. The latter was selected in lieu of gilding, which was judged less durable and more expensive to maintain.

CHURCH FURNISHINGS

Church furnishings were important components of the Martin redecoration scheme, and they were the subject of narratives in the *Centenary Manual* and *St. Vincent de Paul Church: Art and Architecture*. In these works, Martin discussed nineteen ceremonial and decorative objects. Selected earlier church furnishings that were compatible with the design principles were retained. Liturgy and fashion dictated the selection of appropriate fixtures.

Church furnishings can be divided into three functional categories: (1) permanent furnishings, (2) ceremonial objects, and (3) church accessories. Permanent furnishings at St. Vincent's included the altar, the sanctuary railing, pews and kneelers, confessionals, an organ, a baptistry, and a font. The main altar and tabernacle, the focus of the building, were modified slightly as described above. The altar incorporated portions of the simple 1841 fixture and retained features of the elaborate baldachino erected under Father Didier.

A mahogany railing ornamented by gilded cast-iron crosses and fili-gree panels defined the spatially reduced sanctuary. The railing delineated the ceremonial center of the building from the congregation seated in the pews. The church's existing pews, constructed of heart pine with ma-hogany trim, were retained; however, the numbered paneled pew doors were removed and installed as wall paneling in the adjoining rectory. The removal of the numbered pew doors is documented by Martin, and re-flected the general trend toward abandoning pew rents as an economic mainstay of church support, and emphasized the trend toward open seat-ing. Envelope collections generally replaced pew rents in the archdiocese when pew subscriptions fell with the economic depression of the 1930s. However, envelope collections were not used by St. Vincent's Parish to raise revenue.[17]

Church confessionals located at the rear of the nave were expanded and refurbished. The wood-paneled cubicles included "opaque odor and germ-proof grills" as an added incentive to potential penitents.

A new church organ, a Hammond Model E electric organ, replaced the instrument housed in the rear gallery. The existing organ front was re-tained and slightly recessed to provide additional space in the confined upper level. The gilding on the case of the instrument was softened to an "antiqued" finish. According to the detailed description of the instrument contained in the *Centenary Manual,* the "organ cannot be played off pitch, requires no tuning, is impervious to extremes in temperature and humid-ity, and due to the millions of tonal qualities possible, the organist is en-abled at all times to voice the organ at will according to his taste with in-stantaneous results."

The baptistry was installed in the building wing connecting the church with the rectory. City map data document that this wing was in place by 1890. The baptistry contained an early zinc font that originally incorpo-rated a conical top and ornamental base figures; these latter elements were eliminated in the redecoration.

Ceremonial objects included in the redecoration program included the church crucifix, reliquaries, bells, brass candlesticks, credence table, bench, statuary, pulpit, lanterns, and poor boxes. The crucifix was of "bounty" design as depicted by the archdiocesan shield and seal. Prior to the redecoration, the cross that had hung on the wall adjoining the narthex was relocated to accommodate a new confessional. Two reliquaries, fabricated in Mexico, were installed on the altar. These wood and brass elements contained the relics of St. Vincent de Paul and St. Felicity.

Four statues were documented in 1940. The Sacred Heart and Our Lady of Victory were executed in Carrara marble; St. Joseph was carved in alabaster; and St. Vincent was depicted in marble-dust composition. The credence table, bench, and pulpit were movable wooden furnishings. The table and bench predated the redecoration. The white oak pulpit, installed in the church in 1895, was refinished to imitate mahogany.

The condition of the electric lighting system identified in the 1940 insurance assessment appears to have been addressed under Martin's project. Martin's articles specifically mentioned bronze lanterns with upper and lower units to diffuse light. It is doubtful that these new fixtures would have been added to the existing wiring system.

Church accessories included curtains and floor coverings. American carpets of Oriental design were selected for the sanctuary while the aisles and the choir loft were accented by red carpeting. Curtains installed behind the altar and confessional were simple unbleached monkscloth.

The 1941 redecoration of the church sought to establish artistic, architectural, and liturgical harmony in the church. In addition, the redecoration was intended to provide religious instruction and inspiration to the congregation. The redecorating program recognized the significance of the original architecture and sought interior treatments that were compatible with the classical prototypes echoed on the exterior of the building. These interior treatments fulfilled the aesthetic criteria developed by Father Martin through color, restrained ornamentation, and structural emphasis. The overall 1895 framework of plan, spatial divisions, and furnishings was retained. The particulars of color, finish, and ornamentation were manipulated to suit the aesthetics of the period and the functional requirements of the building. The redesign of St. Vincent's physical framework to meet the functional requirements of use would be addressed during the second major twentieth-century renovation of the building.

THE PRESERVATION
AESTHETIC

1973–1990

By the early 1990s, the area surrounding St. Vincent de Paul Church bore little resemblance to the affluent residential neighborhood that originally supported its construction. Urban redevelopment, building demolition, and new construction physically had isolated the church and its rectory. The orphanage and the annex were demolished in 1967, and the lots were donated to the city as park land. A parking lot, incorporating contemporary statuary commissioned by the parish, was located north of the rectory on land previously occupied by dwellings.

Road construction also had an effect on both the appearance and the accessibility of the neighborhood. Fayette Street had been expanded to a major city artery while Front Street diminished in importance. Jones Falls, the historic rear boundary of the core church complex, was contained and paved; its location was marked by the Jones Falls Expressway, an inner-city extension of Interstate 83.

Federal construction had influenced the character of the area in the vicinity of the church. In 1967, Baltimore's main post office was constructed opposite the Front Street entrance of the church. Oriented toward Fayette Street, the Federal complex today occupies an eight-block area that in 1940 contained 212 dwellings.[1] Public housing projects also were built in areas east of the church that previously had been composed of similar blocks of Baltimore's signature brick rowhouses.

St. Vincent de Paul Church and its rectory were isolated historic properties. Clear views of the monumental church front that once dominated the neighborhood had been all but eliminated. While the tower remained an integral part of the Baltimore skyline, the rear elevation of the edifice, viewed from the expressway, was the most visible public image of the landmark.

During these same decades, the archdiocese of Baltimore underwent a transformation reminiscent of its early years under Bishop Carroll. Vatican Council II changed the direction of the church. Among the most important innovations brought on by Vatican II and adopted in the Baltimore archdiocese was the empowerment of the laity. Under the leadership of Archbishop (later Cardinal) Lawrence Shehan, the laity assumed leadership roles through representation on the corporations of parish entities.[2] The laity was encouraged and empowered, mainly through parish councils, to play an active part in determining the structure, future, and programs of the parishes.

As a result of these changes, St. Vincent de Paul was redefined; its status changed from that of a "territorial" parish, drawing membership from within defined geographic boundaries, to a "metropolitan" parish, drawing its congregation from throughout the Baltimore metropolitan area. This important shift was discussed in detail in part 1. In addition to taking a more active role in numerous parish activities, the cosmopolitan membership of St. Vincent de Paul Church, through its parish council and committees, directed plans for the church's rehabilitation to mark its 150th anniversary.

GROUNDWORK

The foundation for the church's rehabilitation predates the construction project by two decades. Maintaining a landmark vulnerable to the physical decay of age and urban encroachment necessitated pro-active strategies. Two elements were constants in decisions related to the church during this most recent phase of parish history: the support of actions through parish consensus and the desire to retain the existing church building.

Both objectives were illustrated in 1973. In that year, Fr. Richard Lawrence, then a newly appointed temporary administrator who later became parish pastor, and two parish corporators, Albert Puliafico and John Bailey, proposed three goals for parish approval: the employment of a coordinator of religious education; the creation of a parish council; and the establishment of a historic trust fund. All three goals were adopted. The historic trust fund established an endowment that provided for the immediate maintenance of the church.

The parish next sought to safeguard the building through public chan-
nels. With the participation of local, state, and federal agencies, the parish
secured official recognition of its church as a Baltimore cultural resource.
The church was documented as a local Baltimore landmark through the
city's Commission for Historical and Architectural Preservation (CHAP).
The church next was nominated for inclusion on the National Register of
Historic Places, the nation's official list of historic properties worthy of
preservation; the church was entered on the National Register on February 12, 1974.

National Register designation was a strategic political maneuver that
offered several advantages. Designation provided public recognition of
the building's significance in addition to its importance to the parish as an
active church. This recognition made church preservation a cause likely
to be supported by Baltimore's broad-based and active historic preservation constituency.

Moreover, recognition of the church imparted consideration in the
planning stages of state and federal projects. Such consideration was a
concern in light of recent construction in the neighborhood and the like-
lihood of continued redevelopment. While National Register listing did
not totally protect the church, it did afford an avenue for meaningful participation.

As a result of National Register listing, the church also became eligible
to compete for federal preservation grants offered by the National Park
Service (NPS) and administered through the Maryland Historical Trust
(MHT). Funding for continued building maintenance was an ongoing
concern, despite the financial support of St. Vincent's own historic trust.
Matching grants expanded the reach of maintenance dollars. St. Vincent's
was awarded a $30,000 grant during the 1978–80 funding cycle to sup-
port, in part, the installation of a new roof and rehabilitation of the
church tower. The balance of the $102,000 project was raised by the
parish through its historical trust and a project-specific fundraising
campaign.

DESIGN RULES

In return for grant monies, the parish agreed to undertake all work on
the church in compliance with the *Secretary of the Interior's Standards for
Rehabilitation and Guidelines for Rehabilitating Historic Buildings* (36 CFR
67).[3] A Historic Preservation Easement also was conveyed to the Mary-

land Historical Trust. These concessions had an important impact on defining the types of changes that the parish could undertake, both for projects underwritten by grants and for future privately financed work. Three approaches to the building were possible:

1. Preservation, or "applying measures to sustain the existing form, integrity, and material" of the church;
2. Restoration, or the "process of accurately recovering the form and details of a property and its setting as it appeared at a particular period of time by means of the removal of later work or by the replacement of missing earlier pieces"; and
3. Rehabilitation, or the "process of returning a property to a state of utility through repair or alteration which makes possible an efficient contemporary use while preserving those portions or features of the property which are significant to its historical, architectural and cultural values."

Of the three historic preservation approaches, rehabilitation offered the most flexibility in modifying the historic building for new or continued service.[4] The intent of this approach is to ensure that modifications to historic properties are sensitive to historic features.

During the 1970s, recognition of the architectural significance of the church was achieved, participation in federal and state project planning was guaranteed, and the rules for future modifications to the design of the church were established. The parish next focused its attention on the ability of the existing building to meet its current needs through a process that involved the full parish membership. As in the case of earlier building renovations, liturgy, fashion, and the existing structure influenced the development of the design. In contrast to earlier building campaigns, credit for the resulting rehabilitation cannot be assigned to one individual. The parish achieved design through consensus, a formal process that had become an operational principle of parish action.

However, despite this design by committee, the project followed an efficient four-phase pattern common to the majority of such successful projects. In the first stage, analysis of use determines that the existing design does not serve the contemporary use of the building adequately. In stage 2, new aesthetic, functional, and spatial priorities are established. In stage 3, priorities are translated to specific design proposals within the context of the historic building fabric. The final stage of a rehabilitation project involves the execution of the approved design.

ARCHITECTURAL PROGRAMMING: THE ART AND
ARCHITECTURE COMMITTEE

The Art and Architecture Committee, as directed by the Parish Council, served as the task force to develop the renovation program for St. Vincent de Paul Church. Members of each of the liturgical communities, the
Liturgy Committee, the Education Committee, and the Parish Council
formed the subcommittee. The committee held its first meeting on August 16, 1983, to develop a procedure to achieve consensus on church renovation. The committee designed a six-step strategy that included: (1) fa-
miliarization of parish members with the importance of liturgical space;
(2) development of a vision statement, taking into consideration the comments of parish members; (3) consultation with a design professional to
develop the vision statement; (4) circulation of the schematic plans
among parish members for review and comment; (5) assessment of plan
suitability and feasibility; and (6) implementation.[5]

The role of architecture and liturgy was explored through analysis and
discussion of the bishops' pastoral letter on art and architecture, *Environment and Art in Catholic Worship*. Four guiding principles and nine target
objectives subsequently were identified for the renovation; all but one of
these principles and objectives were rooted in *Environment and Art*. The
four principles include:

1. A space becomes a church in the presence of a worshipful community; the chief function of the space and its appointments and furnishings should be to facilitate the coming together of the members
   as a worshiping group.
2. The best of the artistic and architectural elements of our historic
   structure should be used/reused to preserve the heritage of the
   church and to respect the footprints of our forbearers.
3. The improvements in the physical conditions of the worship space
   should reflect our self-image to ourselves and to others.
4. Renovations in the physical conditions of the worship space should
   enhance the aesthetic and functional aspects of worship; they should
   also reflect an awareness of the spiritual and practical needs of
   others.[6]

The nine target objects developed were:

1. Within the structure, the primary space should be a place in which
   the community gathers for liturgical worship.

2. At times when one person speaks for or to the community, such as when a reader proclaims the Sacred Scripture or the celebrant says the eucharistic prayer, each member of the community should be able to make eye contact with that person.

3. At times when the whole community prays together, such as when a song is sung or the Lord's Prayer recited, each member of the community should be able to make eye contact with a representative number of other members of the community.

4. The central focal area (the bema) should provide for a variety of uses; appointments and furnishings should be flexible. The central area should also allow for a variety of enhancements of liturgical celebration, such as music, dance, drama, and audiovisuals.

5. The primary actions of our worship are the Liturgy of the Word and the Liturgy of the Eucharist. The space should make these actions distinct and equally prominent.

6. The space should provide a place for greeting, meeting, and hospitality to strengthen and build the reality of community.

7. The sacraments, particularly baptism, are a fundamental part of our communal, liturgical life. Appointments for their celebration should be provided in prominent and convenient places.

8. A space for private devotion and prayer, especially in relation to the Blessed Sacrament, should be provided.

9. Consideration of the handicapped should be included in all renovation plans.[7]

Utilizing a town-meeting format, the Art and Architectural Committee presented the renovation principles and objectives to the parish membership for review and comment on two successive weekends in 1984. Each principle and objective was demonstrated, using slides that illustrated its application in other churches. Approval or disapproval ratings for each principle and objective were collected applying a five-point Likert scale.

A total of 175 survey responses were received, and the raw data were analyzed. This analysis incorporated four approaches: simple tabulations were compiled; ratio analysis was undertaken; percentage tabulations were prepared; and dissent responses were analyzed. Survey results were extrapolated from these data and presented as findings in a document entitled *Report on Parish Survey on Renovation Objectives—St. Vincent de Paul Church.*

The results of the survey revealed the priorities of the parish in approaching the renovation project. Principles 1 and 2 were accepted as principles; principle 2, dealing with historic preservation, received the highest overall approval rating. Principle 3 received the lowest approval rating of the four principles and was redefined as a guiding principle to be implemented in subordination to the historic preservation principle. Principle 4 received a lukewarm approval rating, but it was retained in the overall program as a useful principle.

Analysis of the data related to the target objectives revealed enthusiastic support for use, focus, and handicapped accessibility. Objective 5, establishing the primary use of the space for gathering for worship, received high approval ratings. Objective 6, dealing with eye contact with the proclaimer, also was deemed a useful principle; however, objective 7, concerning eye contact with the community, was less favorably received and was judged feasible with conditions. Objective 4, concerning flexibility, was found to be appropriate only if the design adequately avoided the appearance of impermanence. Objective 5, concerning focus for the Word and Eucharist, was approved overwhelmingly, but objective 6, on the creation of a gathering space, was endorsed only upon the condition that the design was compatible with the building's historical design. Objective 7, on space for other sacraments, received solid endorsement. Objective 8, dealing with the position of the tabernacle, was assessed as the most challenging design problem. Objective 9, on handicapped access, also was received and supported enthusiastically.

The process of defining principles, objectives, and achieving consensus for the church rehabilitation was essentially an exercise in traditional architectural programming through which priorities in aesthetics, use, and spatial orientation were established. While the process was driven by liturgical concerns and the need to achieve consensus, the results provided a profile of the architectural patron, the parish, and its design priorities. In addition, the data identified the reasons why the existing church design was inadequate, and they defined the magnitude of building changes necessary for the rehabilitation.

The members of the current parish embraced the existing church design as significant and worthy of preservation. The existing elements of St. Vincent's original design, surviving nineteenth-century alterations, and the early twentieth-century redecoration were recognized as important to parish history. All were integrated in a preservation aesthetic, which served to limit discussion on how best to express the parish's contemporary self-image. The expression of aesthetic preferences became subservient to preservation of the building's existing fabric.

As had been the case with previous designers, renovators, and decorators, the contemporary parish viewed the church as a series of hierarchical spaces specialized by function. However, the contemporary parish differed from its design predecessors in its emphasis on the spatial requirements for community and interaction. These priorities impacted the existing plan in three ways. First, they necessitated the addition of a space designed to promote social cohesion. Second, they required the restructuring of the nave and aisles to promote worship as a community, while affording flexibility and maintaining "distinct" and "prominent" areas for the Liturgy of the Word and the Liturgy of the Eucharist. Finally, they required the removal of obstacles in the existing design that would exclude or make handicapped members of the current or future parish appear to be conspicuous.

Based on the results of the survey, the Art and Architecture Committee proceeded with the next stage of its strategy. This stage involved the assistance of a liturgical space planner to give substance to the principles and objectives developed for the renovation program.

GOALS REFINED

In keeping with the direction established by the Parish Council, the parishioners of St. Vincent de Paul Church were the principal architects in the church renovation. In May 1986, the Art and Architecture Committee established specific design goals for the worship space, adjacent spaces, and finishes of the church. These thirteen goals were detailed, concise, and practical, and they reflected a desire to reinforce community, establish a functional worship area, accommodate the sacraments, and preserve the architectural character of the building.[8]

The services of Rev. John Buscemi, St. Mary's Church, Janesville, Wisconsin, a liturgical consultant and designer, were enlisted to assist in developing schematic renovation designs related to liturgical concerns. Correspondence between Father Buscemi and St. Vincent's Art and Architecture Committee for the period July 1986 to September 1987 documents the development, revision, and refinement of the renovation design. Schemes for the treatment of the high altar, the design of the sanctuary, seating capacity, pew arrangement, the location of the baptismal font, the location of the music area, creation of a gathering space, and handicapped access were discussed at length.

The degree of detail and plan development was reflected in a floor plan

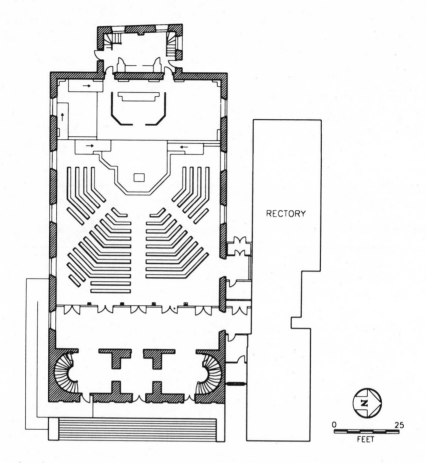

RECTORY

N

0   25
FEET

Plan depicting the interior reconfiguration of St. Vincent de Paul Church in 1990.

developed during the second design revision. A gathering area was created adjoining the narthex wall of the nave. Seating in the worship area was redesigned to facilitate interaction among members of the community, and between the community and the proclaimer. A music area that provided for a song leader was integrated into the seating plan. The sanctuary adopted an asymmetrical design that integrated a spatial hierarchy consisting of a central altar, an ambo, and a chair. The high altar retained its location on the rear wall; a communion rail was used as a device to delineate the high altar and the sanctuary.

The Art and Architecture Committee presented its proposed renovation plan to the church membership on July 17, 1988. The initial presentation was discussed further in a series of three parish "town meetings." Plans also were reviewed by the Archdiocesan Buildings and Properties Commission, by the director of the Archdiocesan Liturgy Office, and by the board of directors of the St. Vincent Historic Trust Fund. A revised renovation budget and final modifications, which incorporated the comments of the parish and archdiocese, were circulated to parish members on September 18, 1988. The document proposed a two-phase construction campaign that would cover the complete renovation of the church. A total revised budget of $492,000 was proposed for implementation of phases 1 and 2.

On September 25 and October 7, 1988, a referendum to decide whether to proceed with the renovation project was conducted. A total of 165 ballots were cast on four questions. Question no. 1, "Shall we proceed with the renovation project?" received an overwhelmingly positive (99 percent) response. Question no. 2, "Is the design as presented and modified satisfactory?" was endorsed by 88 percent of the parishioners who responded. Question no. 3, "Is the suggested phasing plan appropriate?" elicited a positive response from 90 percent. Question no. 4 concerned project funding; 89 percent of those casting ballots preferred funding the project through the historic trust, augmented by a project-specific campaign. After five years of detailed planning, one might have expected lagging enthusiasm for the project. However, while minor disputes regarding particular aspects of the rehabilitation were reflected in the parish consensus process, the overwhelming commitment of the parish to proceed with the rehabilitation was noteworthy.

ARCHITECTURAL PLANS

The Baltimore architectural firm of Murphy & Dittenhafer Architects, Inc., was selected to bring the renovation program to fruition. Michael V. Murphy, AIA, served as the project principal while Todd Grove served as the project architect for the firm. Years of planning by the parish simplified the role of the architectural firm. Few previous clients of this firm had displayed such intimate knowledge about their building or had defined their requirements and expectations so carefully.

Historic rehabilitation projects are notorious for their unpredictability. Structural problems frequently are hidden by sound materials. Existing conditions assessments are, therefore, critical to avoid unexpected discoveries during the course of construction that can result in delays and unanticipated costs. On-site investigation was undertaken by the architects to assess conditions and to develop construction strategies for implementing the architectural program adopted by the parish. Progressive stages of architectural design were documented through project drawings of increasing refinement. These drawings reflect a logical and well-organized approach to the rehabilitation, as well as acuity in anticipating problems and dealing with historic building fabric.

Areas affected by the proposed work or "as-builts" were documented through drawings in March 1988. Schematic designs and improvement schedules were completed in August 1989. Comprehensive architectural plans and construction specifications were refined by the spring of 1990. The sixteen-sheet set of construction plans was prepared by April 2, 1990, for use in conjunction with the March 27, 1990, project manual. In addition to the title page, the drawings included a demolition plan, a floor plan, sections, details of the new glazed wall, miscellaneous details, pew details, handicapped ramp details, a power and lighting plan, altar modification work, and a framing plan.

The final renovation design realized by Murphy & Dittenhafer Architects incorporated many of the design solutions that the parish had developed in consultation with Rev. John Buscemi. The church nave and rectory building wing were redesigned to accommodate a gathering area adjoining and extending into the nave. The assembly space integrated an irregular seating arrangement of four groupings. The original church pews were reconfigured to conform to the radiating seating plan. The asymmetrical sanctuary plan was refined from the preliminary schematic designs and was elevated above the main floor. The reconfigured high altar retained its prerenovation position but was elevated from the new sanctuary by a riser. A complex design of handicapped-access ramps was integrated inconspicuously into the design of the elevated platform for both the sanctuary and the high altar. The confessionals that occupied the rear of the nave were removed and replaced by a reconciliation room in the building wing connecting church and rectory. A handicapped-accessible restroom and preparation area were located on the opposing end of the connection.

The renovation project manual adopted the standard format of the Construction Specifications Institute. In addition to bidding requirements, contract forms, and conditions, the manual addressed general specifications, selective demolition, masonry, metals, wood and plastic work, thermal and moisture protection, doors and windows, finishes, and electrical work. As summarized in the project specification manual, the project encompassed the following tasks:

- Installation of exterior handicapped-access ramp
- Modification to exterior doors
- Alterations to vestibule area, including enlargement of existing masonry openings
- Construction of new enclosed gathering space
- Modifications to the existing worship space, including new and refinished floors, new sanctuary platforms and ramps
- Modifications to existing marble altars
- Associated modifications to the existing mechanical and electrical systems
- Improvements to the "bridge" area between the existing church and rectory, including a new handicapped-accessible toilet room, sacristy, storage closet, and reconciliation room.

Provisions for regular progress meetings were included as part of the project specifications. Sealed bids for demolition and general construction were received by Rev. Richard Lawrence at the St. Vincent de Paul rectory on April 18, 1990.

Tamarack Construction Company, Inc., Glen Arm, Maryland, was awarded the contract for demolition and construction. Fourteen subcontractors were included on the Tamarack project team.

Redesign of the church pews to accommodate the new seating arrangement was awarded to Augustus Woodworking. Elizabeth Faas served as project conservator for the Augustus work. The project preconstruction meeting was held on June 6, 1990, and a schedule of biweekly progress meetings was established. A construction completion schedule was developed covering successive stages of demolition, structural framing, trim out, and final finishes for twenty-three related tasks, including pew removal and reinstallation. The project was scheduled for completion in the fall of 1990.

The building remained in service as a church throughout the rehabilitation process. Parish activities, including mass, were temporarily relocated to the church basement, or undercroft, where they remained for the duration of the project.

THE WORK

Murphy & Dittenhafer Architects continued in their role as supervising project architects during construction. In addition, Fr. Richard Lawrence, pastor of St. Vincent's, assumed the traditional role of "clerk of the works" and provided on-site supervision and oversight. Lou Baird and Rose McNally represented the interests of the archdiocese in monitoring the project. Mark Hoffman served as project manager for Tamarack Construction, Inc. Randy Twinning was the on-site superintendent. Greg Butcher coordinated the work for Augustus Woodworking.

Three major categories of work were identified in Tamarack's project schedule to accomplish the twenty-three distinct tasks. These categories were demolition, rough-in, and trim-out. The majority of work was confined to the interior of the church narthex, nave, and wing connection to the rectory. Exceptions included the exterior handicapped-access ramp and mechanical systems. Stripping away the successive layers that had been added to the building over the years provided a rare opportunity to document clues to its early appearance. This evidence was used, in conjunction with archival research, to develop the sequence of design and construction presented in this study.

The existing pews first were removed for reconfiguration by Augustus Woodworking. This exacting job required that the existing benches be rejoined in combination using acute angles to achieve a radiating seating plan. The reconfigured pews then were refinished and reinstalled at the conclusion of the rehabilitation project.

Once the pews were removed, work on the church began in earnest. Demolition accounted for the majority of work during the initial stage of the project. Minor modifications were made to the three-cell narthex. The textured off-white cladding, which had been installed on the walls and ceiling to conceal cracked original plaster, was removed. Wall and ceiling surfaces were inspected and selectively repaired, as required. All plaster work was completed by Sonny Carter of Joppa, Maryland; painting was completed by D & M Painting and Drywall, Inc.

Despite its 150 years of service, the majority of the original plaster was attached securely to the load-bearing brick walls. The historic plaster had utilized a mix incorporating animal-hair binder. Plaster was applied directly to the brick walls in successive coats, ending with a regular finish coat to which pigment was applied. Interior doors, woodwork, and decorative grapevine motif ornamentation were carefully disassembled and stored for reuse.

Structural changes were made in the end stairhalls of the narthex where the entrances to the nave were enlarged. The expansion of these bays required the removal of the two monuments that adjoined the nave entrances in each of the cells. Both monuments were retained in the rehabilitation, and were reinstalled in their present location on the interior wall perpendicular to their original site. The southern monument, which adopts a bracketed shelf design, was reinstalled intact. The project was used as an opportunity to expand the northernmost monument, which records the church's sequence of pastors. The monument adopts a design similar to an engaged column and incorporates a base, a shaft, and a cornice. Inscriptions are confined to the shaft; an additional tablet was added above the base. Work on the monuments, as well as the altar work discussed below, was completed by Hilgartner Stone Co., Inc., of Baltimore.

Heating registers located in the floors of the stairhalls were removed and new floor registers were installed, following improvements to the concealed ductwork. Mechanical systems supplemented during the project included electrical work and fire alarms, executed by Budd Electrical Service Company, and plumbing and HVAC work, executed by B. J. Kirkwood & Co., Inc., both of Baltimore.

Alterations to the church nave and sanctuary were the most extensive changes in the rehabilitation project. Again, work during the initial months of the project focused on demolition. The removal of the late nineteenth-century side altars and the redesign of the main altar were among the first items of work. The secondary side altars were dismantled and their materials were stored on site for use in the design of the main altar. The design of the main altar, which had evolved from a simple furnishing to an elaborate feature through successive redesigns, was condensed and simplified. The existing design of the altar served as a dominant feature of the nave. The previous altar design echoed the rituals of earlier liturgy, in which much of the mass was said with the celebrant's back to the congregation.

The existing altar was supported by a brick superstructure and faced with matched white marble slabs. Raised on a platform that extended just over 20 inches from the floor level, the altar integrated an elegant symmetrical design of projecting shelves enlivened by moldings that terminated with the baldachino, which had been added during the late nineteenth century. This design had three components: the back altar, the shelf, and the main altar. The back altar was the tallest element; it was articulated to support the triple columns that supported the rear of the baldachino. This articulation was achieved by visually extending the base of

Interior view looking toward the main altar of the church, 1994.   EDWIN
REMSBURG

the columns through double, two-part base panels. The second major
component, the shelf, projected approximately 20 inches from the back
altar and corresponded to the position of the middle baldachino column.
The shelf served as the base of the twin front baldachino supports that
marked the central tabernacle area. This element was, naturally, the central focus of the overall design and was delineated by a shallow circular
projection. The final element of the existing design was the approximately 8-foot, 10-inch main altar that projected slightly over 25 inches
from the shelf. Stepped approximately 6 inches below the level of the
shelf, the main altar was a flat table-like plane accented by a front that in-

Interior view looking toward the choir, 1994.   EDWIN REMSBURG

corporated pilasters flanking an ornamented central relief panel of contrasting marble.

In the rehabilitation design, the main altar became a backdrop for the community worship that had replaced the single celebrant emphasis of the old order. The design of the feature was contracted to two elements, the back altar and shelf. The stepped platforms that previously had delineated the element were removed, and its height was increased through additions to the base. These additions were necessary to accommodate the new level of the sanctuary floor.

Reworking the floor levels of the nave and aisles to accommodate the new configuration of platforms and handicapped-access ramps was per-haps the greatest construction challenge of the project. The final appear-ance of the nave floor in the rehabilitation design had been a concern from the early stages of project planning. The existing dark finish, ran-dom-width, heart pine floor, with its patterns of wear that documented past building use and configuration, was recognized as an important his-toric feature. Carpeting the room was the most expedient and cost-effec-tive solution to achieving a consistent appearance in the reconfigured floor. However, while this approach was acceptable theoretically under the ground rules of the project, as long as evidence of the original floor finishes was retained, floor carpeting was rejected as an option due to its potential for changing the character of the area. The more expensive, labor-intensive alternative of retaining as much of the original heart pine flooring as possible, supplemented by new flooring of a different wood species, oak, was selected. A uniform tonality was achieved by consistent floor finish.

The new configuration of aisles, platforms, and ramps was achieved applying contemporary construction techniques. The original 3 × 12-inch floor joists spaced at 14-inch intervals (on center) were retained. Batt building insulation with a rating of R 19 was sandwiched between the original structural system and the new platforms. A surface for finish flooring was provided by ⅜-inch exterior-grade plywood, which was in-stalled in staggered sheets to maximize its strength. New flooring com-posed of ¾-inch random-width tongue-in-groove oak and pine was in-stalled in selected areas. Flooring for the project was installed and finished by Danzco Flooring of Baltimore.

As in the case of the narthex, existing wall coverings were removed from the walls of the new assembly space. Original plaster was repaired selectively, and was painted to complete the room.

The architectural programming requirement for a common gathering area, distinct from the assembly space, was achieved through the redesign of the portion of the nave adjoining the narthex below the choir balcony. The existing design had suggested this solution: the cast-iron columns supporting the choir already established a spatial division. Utilization of this space required the removal of the confessionals and the paneled wainscotting along the rear wall, as well as the erection of a frame parti-tion directly behind the existing iron columns. The open visual quality of the area was retained through the integration of five symmetrically placed three-panel double doors in the partition wall. The design of the finished wall, with its doors, glazing, and robust classically derived moldings, is similar in character and compatible with the overall church design. Drywall and framing was completed by R.J.K. Construction, Inc., Kingsville, while mill work and trim were provided by the Reisterstown Lumber Company. Doors, casework, caulking, and glass were provided the respective firms of Building Components Corporation, Cherrywork, Ltd., Thomas McCool, Inc., and Gampel Brothers Glass.

Usable space in the gathering area was maximized further through the enlargement of the entrances to the side narthex stairhalls. Expansion of these secondary doorways required the addition of steel lintels above the doors. The dimensions of the central entry between narthex and nave were retained and served to reinforce the central axis to the nave entrance.

Important clues to the earlier appearance of the church again were discovered during the demolition phase. Remnants of two earlier decorating schemes were uncovered behind the walls of the confessional. The vicinity of the northernmost confessional revealed an intact section of paint suggesting the color scheme adopted during the late nineteenth-century decoration. This surviving sample was cleaned and stabilized by the art conservation firm of Josepha Caraher & Associates, and it was retained in the new gathering area. Evidence of an earlier decoration scheme, consistent with the waterbased paint finishes in use during the period of the church's original construction, also was uncovered behind the center confessional. This sample, described in chapter 9, was in poor condition and occupied an area criss-crossed by electrical conduits.

The interior rehabilitation of the church was extended to the building wing, which connects the church and rectory. In place by at least 1890, the building wing was redesigned to provide special use and service areas for the newly defined assembly and gathering spaces. Segregation between service and private areas was provided by the central passage connecting the church and rectory. Areas west of the hall were devoted to storage and private devotion. Compatible contemporary finishes were used in this less historically sensitive area.

The program for exterior work in the latest building campaign presented one of the most challenging problems in rehabilitation design. Provisions for handicapped access seldom were incorporated in the original designs of older buildings; thus, designs for their later addition have had to address the dual objectives of primary access and design compatibility. Under the objective of primary access, entrances should utilize the main entry to the building in ways that do not distinguish between users. In addition, architectural features important to the building design should be retained intact.

A solution meeting both these criteria was developed for St. Vincent's through the construction of a masonry ramp adjoining the south elevation that terminates at the level of the building's triple front entry. Minimal alteration to the historic fabric was required. The design of the ramp is connected to that of the original building through scale and materials. The veneer face of the masonry ramp is visually similar in construction and materials to the building's raised basement. In addition, iron railings that delineated the side church elevation were reinstalled as part of the design.

CONCLUSION

The latest renovation of St. Vincent de Paul Church was the result of consensus programming by the parish, design by project planners and architects, and execution by construction specialists. The project realized the integration of architectural stewardship with contemporary use through a sophisticated redesign that was deceptive in its logic and simplicity. This design capitalized upon the dynamic quality of the building's architecture, which stemmed from its history of successive building campaigns. In adopting a preservation ethic for its rehabilitation project, St. Vincent de Paul retained the character-defining elements that contributed to its unique architecture, and it adapted those unique elements to enhance the continuation of its ministry to the needs of metropolitan Baltimore.

CONCLUSION

On November 17, 1991, St. Vincent's celebrated its 150th birthday. The mayor was there. Archbishop William Keeler said the mass and delivered the homily. Six priests with ties to St. Vincent's assisted. Seven former teachers at the old parochial school and a good number of former parishioners also attended. The choir under Joe Organ performed magnificently a score composed by him for the occasion.

The 150th differed markedly from the 50th and 100th anniversaries. At the 50th, in 1891, Archbishop Placide Chapelle of Santa Fe said the mass with Cardinal Gibbons presiding. Bishop Keane of the Catholic University delivered the sermon. A choir of sixty sang a Beethoven mass. No civil dignitaries were reported in attendance. At the 100th, in 1941, former parishioners, one a pastor and an assistant pastor, said the mass and delivered the sermon, Archbishop Curley presiding. A mixed choir under Rev. John Sinnott Martin sang a Perosi mass. The governor, the mayor, and a congressman graced the occasion.

All three celebrations had one thing in common: they were all played out in a newly refurbished church. The renovations mirrored, as we have seen, different populations, which, with that of the original building, marked the four ages of the parish: those of the mercantile elite, the immigrant community, the largely transient middle class, and the body of postconciliar Catholics who, in the process of redesigning their home, approached a redefinition of parish.

An important change in parish ministry, however, had occurred. A significant portion of the Catholic laity in the generation before Vatican Council II had responded to the church's call to Catholic Action, to a more productive participation in the mission of the church. But they had looked to extraparochial organizations, or "interest communalities," for such involvement—the Christian Family Movement, the Cana Conference, the Catholic Interracial Council, the Catholic Worker houses, to name but a few.[1] After Vatican Council II, however, Catholics had returned to the parish as the focus of a more active role in the social, educational, and organizational life of their church. There occurred, in fact, what one historian called "the lay ministry explosion."[2]

St. Vincent's with its meager resources could play but a limited role in such an explosion. Yet it was able to signal, especially to downtown parishes, new strategies that would enable them to achieve the traditional goals of their church. While most of the ministries at St. Vincent's seemed new, they represented a return to those undertaken in its heyday in other guises. The new styles of ministry reflected changes in the church and society at large. In the nineteenth and early twentieth centuries the object of such ministries was almost always Catholics—Catholic children in need of an education, Catholic orphans in need of a home, Catholic men addicted to drink. Strictly Catholic institutions were created to serve them—the parochial school, the orphanage, the temperance society. St. Vincent's had had them all.

Today the problems remain, but the parameters have changed. The Catholic population has, for the most part, assimilated itself into the larger, middle-class community. The walls have collapsed. The parish no longer serves as the primary social reference group. The numerical decline of religious orders, moreover, has all but eliminated the virtually free staff on which most parishes depended. Today there are new players in the game. Governmental funding and foundation and corporation grants are available for any number of worthy causes, though often not for those of churches or church institutions as such. All this has dictated a change in strategy. Although goals and missions remain the same, new skills in networking and leverage have been adopted.

While its orphanages are gone, St. Vincent de Paul still concerns itself with poor and neglected children. Through the neighborhood association it helped found, the Jonestown Planning Council, it created in 1981, as we have seen, the Jonestown Day Care Center, Inc. The pastor and two professional laymen from St. Vincent's are numbered among the center's six-member board. The center has come to serve annually well over a hundred poor children from the neighborhood, only two or three of them Catholic.

While it can no longer support a parochial school, St. Vincent's, in conjunction with five other parishes, cosponsored in 1989 the Queen of Peace Interparochial School. At two locations—one at the former St. James and St. John Parochial School, the other at the former St. Katharine of Siena's Parochial School—it now educates over 600 children a year, more than two-thirds of them poor, only 15 percent of them Catholic. Each of the six parishes contributes 5 percent of its offertory collections for tuition assistance grants. The school also obtains tuition assistance from the archdiocesan Lawrence Cardinal Shehan Scholarship Fund and from the Archbishop's Lenten Appeal.[3] St. Vincent's pastor and two of its lay parishioners are on the school's board of directors. Thus St. Vincent's contributes people, time, talent, and money to a joint venture to do what the parish alone could not do.

The understanding and treatment of alcoholism has changed considerably since the days of the St. Vincent's temperance societies. Today alcoholism is treated most effectively in an in-patient setting with a professional staff, a program that St. Vincent's itself could not afford. Again, however, it helped save, as we have seen, a detoxification, treatment, and aftercare complex called East End Hotel and remained a part of its governance even after it moved from within the parish boundaries. The parish also offered its own facilities to two different groups of Alcoholics Anonymous.

With such networking and leverage St. Vincent's has continued to fulfill its own 150-year-old mission of *diakonia*. It has demonstrated how a Catholic parish could, with imagination and determination, continue to provide the works of charity that are incumbent on every parish as "church."

The concept of "parish" is under reexamination. As early as 1951 a priest-scholar called for "a complete rebirth from the source."[4] St. Vincent's has recaptured the threefold mission of the primitive church mentioned at the outset—proclamation, community building, and service—not only through its new strategies but also through the process of renovating its home.

The process itself (described in the final chapter) created a greater sense of community building. The end product created a more effective setting for proclamation. A reconfiguration of the pews wrapped the people around a bema where the central acts of the liturgy occurred, thus virtually eliminating the clear demarcation between sanctuary (now enlarged) and nave (now abbreviated). The community became the subjects, not the objects, of the liturgy. At St. Vincent's the building remained the house of God as well as the house of "the people of God," a concept that determined the renovations of other church buildings. The tabernacle stayed where it has always been. The new narthex, moreover, brought the gathering space closer to the worshiping space.

In all its altered forms St. Vincent de Paul Church has served as a tangible link among the tastes, aspirations, and priorities of past and present generations. The history of St. Vincent's parish and church has provided an excellent opportunity to examine the historical evolution of the parish as an active religious community in a dynamic urban context. The parish and church have witnessed and successfully adapted to major demographic, social, and political changes in both American Catholicism and American secular society. Two constants have been strong leadership and a clear imaging of community, both reflected in the building itself.

The architecture of St. Vincent de Paul, through the original design and successive modifications, well documents the evolving character of a uniquely American Catholicism: it integrates popular styles, theological concepts, and parish hierarchy. The history of parish and church, the people and their home, is marked by strong personalities, perseverance, dedication, and faith. These factors have made constructive changes possible in the past and will continue to influence the direction of the parish in the future.

PASTORS AND ASSISTANT PASTORS

PASTORS

John Baptist Gildea	1841–45	John Daniel Boland	1892–1903
Peter Stanislaus Schreiber	1845	Desiderius Constantin	
Charles Ignatius White	1845–46	DeWulf	1903–11
John Philip Donelan	1846–51	Philip Bernard McGuire	1912–39
Leonard Ambrose		John Sinnott Martin	1940–65
Obermeyer	1851–60	Edmond John Stroup	1966–73
Henry Myers	1860–73	Richard Thomas Lawrence	1973–
Edmund Didier	1873–92		

ASSISTANT PASTORS

Peter S. Schreiber	1841–45	Joseph L. Andreis	1874–80
Charles C. Brennan	1845	George H. Nyssen	1878–79
William D. Parsons	1845–46	John C. Ahern	1879–83
Michael Slattery	1846–49	James A. Cunningham	1881–83
John F. Hickey	1849–55	Joseph A. Gallen	1883–88
William D. Parsons	1855–59	Thomas E. Stapleton	1887–96
John J. Byrne	1858–59	James A. Cunningham	1888–92
George Flaut	1859–60	Joseph A. Thornton	1896–98
Peter F. McCarthy	1860–62	Hugh A. Curley	1898–1904
John J. Dougherty	1862–66	Patrick S. Flood	1904–7
Thomas Sim Lee	1866–68	Joseph H. Flottemesch	1907–8
Lewis A. Morgan	1868–70	John T. Coolahan	1908–12
Alphonse Coppens	1870–71	Angelo Romeo	1928–43
Michael Dausch	1871–78	Francis J. Egan	1943–46
Edmund Didier	1871–73	David W. Shaum	1946–50

John J. Hart	1946–52	Thomas J. Penn	1959–61
William F. Reilly	1951–53	Maurice J. Wolfe	1961–64
Thomas J. Fannon	1953–55	Edmond J. Stroup	1961–66
William K. Dunn	1955–56	Joseph R. Wenderoth	1966–70
Clare J. O'Dwyer	1956–59	Charles J. Canterna	1976–83
Donald P. Croghan	1957–61		

INCORPORATION OF THE CHURCH OF ST. VINCENT OF PAUL

1841

Constitution of the Association of the Church of St. Vincent of Paul in the City of Baltimore, To all whom these presents shall come, We the Reverend John B. Gildea, Frederick Crey, Benedict I. Sanders, John D. Danels, Patrick McKew, John I. Gross, Charles Pendergast, John McColgan, George C. Collins, John Fox, Daniel Coonan, and James Fortune all members of the Roman Catholic Church and citizens of Baltimore send greeting. Whereas we have associated for the purpose of erecting a church for the worship of God according to the Faith and Discipline of the Holy Catholic Church on the lot of ground on Front Street in the City of Baltimore with the sanction of the Most Reverend Archbishop of Baltimore we have made progress in our undertaking and now desire to be incorporated according to the provisions of the Act of the General Assembly of Maryland passed at the November sessions in the year 1802 Chapter III and we have agreed upon the following articles viz:

ARTICLE I

This corporation shall be known by the name of the Association of the Church of Saint Vincent of Paul in the City of Baltimore and shall be composed of the Reverend Pastor whom the Archbishop may appoint for the said Church and the 11 lay members above named.

ARTICLE 2

The officers of this Association shall consist of a President, a Vice President, a Treasurer and a Secretary.

ARTICLE 3

The officers of the Association shall be chosen annually except the Reverend Pastor who shall be appointed as above and shall always ex officio be President of the Association.

The President shall preside at all of the meetings of the Association, in his absence the Vice President and in the absence of both, a president pro tem may be chosen, all contracts and agreements for the use and benefit of the Association, all drafts drawn or bills or orders to be paid must be signed by the President.

The treasurer shall receive all funds belonging to or that may be collected for the corporation and shall deposit and keep all such funds as the Association may direct until appropriated by the same. Treasurer shall also make quarterly reports of the state and condition of the treasury to the Association.

The Secretary shall keep a record of all the proceedings of the Association and shall serve all notices for their meetings.

A quorum to transact business shall consist of the President and three members or three members with the Vice President or a president pro tempore.

No vacancy that may occur in the Association by the death or resignation or otherwise of any lay member shall be filled until the present number of lay members shall be reduced to five, and any vacancy which may occur after that number has been reduced shall be filled by the whole of the remaining number but the number five not be increased.

The stated meetings shall be held on the first Monday of every month at seven o'clock at such place as the Association may determine, the President on his absence the Vice President may call Special meetings.

Whenever the debts due or hereafter to be contracted for building, improving or finishing said Church shall be paid or this Association relieved of the responsibility incurred by the Archbishop or Pastor as they may otherwise devise assuming the debts, then the said Association for the time being shall cease to exist as a body corporated and shall relinquish all claims to said building and shall convey all rights and title they may have to the same to the Archbishop and his successors according to the provisions of an Act of the General Assembly of Maryland passed December session 1832 Chapter 308.

ARTICLE 11

This Association shall not interfere with the internal government or management of the Church when completed which shall be left exclusively to the Most Reverend Archbishop and Reverend Pastor.

ARTICLE 12

All the proceeds arising from pews after the current expenses of the Church have been paid shall be appropriated to the liquidation of the debt of the Church and after for the support of the School.

ARTICLE 13

Any amendment to the constitution proposed at a stated meeting in writing may be adopted at the next stated meeting thereafter, provided three quarters of all the members of the Association sanction such amendment. In witness whereof we have hereunto subscribed our names and affixed our seals at the City of Baltimore aforesaid this first day of March, 1841.

John B. Gildea	(SEAL)	Chas. Pendergast	(SEAL)
Frederick Crey	(SEAL)	John McColgan	(SEAL)
Benedict I. Sanders	(SEAL)	Geo. C. Collins	(SEAL)
John D. Danels	(SEAL)	John Fox	(SEAL)
P. McKew	(SEAL)	Daniel Coonan	(SEAL)
J. I. Gross	(SEAL)	James Fortune	(SEAL)

City of Baltimore on the first day of March 1841 before the subscribers, two of the Trustees of the Peace of the State of Maryland in and for the City aforesaid personally appeared the Reverend John B. Gildea, Frederick Crey, Benedict I. Sanders, John D. Danels, Patrick McKew, John I. Gross, Charles Pendergast, John McColgan, George C. Collins, John Fox, Daniel Coonan, and James Fortune, above named and parties to the aforegoing articles of the Association and persons personally and well known to us and severally executed and acknowledged said articles of Association as and for their act and deed for the purpose therein mentioned.

George W. King, Maurice Bush.

Received for record the eighth day of March 1841 at one quarter before 11 o'clock a.m. same day, recorded and examined by Thos Kell.

CURRENT MISSION STATEMENT OF ST. VINCENT DE PAUL PARISH

The purpose of St Vincent de Paul Church is:
To be and increasingly become a Community of diverse groups and persons—
    of those who live here,
        those who work here, and
        those who lived here years ago
    of the poor
        the disaffected, and
        the exiled
    gathered together by God
    to grow and to help each other grow in their discovery of Jesus
        as a person
        as the expression of God's love and
        as a source of life and meaning
    and of themselves
        as children of God,
        worthwhile in themselves, and
        beloved in their Father; and
    to share lively and enlivening liturgies and other celebrations
        which will strengthen in ourselves and communicate to others
        our awareness of God's word and
        our communion with God's people; and
    to serve each other and those we meet,
        those who live in our parish and neighborhood and
        those who live in the larger communities of which we are a part,
        by working as individuals and as a parish community
    to establish and increase freedom, justice and love.

GLOSSARY

ABBREVIATIONS

DOA   Saylor, Henry H., ed. *Dictionary of Architecture*. New York: John Wiley and Sons, 1952.

FGAH McAlester, Virginia, and Lee McAlester. *A Field Guide to American Houses*. New York: Knopf, 1984.

HAS   Harris, Cyril M., ed. *Historic Architecture Sourcebook*. New York: McGraw-Hill, 1977.

IAA   Blumenson, John J.-G. *Identifying American Architecture*. 6th ed. Nashville: American Association for State and Local History, 1986.

NPS   Department of the Interior, National Park Service, *National Register Bulletin 16A: How to Complete the National Register Registration Form*. Washington, D.C.: U.S. Government Printing Office, 1991.

PDA   Fleming, John; Hugh Honour; and Nicholas Pevsner, eds. *A Dictionary of Architecture*. 2d ed. New York: Penguin Books, 1972.

Ambo. A raised stand used for reading the Gospel and Epistle. This feature was common in medieval Italian churches and generally was abandoned in favor of a pulpit during the Renaissance.

Apse. In a church, a semicircular or polygonal termination that usually contains a chancel, a chapel, or the altar complex. (PDA)

Architrave. The lowest of the three main parts of an *entablature*. This term can be used to refer to the molded frame that surrounds a door or window. (PDA)

Art Deco. An architectural style popular between c. 1925 and c. 1940. Art Deco is characterized by a linear, hard-edged or angular composition, often with a vertical emphasis and highlighted with stylized decoration. The façades of Art Deco buildings often are arranged in a series of setbacks that emphasize their geometric form. Strips of windows with decorated spandrels add to the vertical feeling of the composition. Hard-edged, low relief ornamentation is found around door and window openings, along string courses, and along the roof edges or parapet. (IAA)

Balustrade. A short post or pillar in a series that supports a rail or *coping,* thus forming a balustrade. (PDA)

Basilica. An ancient colonnaded Roman hall for public use, later adopted as a building type for early Christian churches. The term indicated function and not form, but ancient Roman basilicas often were oblong buildings with aisles and galleries, and with an apse opposite the entrance. Early Christian churches evolved from public buildings of this type, and by the fourth century they had acquired their essential characteristics: oblong plan; longitudinal axis; a timber roof, either open or concealed by a flat ceiling; a termination, either rectangular or in the form of an *apse;* and usually a *nave* with two or more aisles. (PDA)

Bema. A slightly elevated area that is the focus of a liturgical space.

Cast iron. Iron shaped by pouring into molds. This material was used in buildings, beginning in the late eighteenth century, until it was superseded by steel in the late nineteenth century. (PDA)

Clerestory. The uppermost wall of a church above the aisle roofs that is pierced by windows. (DOA)

Colonial Revival. An architectural style prevalent after 1876. The Colonial Revival style often combined Colonial details with those of contemporary styles. (FGAH and IAA)

Column. A free-standing, slightly tapered, upright building element, circular in cross-section. A column normally serves to support the roof of a building, but it sometimes is erected as an independent monument. Columns of the classic style consist of a shaft, a capital, and, except in *Greek Doric,* a base. (PDA)

Coping. A capping or covering to a wall, either flat or sloped, designed to throw off water. (PDA)

Corbel. A projecting element, usually of masonry, that supports a beam or other horizontal element of a building. A series of corbels, each one projecting beyond the one below, can be used as a cornice and to support a vault or an arch. (PDA)

Corbelling. A series of brick or masonry courses, each built out beyond the one below, a series of *corbels,* that can be used to support a chimney-stack, a projecting window, other building element, or to form a rough arch, vault, or dome. (PDA)

Cornice. In classical architecture, the top projecting section of an *entablature;* also, any projecting ornamental molding along the top of a building, wall, arch, and so on, that finishes or crowns it. If the cornice is located along the sloping sides of a *pediment,* it is known as a raking cornice. (PDA)

Dentil. A small square block used in series in Ionic, Corinthian, Composite, and, more rarely, Doric *cornices.* (PDA)

Dome. A vault of even curvature set on a circular base. In section, a dome can be segmental, semicircular, pointed, or bulbous. If a dome is erected on a square base, structural elements must be interpolated at the corners to provide a transition between the square and the circle. Domes can be placed directly on a circular base-line, or on a drum, which usually is pierced with windows. (PDA)

Elevation. The external faces of a building; also a measured scale drawing made to show any one side (or elevation) of a building. (PDA)

Entablature. The upper part of an *order,* consisting of an *architrave, frieze,* and *cornice.* (PDA)

Façade. The front or face of a building, emphasized architecturally. (PDA)

Fascia. A plain horizontal band, usually part of an *architrave,* which may consist of two or three fasciae over-sailing each other and sometimes separated by narrow moldings. (PDA)

Federal. An American architectural style characteristic of the period between c. 1780 and c. 1820. Buildings constructed using the Federal style of architecture are typified by a low-pitched roof, a smooth façade, large areas of windows, and elliptical fan lights with flanking slender side lights. Geometric forms such as polygonal or bowed bays accentuate the rhythm of the exterior, and serve to demarcate interior spaces. Ornamental elements found on many of the buildings constructed in this style were derived from the work of the designers, the Adams brothers. (IAA)

Finish. The treatment applied to an exterior or interior surface, such as paint, stucco, paneling, and the like.

Frieze. (1) The middle division of an *entablature,* between the *architrave* and *cornice;* usually decorated but may be plain. (2) The decorated band along the upper part of an internal wall, immediately below the *cornice.* (PDA)

Gable. The triangular upper portion of a wall at the end of a pitched roof that corresponds to the pediment in classical architecture. It normally has straight sides, but there are variations. For example, the uppermost portion of a hipped gable is sloped back, while a shaped gable has multicurved sides. (PDA)

Gallery. In church architecture, an upper story over an aisle that opens onto the nave. In secular architecture the term *gallery* is used to describe a similar platform or mezzanine supported on columns or brackets which overlooks the main interior space of a building. (PDA)

Georgian. The prevailing high architectural style of the eighteenth century in Great Britain and the North American colonies, so named after kings George I, II, and III (1714–1820). It is characterized by a formal arrangement of parts employing a *symmetrical* composition enriched with classical detail. (HAS and IAA)

Gothic arch. A generic term that refers to a *pointed arch.* (HAS)

Gothic Revival. The popular Gothic Revival style (c. 1830) was used for everything from picturesque timber cottages to stone castles, and churches to public buildings. In ecclesiastical architecture, Gothic Revival churches adopted architectural details and principles associated with medieval European cathedrals, including steeply pitched roofs, extreme verticality, the "Gothic" or pointed arch, and liberal use of carved and colored glass ornamentation. (IAA)

Greek Revival style. Popular between c. 1820 and c. 1860, the Greek Revival architectural movement was based on the use of pure Greek forms. The movement mirrored a renewed interest in Greek antiquities and in the United States was thought to represent the democratic ideals of the American Republic. (HAS, DOA, and IAA)

Haunch. That portion of an *arch* that is located roughly midway between the spring line and crown, where the lateral thrust is strongest. (DOA)

Impost. A structural element of a wall, usually formed of a projecting bracket-like molding, on which the end of an arch appears to rest. In Gothic architecture, the moldings of an arch sometimes continue without break to the floor, and are called *continuous imposts.* (PDA)

Italianate. An eclectic form of design, fashionable in England and the United States between c. 1840 and c. 1880, that is characterized by low-pitched, heavily bracketed roofs, square towers, and, frequently, by round-arched windows. (HAS and IAA)

Jamb. The vertical part of an archway, doorway, or window. The part of the jamb between the window or door frame and the outer wall-surface is called a *reveal.* (PDA)

Keystone. The central stone of an arch or rib vault; sometimes carved. (PDA)

Lantern. A small circular or polygonal turret encircled with windows that crowns a roof or dome. (PDA)

Light. The spaces, generally filled by panes of glass, between the *muntins* of a window. (PDA)

Lintel. A horizontal beam or stone that bridges an opening, such as a door or a window. (PDA)

Massing. A term used to describe the arrangement of the major geometrical forms or the various components of a building.

Materials. Refers to the components used to execute the engineering and the architectural design of a building or structure. Masonry, cast iron, structural steel, and wood are the most commonly used architectural materials.

Meetinghouse. A house of worship derived from the basilica form. The meetinghouse form generally refers to a house of worship that has a simple design and rectangular ground plan. (HAS)

Metope. The square space between two *triglyphs* in the *frieze* of a Doric order; it may be carved or left plain. (PDA)

Monumental scale. Refers to the size of very large buildings or structures that generally serve public functions and that accommodate large numbers of people. Cathedrals, arenas, multistory commercial office and industrial buildings, and major government structures all are examples of monumental scale architectural designs.

Muntin. An element that divides a window or other opening into two or more *lights*. (PDA)

Narthex. In a general sense, an enclosed covered antechurch located between the main entrance to the church and the entrance to the nave of the church. (PDA)

National Register of Historic Places. The official federal list of districts, sites, buildings, structures, and objects significant in American history, architecture, archaeology, engineering, and culture. National Register properties contribute to an understanding of the historical and cultural foundations of the nation. (NPS)

Nave. That portion of a church between the altar rail and the entrance that normally is occupied by the congregation. (PDA)

Neoclassical. An architectural style prevalent between c. 1900 and c. 1920. Neoclassicism is based on Greek and Roman architectural designs. It is distinguished by symmetrically arranged buildings of monumental proportions that are finished with a smooth or stone surface; strict use of the classical orders; and restrained use of ornamentation. (HAS and IAA)

Newel. The principal post at the end of a flight of stairs. (PDA)

Order. In classical architecture, a column with base (usually), shaft, capital, and entablature, decorated and proportioned according to one of the accepted styles: Doric, Tuscan, Ionic, Corinthian, or Composite orders. (PDA)

Ornamentation. In architecture, those details of shape, texture, and color that are exploited or added deliberately to attract an observer. (HAS)

Pediment. In classical architecture, a low-pitched *gable* above a *portico,* formed by running the top member of the *entablature* along the sides of the gable; also a similar feature above doors, windows, and so on. It may be straight-sided or curved. (PDA)

Pier. (1) A solid masonry support for a building, as distinct from a *column*. (2) The solid mass between doors, windows, and other openings in buildings. (PDA)

Pilaster. A shallow *pier* or rectangular column that projects from a wall, and is added for architectural effect. In classical architecture, a pilaster generally conforms with one of the *orders*. (PDA)

Plan. The horizontal arrangement of the parts of a building, or a drawing or diagram showing such arrangement as a horizontal section. (PDA)

Pointed arch. Any arch with a point at its apex, characteristic of Gothic architecture.

Portico. A roofed space, open or partly enclosed, that forms the entrance and centerpiece of the façade of a temple, house, or church. It often features detached or attached columns and a *pediment*. (PDA)

Proportion. A mathematical concept providing, in architecture and the visual arts, a set of norms comparable to meter in poetry and music. In architecture, proportion defines the ratio of space between the elements of a building, such as the height-to-width ratio of doors, windows, and the like. (PDA)

Romanesque Revival. The re-use, during the late nineteenth century (c. 1880–c. 1910), of massive forms, particularly for monumental scale architecture. Patterned after early medieval European cathedrals and structures, Romanesque Revival buildings are particularly characterized by the use of the round arch for window and door openings. (HAS and IAA)

Round arch. A semicircular element used as a support over an open space, such as a bridge or a doorway.

Sacristy. A room in a church near the *chancel,* where the vestments and altar vessels are stored, where the clergy vest themselves for services, and where some business of the church may be done. Usually a single room, but sometimes a very large one. (HAS)

Scale. In architecture, the relationship of the parts of a building to one another, and to the human figure; an expression of proportion and size. (DOA)

Sill. The horizontal element at the base of a timber framed wall, into which the posts and studs normally are fastened. Also, the horizontal member at the bottom of a window opening or a door frame. (PDA)

Spring line. The level at which an arch unites with its supports. (PDA)

Springer. The point at which an arch unites with the piers or structure that supports it.

Stilted arch. An arch with a spring line raised by vertical *piers* above the *impost* level. (PDA)

String course. A continuous horizontal band, usually molded, that is set in the surface of an exterior wall or projects from it. (PDA)

Stringers. The two sloping members that carry the ends of the treads and risers of a staircase. (PDA)

Symmetrical. Having identical forms or masses on either side of a center line. (DOA)

Temple form. Basic building form developed first by the ancient Greeks as a sacred place of worship and ritual. It is characterized by a rectangular footprint. The single rectangular interior room housed sacred shrines and objects or the performance of sacred rituals. The exterior entrance porch, positioned across the width of the building, generally was supported by columns, which sometimes were continued as a series (colonnade) around all sides of the building.

Transept. The transverse wings of a church flanking the main axis at a right angle to produce a cruciform plan.

Triglyphs. Blocks separating the *metopes* in a Doric *frieze.* Each one has two vertical grooves or glyphs in the center and half grooves at the edges. If the half grooves are omitted, the block is called a diglyph. (PDA)

Tympanum. The triangular or segmental space enclosed by the moldings of a *pediment.* (PDA)

Undercroft. (1) The vaulted basement of a church or secret passage, often wholly or partially below ground level. (2) A crypt.

Vernacular architecture. A recent term coined to designate building designs of indigenous style that are constructed from locally available materials and that follow traditional building practices and patterns. Vernacular buildings are not designed by professional architects. (PDA)

Wainscot. A timber lining applied to interior walls. The term is also applied to the wooden paneling of pews. (PDA)

NOTES

Abbreviations

AAB Archives of the Archdiocese
of Baltimore
ASV Archives of St. Vincent de Paul Parish
BCR Baltimore Catholic Review
CA Catholic Almanac and Laity's Directory
CM Catholic Mirror

CR Catholic Review
MCA Metropolitan Catholic Almanac
MHM Maryland Historical Magazine
SAB Sulpician Archives of Baltimore
SVN "St. Vincent's Notebook"
USCM United States Catholic Magazine

Preface and Acknowledgments

1. Jay P. Dolan, ed., *The American Catholic Parish: A History from 1850 to the Present,* 2 vols. (New York: Paulist Press, 1987), 1:2.
2. Outstanding works that have utilized parish records are Jay P. Dolan, *The Immigrant Church: New York German and Irish Catholics, 1815–1865* (Baltimore: Johns Hopkins University Press, 1975); Robert A. Orsi, *The Madonna of 115th Street: Faith and Community in Italian Harlem, 1880–1950* (New Haven: Yale University Press, 1985); and Stephen J. Shaw, *The Catholic Parish as a Way-Station of Ethnicity and Americanization: Chicago's Germans and Italians, 1903–1939* (Brooklyn, N.Y.: Carlson Publishing, 1991).
3. See n. 1. The work is divided into six regional studies by as many historians.
4. Examples of recent scholarly parish histories are Joseph M. White, *Sacred Heart Parish of Notre Dame: A Heritage and a History* (Notre Dame, Ind.: Sacred Heart Parish, 1992), and Morris J. MacGregor, *A Parish for the Federal City: St. Patrick's in Washington, 1794–1994* (Washington, D.C.: Catholic University of America Press, 1994).

Introduction

1. For brief histories of parishes in Europe see W. Croce, "The History of the Parish," and J. Homeyer, "The Renewal of the Parish," in Hugo Rahner, ed., *The Parish from Theology to Practice,* trans. Robert Kress (Westminster, Md.: Newman Press, 1958), 9–22, 122–39.
2. Thomas W. Spalding, *The Premier See: A History of the Archdiocese of Baltimore, 1789–1989* (Baltimore: Johns Hopkins University Press, 1989), 25–36 and passim. See also Gerald P. Fogarty, "The Parish and Community in American Catholic History," *U.S. Catholic Historian* 4 (1985): 233–57.

3. The best treatment of trusteeism is Patrick W. Carey, *People, Priests, and Prelates: Ecclesiastical Democracy and the Tensions of Trusteeism* (Notre Dame, Ind.: University of Notre Dame Press, 1987).

4. Fogarty, "Parish and Community," 254.

5. Spalding, *Premier See*, 418–19, 446–47, 479–80.

6. The downtown parishes that survived were, besides St. Vincent's, the Cathedral of the Assumption, St. Alphonsus, St. Ignatius, and St. John the Baptist. The latter, however, surrendered its parochial status to become St. Jude's Shrine.

7. ASV, Oddi to Borders, Rome, March 30, 1982 (copy).

8. Ibid., "The Urban Parish" and "Quaestiones de Paroecia Urbana" (copy). The statement offered three possible alternatives to existing territorial parishes: the elective parish, a parish coterminous with the city, or the territorial parish with "internal cell-like entities."

9. ASV, "Response of the Archdiocese of Baltimore to the Sacred Congregation of the Clergy on the Theology and Life of the Parish in the Great Cities of the World." The other members of the committee were Rev. F. Joseph Tinder of St. Joseph's Parish, Fullerton; Rev. Edward M. Miller of St. Bernardine's Parish, Baltimore; and Rev. Michael J. Roach of St. Peter the Apostle Parish, Baltimore.

10. The videotape is still available at St. Vincent de Paul Parish and the Catholic Center in Baltimore.

11. ASV, "Parish as Church," a paper delivered September 27, 1992, in Washington, D.C. The work of Avery Dulles, SJ, cited is *Models of the Church: A Critical Assessment of the Church in All Its Aspects* (Garden City, N.Y.: Doubleday, 1974).

12. See chapter 1 for the development of early Baltimore.

13. *The Sun*, March 9, 1950.

14. U.S. Department of Transportation et al., *Final Environmental Impact Statement* (July 1983), II–43, III–5.

CHAPTER 1. Convergence

1. USDOT, *Final Environmental Impact Statement*, III–24.

2. J. Thomas Scharf, *Chronicles of Baltimore* (Baltimore: Turnbull Bros., 1874), 1–18; Thomas O'Brien Hanley, *Charles Carroll of Carrollton: The Making of a Revolutionary Gentleman* (Washington, D.C.: Catholic University of America Press, 1970), 11–12.

3. Garrett Power, "Parceling Out Land in the Vicinity of Baltimore: 1632–1796," pt. 1, *MHM* 87 (1992): 458–61, 464–65.

4. The building is identified by one authority as that numbered 19 at South Lane and Sharping Lane on Moale's map of 1752. See Clarence V. Joerndt, *St. Ignatius, Hickory, and Its Missions* (Baltimore: privately printed, 1972), 34, 83.

5. Power, "Parceling Out Land," pt. 2, *MHM* 88 (1993): 151–52; Suzanne Ellery Greene, *An Illustrated History of Baltimore* (Woodland Hills, Calif.: Windsor Publications, 1980), 4–5.

6. Scharf, *Chronicles*, 32; Sherry H. Olson, *Baltimore: The Building of an American City* (Baltimore: Johns Hopkins University Press, 1980), 8.

7. *First Records of Baltimore Town and Jones Town, 1729–1797* (Baltimore: King Bros., 1905), 1–20.

8. Scharf, *Chronicles*, 10. Front Street was actually the southernmost of three segments of the same street, all of which would acquire the name. The northernmost was originally called Jones Street and the middle one Short Street.

9. Olson, *Baltimore*, 10.

10. Scharf, *Chronicles*, 53–54.

11. Norman G. Ruckert, *The Fells Point Story* (Baltimore: Bodine & Associates, 1976), 11–17.

12. Robert J. Brugger, *Maryland: A Middle Temperament, 1634–1980* (Baltimore: Johns Hopkins University Press, 1988), 63–70; Olson, *Baltimore*, 4–7.

13. Hamilton Owens, *Baltimore on the Chesapeake* (Garden City, N.Y.: Doubleday, 1941), 69–70.

14. Kenneth Roberts and Anne M. Roberts, trans. and eds., *Moreau de St. Mery's American Journey* (Garden City, N.Y.: Doubleday, 1974), 76–81.

15. Emily Emerson Lantz, "Front Street," in Joseph B. Legg, comp., "Baltimore Streets," unpaginated typescript at the Enoch Pratt Free Library; Letitia Stockett, *Baltimore: A Not Too Serious History* (Baltimore: Norman, Remington Co., 1928), 43, 157ff.

16. *A Centenary Manual: Church of St. Vincent de Paul, Baltimore, 1841–1941* (n.p., [1941]), unpaginated (hereafter *Centenary Manual*).

17. William Bruce Wheeler, "The Baltimore Jeffersonians, 1788–1799: A Profile of Intra-factional Conflict," *MHM* 66 (1971): 166.

18. William J. Kelley, *Brewing in Maryland* (Baltimore: n.p., 1965), 83–87.

19. Richard M. Bernard, "A Portrait of Baltimore in 1800: Economic and Occupational Patterns in an Early American City," *MHM* 69 (1974): 348.

20. Eugene Lemoine Didier, *Poe Memoir* (New York, 1877), later expanded to *The Poe Cult, and Other Poe Papers, with a New Memoir* (New York: Broadway Publishing, 1909). Edgar Allan Poe was a frequent visitor to Old Town, on the outskirts of which he had lived in his early years. The bell in St. Vincent's tower may have been the inspiration for his "Hymn of the Angelus." In 1849 he was found near death not far from the church.

21. Andrew Skeabeck, "Most Rev. William Gross: Missionary Bishop of the North," *Records of the American Catholic Historical Society of Philadelphia* 65 (1954): 13–15, 22 n. 4.

22. Fred Hopkins, "For Flag and Profit: The Life of Commodore John Daniel Danels of Baltimore," *MHM* 80 (1985): 392–401; Kelley, *Brewing in Maryland*, 87–90.

23. Interview with Sr. Annella Martin, RSM.

24. Research by the staff of the Baltimore City Life Museums and Dean Krimmel of the Peale Museum.

25. [Michael J. Riordan], *Cathedral Records from the Beginning of Catholicity in Baltimore to the Present Time* (Baltimore: Catholic Mirror, 1906), 6–8.

26. Thomas W. Spalding, "'A Revolution More Extraordinary': Bishop John Carroll and the Birth of American Catholicism," *MHM* 84 (1989): 195–97.

27. Terry D. Bilhartz, *Urban Religion and the Second Great Awakening: Church and Society in Early National Baltimore* (Rutherford, N.J.: Fairleigh Dickinson University, 1986), 19–20 and passim.

28. Ibid., 19–27, 149.

29. Whitman H. Ridgeway, *Community Leadership in Maryland, 1790–1840: A Comparative Analysis of Power in Society* (Chapel Hill: University of North Carolina Press, 1979), 122. Among the Catholics of Baltimore not identified as such by Ridgeway in his appendices, 215–76, are James Barry, Thomas Hillen, and Richard Lilly.

30. Spalding, *Premier See*, 29, 57–58; Ridgeway, *Community Leadership*, 215–40.

31. Spalding, *Premier See*, 28–31; [Riordan], *Cathedral Records*, 19–41, 50–51.

32. Spalding, *Premier See*, 81–83, 88–92, 116–17.

33. Brugger, *Maryland*, 148–49; Scharf, *Chronicles*, 43, 123, 239.

34. Charles Warren Currier, *Carmel in America: A Centennial History of the Discalced Carmelites in the United States* (Baltimore: John Murphy, 1890; rpt., Darien, Ill.: Carmelite Press, 1989), 184.

35. SAB, RG 1, Box 1A, Diary of Louis Regis Deluol translated (hereafter Deluol diary), May 1, 1835.

36. Deluol diary, June 11, 1834.

37. *USCM* 4 (1845): 202.

38. AAB, 23-I-2, Gildea to Whitfield, Martinsburg, October 21, 1832.

39. Ibid., 23-I-4, Gildea to Whitfield, n.p., n.d.

40. Deluol diary, May 14, 1835.

41. Ray Allen Billington, *The Protestant Crusade, 1800–1860: A Study of the Origins of American Nativism* (New York: Macmillan, 1938), 32–55.
42. Spalding, *Premier See,* 114–15.
43. Deluol diary, May 18, 1835.
44. Ibid., May 20 and 22, 1835.
45. Ibid., May 28, 1838, July 3 and 24 and September 14 and 15, 1840. In 1840 the Sisters of Charity would leave Maryland Hospital to begin Mount St. Vincent Hospital opposite St. Vincent de Paul Church but would in 1844 acquire Mount Hope College and move the hospital there.
46. AAB, Deeds, St. Vincent de Paul.
47. See chapter 9 for a consideration of Gildea as an architect.
48. *CA* (1839), 98. This was the first year such organizations were listed in the *Catholic Almanac* for the archdiocese of Baltimore. See also [Riordan], *Cathedral Records,* 106.
49. *CA* (1840), 74.
50. SAB, RG 26, Box 9, a prospectus that includes the constitution introduces a series of bound tracts.
51. Ibid., White's address presented at the first annual meeting of the society.
52. AAB, Deeds, St. Vincent de Paul.
53. The minutes now lost were evidently in the hands of the pastor, Rev. John Sinnott Martin, when he authored the *Centenary Manual* (see n. 16 above) in 1941 and "St. Vincent de Paul Church: Historical Sketch" published anonymously in the "St. Vincent's Notebook" (SVN, no. 153). They were also quoted in *The Sun,* November 23, 1941, in an article entitled "St. Vincent's Asylum, Century Old."
54. AAB, Deeds, St. Vincent de Paul. The ground rent system, wherein a person could own his home but not the land on which it stood, was peculiar to Baltimore.
55. One of the best biographies of the saint is Pierre Coste, *The Life and Works of St. Vincent de Paul,* trans. Joseph Leonard, 3 vols. (Westminster, Md.: Newman Press, 1952). A popular biography is Henry Daniel-Rops, *Monsieur Vincent,* trans. Julie Kernan (New York: Hawthorn Books, 1961).
56. Olson, *Baltimore,* 91
57. Michael J. Curley, *The Provincial Story: A History of the Baltimore Province of the Congregation of the Most Holy Redeemer* (New York: Redemptorist Fathers, 1963), 1–55. St. Alphonsus Liguori was the founder of the Redemptorists.

CHAPTER 2. Foundation

1. Scharf, *Chronicles,* 501, 502.
2. *United States Catholic Miscellany,* May 30, 1840.
3. *American and Commercial Daily Advertiser,* May 22, 1840. The cornerstone has not to date been found. Presumably it was covered by construction work.
4. *United States Catholic Miscellany,* May 30, 1840.
5. See chapter 1, n. 53.
6. Baltimore City Chattel Records T.K., 63–154. In the original copy, AAB, Deeds, St. Vincent de Paul, there are three differences: (1) the article concerning the application of the income from pew rents is not in the original; (2) there is a twelfth incorporator: James Roche; (3) the day and month of incorporation have been left blank.
7. Spalding, *Premier See,* 88–89, 91–92, 141.
8. Deluol diary, December 15 and July 19, 1841.
9. [Joan Mary Crumlish], *1809–1959* (Emmitsburg, Md., 1959), 32.
10. Deluol diary, November 1, 1841; *American and Commercial Daily Advertiser,* November 5, 1841.
11. Deluol diary, November 7, 1841.

12. ASV, typed account, source not indicated but obviously from a contemporary newspaper.
13. SVN, no. 153.
14. SAB, RG 26, Box 10, a receipt among the papers relating to the settlement of the estate of John Baptist Gildea by Alexius J. Elder, SS. These papers will hereafter be cited as Gildea estate.
15. Gildea estate, papers beginning "The following is a Copy of one page of Cash Book, kept by the late Revd. J. B. Gildea," and "Amount Loaned to St. V.B.A [Benevolent Association]." Another list signed by those who promised to pay a certain amount shows that Daniel Coonan also purchased $2,391 worth of stock and Ferdinand Brandel $1,100.
16. *The Sun,* August 15, 1905.
17. Deluol diary, September 29 and 30, October 1, 1845. On February 7, 1847, Mary Rubina, daughter of Solomon and Emily Hillen, was baptized at St. Vincent's, Mrs. Jeannette Hunter (sister of Solomon) her sponsor.
18. Ann C. Van Deventer (organizer), *"Anywhere So Long as There be Freedom": Charles Carroll of Carrollton, His Family, and His Maryland* (Baltimore: Maryland Historical Society, 1975), 31, 250.
19. *Biographical Encyclopedia of Representative Men of Maryland and the District of Columbia* (Baltimore: National Biographical Publishing, 1879), 193.
20. Edward Felix Jenkins, *Thomas Jenkins of Maryland 1670: His Descendants and Allied Families* (Baltimore: Maryland Historical Society, 1985), 97.
21. Hopkins, "For Flag and Profit," 400. Minutes of the faculty meeting of St. Mary's Seminary for July 3, 1826, read: "Since there is no doubt that Emmanuel and Thomas Paez are colored, and that, consequently, their presence in the College would harm its reputation, we decided that the President should notify their guardian that he is to withdraw them at the latest next September, at the beginning of the school year, a year after they have been admitted." The bills were paid by Commodore Danels. SAB, Finance Records.
22. Scharf, *Chronicles,* 622–23.
23. At the outbreak of the Civil War Lt. Joseph Danels resigned his commission but soon regretted the decision and sought reinstatement. As a volunteer lieutenant-commander he led the attacks on Fort Fisher while critically ill. He died before his commission as lieutenant-commander in the regular navy arrived, and his widow placed it in his hands before he was buried. "Some Catholic Names in the U.S. Navy List," *Historical Records and Studies* 6, pt. 1 (1911): 190–93.
24. Clippings and other information from the Dielman-Hayward File at the Maryland Historical Society.
25. *CM,* March 23, 1861.
26. Information taken mostly from *Matchett's Baltimore Directory.*
27. Gerald W. Johnson et al., *The Sunpapers of Baltimore* (New York: Knopf, 1937), 19n, 60; Harold A. Williams, *The Baltimore Sun* (Baltimore: Johns Hopkins University Press, 1987), 16.
28. Children baptized at St. Vincent's 1841–1853 were Robert Arunah, George William, Charles, Walter Robert, and Agnes Frances. John Fox was sponsor for Robert and Margaret Fox, his wife, for Charles.
29. Information on the Clagett family from Brice M. Clagett.
30. John Tracy Ellis, *The Life of James Cardinal Gibbons, Archbishop of Baltimore, 1834–1921,* 2 vols. (Milwaukee, Wis.: Bruce, 1952), 1:3–23, and passim.
31. Patrick Henry Ahern, *The Life of John J. Keane: Educator and Archbishop, 1839–1918* (Milwaukee, Wis.: Bruce, 1954), 1–8.
32. Gildea estate, receipt of March 1840 signed by Mary F. Hollan acknowledging payment by Gildea of $25 as interest on a loan made him by the Tobias Society and another of April 25, 1843, signed by same for $45 interest.

33. Ibid., "Account opened with St. Vincent's mutual relief Society of Coloured persons commenced May eight 1843." On December 3, 1843, the Society of Colored People, later called the Holy Family Society, was organized at Calvert Hall. It counted some 270 members. John Noel was elected president and "Mary Holland" first counselor. See Cyprian Davis, *The History of Black Catholics in the United States* (New York: Crossroad, 1990), 86–88. The St. Vincent's Mutual Relief Society of Colored Persons may have merged with this society, but it continued to deposit sums with Gildea under its original title until 1845. It may have been an extension of the Tobias Society.

34. Gildea estate, White to Scott, Baltimore, December 5, 1845; Miles to Association, Baltimore, April 20, 1846; agreement of 1847 signed by John Noel as executor.

35. *United States Catholic Miscellany,* October 1, 1842.

36. *Religious Cabinet* 1 (1842): 190.

37. *The Sun,* November 23, 1941.

38. *MCA* (1842), 72; (1845), 71.

39. Although the names are from reports that begin in 1850, there can be little doubt that these same women were active from the beginning.

40. Archives of the Sisters of Charity, Emmitsburg, Gildea to "Esteemed and Respected Mother," Baltimore, April 21, 1842.

41. *MCA* (1844), 73–74.

42. *USCM* 2 (1843): 447; 4 (1845): 334–35.

43. Brother Angelus Gabriel, *The Christian Brothers in the United States, 1848–1948* (New York: Declan X. McMullen, 1948), 72–79; Spalding, *Premier See,* 142–43.

44. J. Devadder, *Rooted in History: The Life and Times of T. J. Ryken, Founder of the Xaverian Brothers,* 2 vols. (Bruges, Belgium: privately printed, 1987), 1:455–58.

45. SAB, RG 26, Box 10, bound collection of tracts of the Catholic Tract Society.

46. Gildea estate, inventory submitted by Thomas C. Dunlevy and John Baker on March 6, 1845. Gildea's personal estate was valued at $1,162.65, which did not include $92.06 on deposit at the Chesapeake Bank.

47. Ibid., decree in chancery, December Term, Ann Campbell v. Peter Kees et al.

48. The "Historical Sketch" of St. Vincent's by Rev. John Sinnott Martin in SVN, no. 155, says that the house was built about 1825 by a contractor, who also resided there, but no evidence has to date been found for this.

    The inventory, which describes the contents of each room of the rectory, is not entirely in agreement with Father Martin's description in SVN, no. 155; he indicates that the dining room was in the back building and that there were two bedrooms in the garret. The inventory does not mention contents of a basement.

    A receipt dated October 11, 1839, in the papers of the Gildea estate signed by Jeanette H. Hunter reads: "Received of John B. Gildea Sixty dollars for one years hire of Rose Jones coloured woman."

49. Gildea estate, a bill for advertisements in the *American* from March 1840 to January 1843 and a note to Angela Mudd, superior of the Carmelites, for $400 dated February 12, 1841. Gildea had a running account with the publisher Fielding Lucas Jr., going back to 1834, that he apparently never paid.

50. Deluol diary, October 28, 1844, and November 24 and 25, 1845.

51. *CM,* November 14, 1891.

52. Deluol diary, January 31, 1845.

53. AAB, Deeds, St. Vincent de Paul.

54. Deluol diary, February 18, 19, and 20, 1845.

55. *USCM* 4 (1845): 334–35.

56. Ibid., 380–81.

57. Ibid., 677–78.
58. Deluol diary, September 11, 14, 15, and 16, 1845.
59. Ibid., October 24, 1845.
60. Helene Philibert, Estelle Philibert, and Imogene Philibert, *St. Matthew's of Washington, 1840–1940* (Baltimore: A. Hoen, 1940), 42–44, 142–43; [Riordan], *Cathedral Records,* 60–61.
61. Deluol diary, January 21, 1846.
62. Ibid., August 6 and September 3, 1846.
63. SVN, no. 154.
64. Spalding, *Premier See,* 141.
65. White as spokesman for the St. Vincent of Paul Benevolent Association contested the claims of four litigants, one of whom was Mary Hollan, for the purchase of stocks. He also claimed that the executor of the estate of John B. Gildea, Alexius A. Elder, SS, had no right to Gildea's unpaid salary. In the last case White contended that Gildea had held funds of the association never accounted for. Gildea estate, White to Scott, Baltimore, December 5, 1845.
66. Gildea estate, decree in Chancery, December Term 1845, Ann Campbell v. Peter Kees et al. The mortgage payments were dated January 13 and March 9, 1846.
67. Edward P. McAdams, *History of St. Charles Borromeo Parish, Pikesville, Maryland, 1849–1949* (Baltimore: Chandler Printing, 1949), 15–23.
68. Deluol diary, July 2, 1848.
69. Philibert et al., *St. Matthew's,* 43.

CHAPTER 3. Transformation

1. Olson, *Baltimore,* 102–3, 116–17.
2. Ibid., 105–8.
3. Spalding, *Premier See,* 121–53.
4. Ibid., 136–39; Olson, *Baltimore,* 123–25.
5. Philibert et al., *St. Matthew's,* 29–30, 141; Thomas J. Stanton, *A Century of Growth, Or the History of the Church in Western Maryland,* 2 vols. (Baltimore: John Murphy, 1900), 1:119.
6. Gildea estate, Donelan to Myles, March 4, 1847.
7. *CM,* September 14, 1850, financial report.
8. Ibid. Among the documents of the Gildea estate is one dated May 31, 1851, in which John McColgan signs as secretary along with Donelan, Bevans, Hartman, and Johnson as trustees.
9. Ibid., January 24, 1852, January 15, 1853, and January 6, 1855.
10. AAB, "St. Vincent de Paul's Graveyard Book" (mislabeled).
11. Several such letters are copied in the back of the "Graveyard Book."
12. Angelus Gabriel, *Christian Brothers,* 86, 272; *CM,* September 21, 1850.
13. *MCA* (1850), 85.
14. Angelus Gabriel, *Christian Brothers,* 273.
15. *CM,* January 24, 1852; SAB, Finance record #56.
16. *MCA* (1849), 98.
17. *CM,* September 21 and March 30, 1850.
18. Ibid, March 8, 1851. The cathedral parish numbered 450 in all, St. Peter's 405, St. Patrick's 354, St. James 258, St. Alphonsus 245, and St. Michael's 225. See Owen B. Corrigan, *The Catholic Schools of the Archdiocese of Baltimore: A Study in Diocesan History* (Baltimore: St. Mary's Industrial School Press, 1924), passim.
19. *MCA* (1852), 76.
20. *USCM* 8 (1849): 30–31; ASV, typed copy of minutes.
21. *CM,* March 30 and May 4, 1850.
22. Gildea estate, Pendergast et al. to Kenrick, 1854 (day and month left blank).

23. SVN, no. 155.

24. MCA (1847), 82; Spalding, *Premier See,* 143–45.

25. MCA (1846), 86.

26. CM, September 21, 1850.

27. USCM 6 (1847): 448; Deluol diary, July 18, 1847.

28. MCA (1850), 85.

29. CM, July 27, 1850.

30. SVN, no. 155, estimates 12,000, but see n. 42 below.

31. Deluol diary, July 11 and August 2, 1848.

32. CM, December 27, 1851.

33. Ibid., March 6, 1852.

34. CR, July 7, 1923. Donelan's friends later installed a memorial that still adorns a wall of the vestibule of St. Vincent's Church.

35. AAB, 30-V-8, Obermeyer to Kenrick, Cumberland, December 13, 1851.

36. Stanton, *Century of Growth,* 1:17–22.

37. Ibid., 1:22.

38. *St. John the Evangelist Church, 1853–1953* (Baltimore: n.p., 1953), 17–54; CM, September 2, 1854.

39. Nicholas Varga, *Baltimore's Loyola, Loyola's Baltimore, 1851–1986* (Baltimore: Maryland Historical Society, 1990), 9–11.

40. The chapel was actually created for Fr. Edward Damphoux after the Jesuits took over his parish, St. Joseph's, in 1849.

41. John J. Ryan, *Chronicle and Sketch of the Church of St. Ignatius of Loyola, Baltimore, 1856–1906* (Baltimore: A. Hoen, 1907), 1–3, 73.

42. CM, September 20, 1856. This was based on an estimate from *DeBow's Compendium* that there were 3.02 births for every 100 persons.

43. CM, July 30, 1853.

44. AAB, Deeds; SVN, no. 155; Jane Bromley Wilson, *The Very Quiet Baltimoreans* (Shippensburg, Pa.: White Mane Publishers, 1991), 47; CM, May 21, 1853.

45. AAB, "St. Vincent de Paul's Cemetery" (ledger).

46. ASV, Burial records.

47. MCA (1856), 77.

48. CM, June 4, 1853; MCA (1854), 76; [Crumlish], *1809–1959,* 40.

49. CM, May 31, 1856, and January 10, 1857. The names of the other incorporators were Richard Lilly, John Eisler, Patrick J. Hedian, Francis Bourquet, William Murray, John Huxley, and James Sloan Jr. When the parochial school was torn down in the 1960s, a marble cornerstone was recovered, which read: "Incorporated/May 1856/[Re]v. L. Obermeyer. Pastor/ Rebuilt June 1865/[Re]v. H. Myers. Pastor/." The claim of Fr. John Sinnott Martin, pastor at the time, that it "marked one of the three homes for working girls in St. Vincent's parish" is certainly incorrect. SVN, no. 135.

50. Archives of the Sisters of Charity, Emmitsburg, Obermeyer to Burlando, July 29 and August 3 and 13, 1858.

51. CM, January 18, 1862.

52. AAB, Deeds, and Notitiae, 1879, 1880.

53. CM, February 11, 1860.

54. Rita Clark Hutzell, *Mother of Churches: A History of St. Mary's Church, Hagerstown, Maryland* (n.p., 1976), 21–22.

55. AAB, 39-P-1, Myers to Spalding, Baltimore, May 3, 1866.

56. From 1850 until 1871 most of the annual reports for St. Vincent's were published in the *Catholic Mirror.* Some are preserved in AAB, Parishes.

57. CM, November 17 and 24, 1860, and January 18, 1862.

58. AAB, 39-P-1, Myers to Spalding, Baltimore, May 3, 1866.

59. *CM*, March 28, 1868.

60. Ibid., November 24, 1860.

61. Owens, *Baltimore*, 260–70; Spalding, *Premier See*, 173–75.

62. Three names of civilians killed correspond to names found in St. Vincent's registers. For a detailed description of the riot, as well as the names, mostly Irish, see Scharf, *Chronicles*, 588–95.

63. Thomas W. Spalding, *Martin John Spalding: American Churchman* (Washington, D.C.: Catholic University of America Press, 1973), chap. 9; *CM*, November 19, 1870.

64. Scharf, *Chronicles*, 684–85; *CM*, July 1, 1871.

65. *CM*, June 24, 1871.

66. Olson, *Baltimore*, 133–34, 162–63, 165–66; Scharf, *Chronicles*, 563, 669–75, 676.

67. St. Vincent's usually followed the cathedral in the highest amounts reported.

68. See appendix A.

69. *CM*, August 2, 1873; *The Sun*, August 30, 1873.

CHAPTER 4. Zenith

1. M. Hildegarde Yeager, *The Life of James Roosevelt Bayley, First Bishop of Newark and Eighth Archbishop of Baltimore, 1814–1877* (Washington, D.C.: Catholic University of America Press, 1947), 1–42 and passim; Spalding, *Premier See*, 207–11.

2. The Notitiae have been faithfully kept by all chancellors, and all through the administration of Cardinal Lawrence Shehan are in AAB.

3. Clarence H. Forrest, *Official History of the Fire Department of the City of Baltimore* (Baltimore, 1898), 132–33.

4. *CM*, May 23, 1903 (obituary); *Grand Official Programme and Souvenir of the Golden Jubilee of St. Vincent de Paul Church* (n.p., 1891), unpaginated (hereafter *Programme and Souvenir*).

5. Thomas J. Stanton, "Old St. Vincent's," in *BCR*, August 8, 1914; *Programme and Souvenir*.

6. *CM*, October 14, 1876.

7. Notitiae, January 1, 1876 and 1877; *CM*, April 6, 1877.

8. *CM*, March 29, 1879.

9. Ibid., April 11 and November 7, 1891.

10. Ibid., February 18, 1888. See also ibid., August 14, 1886.

11. Ibid., December 22, 1877, and July 19, 1876.

12. Ibid., March 30 and April 6, 1878.

13. AAB, 80-R-12, Didier to Gibbons, Baltimore, April 9, 1886, and 85-N-10, Didier to Gibbons, St. Vincent's Church, January 9, 1889.

14. *CM*, February 24, 1872, July 17, 1880, and May 22, 1886.

15. Ibid., January 10, 1874.

16. Ibid., October 19 and November 2, 1878.

17. Carl Bode, *The American Lyceum: Town Meeting of the Mind* (New York: Oxford University Press, 1956); Spalding, *Premier See*, 248–49.

18. *CM*, September 21 and 28, 1878.

19. Ibid., November 30 and April 12, 1878.

20. Ibid., January 29 and April 23, 1881, December 9, 1882, and June 23, 1883.

21. Spalding, *Premier See*, 248.

22. *CM*, July 14, 1883, and March 13 and September 25, 1886.

23. Ibid., December 3, 1887, and February 23, 1889.

24. Ibid., January 4 and April 12, 1879; November 6, 1880; May 24, 1879; April 23, 1881; September 18, November 6 and 20, 1880; January 14, 1882.

25. Ibid., April 24, 1886, March 14 and July 23, 1887, and March 3, 1888.

26. *Programme and Souvenir; CM,* January 12 and March 2, 1889.

27. Spalding, *Premier See,* 248–49; *CM,* May 10, November 8, and December 6 and 13, 1879.

28. *CM,* January 8 and 15, 1881.

29. Ibid., June 9, 1883.

30. Spalding, *Premier See,* 280–81.

31. *CM,* January 23 and 30, 1892.

32. Spalding, *Premier See,* 281, 249.

33. *CM,* March 18, 1871.

34. Spalding, *Premier See,* 218–19, 245–46.

35. *CM,* November 20, 1880; January 15, 1881; July 28, 1883; June 11, 1887.

36. Spalding, *Premier See,* 247–48; Christopher J. Kauffman, *Faith and Fraternalism: The History of the Knights of Columbus,* rev. ed. (New York: Simon & Schuster, 1992), chap. 1.

37. In 1882 and 1883 fifteen branches of the CBL were founded in Baltimore and two in Washington, the latter city preferring the Catholic Knights of America. By 1892 there were nearly forty branches of the CBL spread throughout the archdiocese.

38. *CM,* March 22, 1889. Sometimes there is confusion in the reporting between the Sodality and the League of the Sacred Heart.

39. *Programme and Souvenir.*

40. *CM,* October 3, 1885.

41. *Programme and Souvenir; CM,* October 19, 1889.

42. Daniel T. McColgan, *A Century of Charity: The First One Hundred Years of the Society of St. Vincent de Paul in the United States,* 2 vols. (Milwaukee, Wis.: Bruce, 1951), 1:273.

43. *CM,* March 10, 1875; April 7 and July 21, 1877; April 13, 1878; March 26, 1881.

44. Spalding, *Premier See,* 211.

45. *CM,* June 23, 1883.

46. Ibid., October 12, 1889.

47. Brother Julian [Ryan], *Men and Deeds* (New York: Macmillan, 1933), 84–87.

48. AAB, 74-D-7, Didier to Gibbons, Baltimore, November 26, 1878.

49. *Programme and Souvenir; CM,* February 1, 1890.

50. *CM,* August 4, 1883.

51. Ibid., July 26, 1884.

52. Ibid., August 1 and November 7, 1884.

53. Ibid., January 14, 1888; January 12, 1889; September 26, 1891.

54. Mary Loretto Costello, *The Sisters of Mercy of Maryland (1855–1930)* (St. Louis: B. Herder, 1931), 134–35; *Programme and Souvenir; CM,* September 6, 1890.

55. *CM,* April 16, 1887.

56. AAB, 85-N-10 and 11, Didier to Gibbons, Baltimore, January 9 and 10, 1889.

57. Ibid., 85-O-2, Gibbons to Didier, Baltimore, January 11, 1889 (copy).

58. *CM,* April 6 and July 13, 1889; March 22, 1890.

59. Ibid., October 19 and November 16, 1889.

60. Ibid., September 10, 1887.

61. Ibid., January 23, 1892.

62. Ibid., April 14, 1894; November 16, 1901.

63. Ibid., December 10, 1892; February 4 and March 18, 1893; June 10, 1899; October 13, 1900.

64. *Church News* (Washington), December 17, 1898; *CM,* April 8, 1899.

65. AAB, 98-H-5.1, O'Brien to Didier, Baltimore, September 23, 1900 (copy).

CHAPTER 5. Decline

1. Ellis, *Life of Gibbons,* 2:369–537 and passim; Spalding, *Premier See,* 316–17.

2. *Wood's City Directory,* 1881 and *Sheriff and Taylor's Baltimore City Directory,* 1885; information from several issues of the *Catholic Mirror.*

3. In the years 1874–80 Rev. Joseph Andreis recorded the native towns of the parents of children of Italian extraction he baptized. Of the twenty-five recorded in 1874 all fathers were born in Italy, over half in or near Genoa and only one from southern Italy (Marsicovetri near Naples). Mothers were usually from the same area as the father, but four were recorded as from Baltimore, Germany, England, and Virginia, respectively. Of the twenty-one baptisms recorded in 1878 sixteen were from northern Italy, mostly near Genoa, and the other five from Sorrento, Marsicovetri, Corsica, Cefalù, and New York City.

4. *Sheriff and Taylor's Baltimore City Directory* for 1881 and 1885. See also Gilbert Sandler, *The Neighborhood: The Story of Baltimore's Little Italy* (Baltimore: Bodine & Associates, 1974), especially 23–26.

5. AAB, 74-R-4, Andreis to Gibbons, Baltimore, September 11, 1879.

6. *The Church of St. Leo the Great, 1881–1981: The Heart of Little Italy* (Baltimore: St. Leo the Great Press, 1981), 3–7.

7. AAB, 75-J-5, 75-Y-10, and 76-H-14, Didier to Gibbons, Baltimore, September 24, 1880, June 24, 1881, and November 15, 1881.

8. Ibid., 76-S-7, Andreis to Gibbons, Baltimore, July 28, 1882.

9. *CM*, September 9, 1882.

10. Ibid., April 14, 1888.

11. Included in the receipts of 1890 were $300 from "A person, conscience money returned" and a $487.50 legacy from Mary McManus. Most of the legacies were from widows.

12. *CM*, July 28, 1877.

13. Edward K. Muller and Paul A. Groves, "The Changing Location of the Clothing Industry: A Link to the Social Geography of Baltimore in the Nineteenth Century," *MHM* 71 (1976): 403–20.

14. *Baltimore American*, February 17, 1935.

15. *Evening Sun*, March 14, 1944, and other clippings in the Enoch Pratt Free Library. Possible Catholics on the original board of directors were John Donnelly and George A. Vernetson.

16. Although Didier gave 3,000 as the parish population in his first three annual reports, the 4,983 for 1876 was probably closer to the fact. Five times he gave the number of children in the parish in exact figures rather than round numbers: 1,183 for 1876, 1,166 for 1878, 1,423 for 1880, 867 for 1881, and 636 for 1885. Only once did he give exact figures for women—2,318 in 1877—and only once for men—1,696 in 1879. In these two years the number of children appeared in round numbers, 800 and 1,000 respectively.

17. Owens, *Baltimore*, 301.

18. Lawrence H. Larsen, *The Rise of the Urban South* (Lexington: University of Kentucky Press, 1981), 139–40.

19. *Baltimore American*, March 3 and June 9, 1935. In the *Baltimore City Directory* for 1885 saloons were conducted by Patrick Roddy at 147 N. Front, Thomas Roddy at 148 N. Front, John Roddy at 154 N. Front, and Bernard Roddy at 4 W. Centre, and a liquor store by Michael J. Roddy at 186 N. High.

20. *CM*, July 23, 1887.

21. Ibid., June 2, 1888.

22. Ibid., November 22, 1888, and editorials of January 25, February 15, March 8, 15, and 29, and April 5, 1890.

23. Ibid., June 29 and October 12, 1889, July 30, 1887, and March 17, 1888.

24. *Programme and Souvenir.*

25. For the Gorman-Rasin machine see Brugger, *Maryland*, 385–95.

26. He was baptized August 6. His godparents were Robert White and Rose Bannon.

27. "The Autobiography of a Baltimore Boss" was carried by *The Sun* each Sunday of October 1922.

28. *Biographical Encyclopedia of Representative Men of Maryland and the District of Columbia,* 305.

29. *Baltimore American,* February 17, 1935, and January 27, 1952.

30. AAB, 73-K-7 and 73-Y-3, Didier to Gibbons, Baltimore, December 26, 1877, and September 27, 1878.

31. Ibid., 75-J-5, 76-N-2, 80-R-12, 89-H-9, September 24, 1880, February 4, 1882, April 9, 1886, and January 11, 1892.

32. *CM,* October 2, 1886.

33. AAB, 88-B-4, Didier to Gibbons, Baltimore, October 29, 1890.

34. "Old St. Vincent's," *BCR,* August 8, 1914.

35. *CM,* October 26, 1895.

36. Corrigan, *Catholic Schools,* 42.

37. Costello, *Sisters of Mercy,* 137–38.

38. *CR,* September 19, 1941; *The Sun,* November 23, 1941.

39. Joerndt, *St. Ignatius, Hickory,* 430–32; McAdams, *St. Charles Borromeo Parish,* 68.

40. Isador Blum, *The Jews of Baltimore: A Historical Sketch* (Baltimore: Historical Review Publishing, 1910), 28–31; Isaac M. Fein, *The Making of an American Jewish Community: The History of Baltimore's Jewry from 1773 to 1920* (Philadelphia: Jewish Publication Society, 1971), 141ff.

41. Fein, *American Jewish Community,* 204.

42. *The Catholic Red Book of Baltimore-Washington and Environs: A Catholic Directory* (Baltimore: Red Book Society, 1908), 477–78.

43. Costello, *Sisters of Mercy,* 136–38.

44. ASV, transcript of a news item from the *Baltimore News-Post* dated November 7, 1911.

45. See SVN, no. 157.

46. *BCR,* August 8, 1914.

CHAPTER 6. Revival

1. ASV, a small notebook of clippings collected by George Rohleder (hereafter Rohleder clippings), clipping dated 1916. Newspapers are not identified, nor are day and month of issue.

2. AAB, Deceased Priests files.

3. Ibid.; Joerndt, *St. Ignatius, Hickory,* 460–63.

4. SVN, no. 148.

5. Rohleder clippings, 1910 [sic], 1913, 1914.

6. Ibid., 1915 and 1916 (two clippings from each); *CR,* January 15 and February 28, 1916.

7. Ibid., 1910, 1915, 1917, 1926; SVN, no. 124.

8. *CR,* April 21, 1950. No correspondence on the indult has been located in the AAB.

9. Rohleder clippings, 1914, 1915; *CR,* April 21, 1950. In 1919 an indult was also granted for a printers' mass at St. Patrick's in Washington, D.C.

10. Rohleder clippings, 1914.

11. The other sources of income listed in the Notitiae of January 1, 1922, were $976 from extraordinary collections, $600 from diocesan collections, $440 from the cemetery, $278 from the sale of newspapers, and $66 from pew rents.

12. Spalding, *Premier See,* 326.

13. Ibid., 325–57.

14. ASV, undated clipping (obituary); undated clipping from the Sisters of St. Francis.

15. *Evening Sun,* July 17, 1978.

16. SVN, no. 158.

17. The 1926 number had also been repeated in the Notitiae until 1930.

18. AAB, M-775, Curley to McGuire, February 18, 1930 (copy).

19. SVN, no. 159.

20. *Church of St. Leo,* 15–19.

21. SVN, no. 158.

22. The Notitiae for 1927 and 1928; SVN, no. 158, which says that the entire cost of the undertaking was $200,000.

23. ASV, "Echos from the Past," a typed paper unattributed.

24. SVN, no. 158.

25. AAB, M-776, Curley to McGuire, May 9, 1933 (copy).

26. ASV, "Historical Sketch," 31, the original manuscript of Rev. John Sinnott Martin's history of the parish published in SVN, but with this part omitted.

27. SVN, no. 159; *Centenary Manual*.

28. AAB, Roman Correspondence, Curley to Cardinal Prefect, November 14, 1930 (copy).

29. SVN, no. 160.

30. Albert Puliafico, interview with author.

31. AAB, Deceased Priests files, Martin to Curley, Randallstown, December 29, 1939; Curley to Martin, January 2, 1940 (copy).

32. SVN, no. 159; AAB, Deceased Priests files.

33. Puliafico interview.

34. *Centenary Manual*.

35. AAB, Chancery files, Martin to Curley, Baltimore, October 7, 1943.

36. Ibid., Curley to Martin, October 9, 1943, March 3, 1942, and January 23, 1945 (copies).

37. ASV, "Historical Sketch," 31, omitted in the SVN history. The Italians may not have liked the pastor's transferring their annual procession from the Feast of St. Vincent to the centennial celebration in October. The Notitiae showed a membership of 62 in 1941. Thereafter the count declined rapidly, numbering "about 20" for most of the years before it disappeared in 1956.

38. These appear only in the Notitiae submitted by Father Romeo as acting pastor at the end of 1939 except for the Girls Club, which was listed for three more years.

39. *Centenary Manual*.

40. Ibid., which carried items from earlier "Notebooks," now lost.

41. SVN, nos. 36, 117, 112.

42. *Centenary Manual* (from the "Notebooks").

43. SVN, no. 125.

44. Ibid., no. 160.

45. Until 1952 Martin initialed most of his editorials.

46. CR, January 19, 1950.

47. Spalding, *Premier See*, 398–99.

48. *The Sun*, December 20, 1965. Criticism of gambling in Ocean City brought a summons to appear before a grand jury in Worcester County. *CR*, December 24, 1965.

49. Interview with Fr. Edmond Stroup. Mrs. Ruth Martin, sister-in-law of Father Martin, remembers his exasperation at the archbishop's habit of holding up a story until it was "stale."

50. Often a guest speaker, Martin predicted at a high school commencement in 1949 that many of the graduates would end up dishonest businessmen, many crooked lawyers, many quack doctors, and many corrupt politicians, prompting Bishop Lawrence Shehan, the presiding prelate, to whisper to the principal: "I thought he could have at least held out hope for a few of them."

51. AAB, Chancery, Curley to Martin, January 25, 1944 (copy).

52. SVN, no. 161. See appendix A.

53. AAB, Deceased Priests files, Martin to (Bishop Austin) Murphy, Baltimore, May 14, 1964.

54. SVN, no. 159.

55. Ibid., nos. 120, 123, 125, 128.

56. G.W.L., "Death of a Church," *Architect's Report* 4 (1962): 4.

57. AAB, Chancery files, Gallagher to Shehan, Baltimore, April 9, 1963.
58. SVN, nos. 120, 161. As late as 1964 the SVN, no. 133, reported: "Talk of razing or removing St. Vincent's keeps cropping up in the press, until one might think this is the main reason for finishing the Jones Falls Expressway. It couldn't be moved; would be costly to raze, would cost a million dollars to rebuild."
59. Ibid., nos. 160, 161.
60. Ibid., no. 125.
61. Fr. Edmond Stroup, interview with author.
62. AAB, Chancery files, Gallagher to Shehan, January 2, 1962, and "Needed Repairs and Improvements," July 6, 1962.
63. SVN, no. 129.
64. Ibid., nos. 118, 123.
65. In 1961 the income was $116,051 and expenses $114,824, but this included the loan and the expenditures for air conditioning.
66. SVN, nos. 123, 137, and 138.
67. *CR,* December 24, 1965.

CHAPTER 7. Revolution

1. Interview with Father Stroup, who supplied many of the details of this chapter.
2. SVN, no. 150.
3. Ibid., no. 147.
4. Ibid., no. 151.
5. *The Sun,* May 27, 1968, and August 2, 1969.
6. Mikulski to the author, Washington, D.C., March 25, 1993.
7. Fr. Joseph Wenderoth, interview with author.
8. SVN, no. 159.
9. AAB, Parish files, Armstrong to Gossman, Baltimore, October 15, 1970.
10. Stroup interview.
11. *Baltimore Urban Parish Study* (Baltimore: Archdiocese of Baltimore, 1967), 8.
12. Ibid., 43–44.
13. Stroup and Wenderoth interviews; *The Sun,* April 7, 8, and 9, 1968; *Evening Sun,* April 8, 1968.
14. *The Sun,* April 10, 1968; Olson, *Baltimore,* 383–84.
15. *CR,* April 26 and May 3, 10, and 24, 1968.
16. *The Sun,* October 12, 1970.
17. Stroup interview.
18. Ibid.
19. AAB, Parish files, Stroup to Shehan, Baltimore, June 13, 1969.
20. SVN, no. 156.
21. ASV, printed questionnaire.
22. SVN, no. 159.
23. The annual report of 1971 was a new form no longer headed "Notitiae." Beginning in 1969 the annual report covered July 1 to June 30.
24. *The Sun,* January 23, 1971; Francine du Plessix Gray, *Divine Disobedience: Profiles in Catholic Radicalism* (New York: Knopf, 1970), 109–11.
25. One of the best accounts of the movement is Charles A. Meconis, *With Clumsy Grace: The American Catholic Left, 1961–1975* (New York: Seabury Press, 1979). For a brief treatment see Spalding, *Premier See,* 439–42, 457–58.
26. Wenderoth interview.
27. ASV, statement with photo published by the Philadelphia Resistance Press.

28. Ibid., memorandum of assistant chancellor, March 2, 1970.
29. *The Sun,* November 27, 29, and 30, and December 4, 1970. See also Jack Nelson and Ronald J. Ostrow, *The FBI and the Berrigans: The Making of a Conspiracy* (New York: Coward, McCann & Geohagan, 1972).
30. *CR,* January 22, 1971.
31. *Sunday Sun,* January 14, 1971; Nelson and Ostrow, *FBI and the Berrigans,* 155–56.
32. He is still (1994) directing Dismas House, a rehabilitation center.
33. AAB, Parish files, "Pastoral Visit—St. Vincent de Paul, October 24–25, 1970."
34. Ibid., Gossman to Stroup, Baltimore, December 24, 1970 (copy).
35. Ibid., Gossman to people of St. Vincent's, Baltimore, December 30, 1970 (copy).
36. *The Sun,* January 13, 1971.
37. *CR,* July 25, 1990.
38. R. Scott Appleby, "Present to the People of God: The Transformation of the Roman Catholic Parish Priesthood," in Dolan, *Transforming Parish Ministry,* 59.
39. Ibid., 60.

CHAPTER 8. Church

1. Much of the material in this chapter is based upon interviews with the present pastor, Fr. Richard Lawrence, and other members of the congregation, especially Albert Puliafico, Anne Freeburger, and Albert Reichelt.
2. These he found mostly at the city's Department of Housing and Community Development.
3. The two corporators were Albert Puliafico and John Bailey. In 1985 Anne Freeburger replaced Bailey.
4. ASV, Annual Report, September 1974.
5. Of the $61,884, $22,706 came from the offertory collections and $21,276 from interest and rents.
6. Eventually the city was induced to maintain the grounds of the cemetery.
7. Much of the information on the activities of the various parish committees is based upon the minutes of the meetings of the parish council, in the SVA, which usually contain the reports of the committees.
8. Maryland Department of Assessment and Taxation, Liber 2156, fol. 128.
9. Ibid., Liber 2524, fol. 10139.
10. SVA, Welsh to Parish Council, November 5, 1980.
11. *Evening Sun,* September 22, 1977.
12. Ramsey Flynn, "God's Fiscal Fireman," *Baltimore Magazine,* July 1984, 71–73, 88–94. See also Spalding, *Premier See,* 465–67, 474.
13. Fr. Charles Canterna, interview with author.
14. In 1984, 1988, and 1991 Father Canterna played an important role in quelling prison riots.
15. Rev. Richard Lawrence, "Easter Flames," *Modern Liturgy* 16, no. 2 (1989): 16. Other commissions were a painting of the Crucifixion by John H. T. Neal Jr., a star by Beverly Lapinski, and a score for Psalm 24 by Joseph Organ.
16. ASV, Lawrence to Kelly, March 9, 1990 (copy).

CHAPTER 9. The Neoclassical Aesthetic

1. The six parishes that were organized prior to St. Vincent de Paul in Baltimore were St. Peter's Pro-Cathedral (c. 1770), St. Patrick's (1792), St. John's (1797), the Cathedral of the Assumption (1821), St. James (1834), and St. Joseph's (1839). Of these six parishes St. Patrick's and the Cathedral of the Assumption still are active.
2. W. Boulton Kelly, Ellen H. Kelly, and Catharine F. Black, "National Register of Historic Places Inventory—Nomination Form: St. Vincent de Paul Roman Catholic Church" (on file at the Maryland Historical Trust, Crownsville, Maryland, 1973).

3. William H. Pierson, *American Buildings and Their Architects: The Colonial and Neo-classical Styles* (New York: Anchor Books, 1976), 3.

4. U.S. Department of Commerce, Bureau of Census, *Baltimore City, Population,* 1840.

5. *Centenary Manual* anniversary program.

6. Thomas T. McCusker, *How Much Is That in Real Money? A Historic Price Index for Use as a Deflator of Money Values in the Economy of the United States* (Worcester, Mass.: American Antiquarian Society, 1992), 327–32.

7. Richard Hubbard Howland and Eleanor Patterson Spencer, *The Architecture of Baltimore* (Baltimore: Johns Hopkins Press, 1953), 18–19.

8. Ibid., 20–22.

9. Kelly, Kelly, and Black, "National Register of Historic Places Inventory."

10. U.S. Department of Commerce, Bureau of the Census, *Baltimore City, Population* (1850).

11. Spalding, *Premier See,* 117.

12. Howland and Spencer, *Architecture of Baltimore,* 20–22.

13. Spalding, *Premier See,* 30–31, 70, 86–87; [Riordan], *Cathedral Records,* 47, 50.

14. Pierson, *American Buildings and Their Architects,* 360–72.

15. Robert L. Alexander, "'Wealth Well Bestowed in Worship': St. Paul's in Baltimore from Robert Cary Long Sr. to Richard Upjohn," *MHM* 86, no. 3 (1991): 123–49.

16. John Dorsey and James D. Dilts, *A Guide to Baltimore Architecture,* 2d ed. (Catonsville, Md., 1982), 107; AAB, 23-E-2, Gildea to Whitfield, September 18, 1830.

17. Phoebe Stanton, *The Gothic Revival and American Church Architecture: An Episode in Taste, 1840–1856* (Baltimore: Johns Hopkins Press, 1968), 7.

18. AAB, 23A-E-3, 23-I-1, Gildea to Whitfield, February 24 and June 8, 1831.

19. SAB, RG 26, Box 10, Gildea estate files.

20. Ibid., receipt dated January 16, 1836; J. Thomas Scharf, *History of Baltimore City and County* (Philadelphia: Louis Everts, 1881; rpt., Baltimore, 1971), 189, 808; [Riordan], *Cathedral Records,* 102.

21. Wilbur H. Hunter, "Robert Cary Long, Jr.," *Journal of the Society of Architectural Historians* 16 (1957): 28–30.

22. Spalding, *Premier See,* 137–39; [Riordan], *Cathedral Records,* 65.

23. SAB, Gildea estate papers.

24. Archives of the Carmelite Monastery in Baltimore, Fenwick to Sister Stanislaus, Boston, October 18, 1841.

25. SAB, RG 26, Box 10, receipt dated June 22, 1841.

26. [Riordan], *Cathedral Records,* 30–44.

27. Dell Upton, *Holy Things and Profane: Anglican Parish Churches in Colonial Virginia* (New York: Architectural History Foundation and MIT, 1986), 28.

28. J. K. Wisner, "Varieties and Manufacture," in *Brick,* a special issue of *Architectural Review* 79, no. 474 (1936): 229–40.

29. Thomas W. Spalding, letter to K. Kuranda, June 14, 1993.

30. Alan Gowans, *Images of American Living: Four Centuries of Architecture and Furniture as Cultural Expression* (New York: Harper and Row, 1976), 191–231.

31. G. E. Kidder-Smith, *The Beacon Guide to New England Houses of Worship* (Boston: Beacon Press, 1989).

32. Alexander, "Wealth Well Bestowed in Worship," 123–49.

33. For a comparison of early Catholic devotionalism to that of the later immigrant church, see Joseph P. Chinnici, *Living Stones: The History and Structure of Catholic Spiritual Life in the United States* (New York: Macmillan, 1989), and Ann Taves, *The Household of Faith: Roman Catholic Devotions in Mid-Nineteenth-Century America* (Notre Dame, Ind.: University of Notre Dame Press, 1986).

CHAPTER 10. The Aesthetic of Presence

1. Dolan, *The Immigrant Church,* 7; Dolan, *The American Catholic Experience,* 127–346.

2. Olson, *Baltimore,* 118–20.

3. Spalding, *Premier See,* 127–229; Michael J. McNally, "A Peculiar Institution: A History of Catholic Parish Life in the Southeast (1850–1980)," in Dolan, ed., *American Catholic Parish,* 117–234.

4. Spalding, *Premier See,* 137.

5. U.S. Department of Commerce, Bureau of the Census, *City of Baltimore, Population* (1840).

6. David O'Brien, *Public Catholicism* (New York: Macmillan, 1989), 38.

7. Stanton, *The Gothic Revival and American Church Architecture,* 246; Talbot Hamlin, *Greek Revival Architecture in America* (New York: Dover, 1944; rpt., 1969).

8. AAB, Notitiae, 1853, 1855; *Centenary Manual,* 1941.

9. *CM,* October 10, 1874.

10. Ibid., September 23 and October 14, 1876.

11. *The Sun,* September 22, 1954.

12. Ibid.

13. Ibid.

14. *CM,* October 14, 1876.

15. Ibid.

16. Ibid., September 23, 1876.

17. Ibid., October 10, 1876.

18. Ibid., June 23, 1883.

19. AAB, Notitiae, 1891.

20. Ibid., 1888.

21. *CM,* April 12, 1890, and November 7, 1891.

22. Ibid., October 28, 1895.

CHAPTER 11. The Aesthetic of Tradition

1. *CR,* March 7, 1941, p. 3.

2. Department of Commerce, Bureau of the Census, "Characteristics of Housing for Census Tracts by Block: 1940," *Sixteenth Census of the United States: 1940* (Washington, D.C.: U.S. Government Printing Office, 1942).

3. Ibid.

4. Department of Commerce, Bureau of the Census, "Years of School Completed, Employment Status, Class of Worker, Major Occupation Group, Country of Birth, and Citizenship, by Sex, by Census Tracts: 1940," in *Sixteenth Census of the United States: 1940.*

5. Brugger, *Maryland,* 506.

6. Tongue, Brooks, and Zimmerman, "Engineering Report: Property of St. Vincent de Paul R.C. Church and St. Leo's Orphan Asylum, Baltimore, Maryland" (1940), unpublished report on file with St. Vincent de Paul Church. The following discussion relies upon data contained in the engineering report.

7. Sanborn-Perris Map Company, *Insurance Maps of Baltimore,* vol. 3 (1902), 258.

8. McCusker, *How Much Is That in Real Money?* 331–32.

9. Ibid.

10. Ruth Martin, telephone interview with Br. Thomas Spalding, 1992.

11. Fr. John Sinnott Martin, *St. Vincent de Paul Church: Art and Architecture* (Baltimore: Frank T. Cimino Co., 1943), 2.

12. Alan Axelrod, ed., *The Colonial Revival in America* (New York: Norton, 1985), 5.

13. Edwin Howland Blashfield, "Mural Painting in America" in ibid., 341–61.

14. Martin, *Art and Architecture*, 2.
15. Ibid., 5–6.
16. Ibid., 6.
17. The removal of the pew doors is documented in ibid., 16. Discussion of the revenue-raising practices of parishes in the Archdiocese of Baltimore is found in Spalding's *The Premier See* (1989).

CHAPTER 12. The Preservation Aesthetic

1. Bureau of the Census, *Population and Housing Statistics for Census Tracts, Baltimore Maryland* (Washington: U.S. Government Printing Office, 1942), 12–13.
2. Spalding, *Premier See,* 430–31.
3. U.S. Department of the Interior, National Park Service, *The Secretary of the Interior's Standards for Rehabilitation and Guidelines for Rehabilitation Historic Buildings* [36 CFR 67] (Washington: U.S. Government Printing Office, 1979; rev. 1983).
4. Ten principles have been developed by the National Park Service to direct rehabilitation projects for historic properties. The Secretary of the Interior's Standards for Rehabilitation (36 CFR 67) require that:

    1. Every reasonable effort shall be made to provide a compatible use for a property which requires minimal alteration to the building, structure, or site and its environment, or to use a property for its originally intended purpose.
    2. The distinguishing original qualities or character of a building, structure, or site and its environment shall not be destroyed. The removal or alteration of any historic material or distinctive architectural features should be avoided when possible.
    3. All buildings, structures, and sites shall be recognized as products of their own time. Alterations that have no historical basis and which seek to create an earlier appearance shall be discouraged.
    4. Changes which may have taken place in the course of time are evidence of the history and development of a building, structure, or site and its environment. These changes may have acquired significance in their own right, and this significance shall be recognized and respected.
    5. Distinctive stylistic features or examples of skilled craftsmanship which characterize a building, structure, or site shall be treated with sensitivity.
    6. Deteriorated architectural features shall be repaired rather than replaced, whenever possible. In the event replacement is necessary, the new material should match the material being replaced in composition, design, color, texture, and other visual qualities. Repair or replacement of missing architectural features should be based on accurate duplication of features, substantiated by historic, physical, or pictorial evidence rather than on conjectural designs or the availability of different architectural elements from other buildings or structures.
    7. The surface cleaning of structures shall be undertaken with the gentlest means possible. Sandblasting and other cleaning methods that will damage the historic building materials shall not be undertaken.
    8. Every reasonable effort shall be made to protect and preserve archeological resources affected by, or adjacent to any project.
    9. Contemporary design for alterations and additions to existing properties shall not be discouraged when such alterations and additions do not destroy significant historical, architectural or cultural material, and such design is compatible with the size, scale, color, material, and character of the property, neighborhood or environment.
    10. Whenever possible, new additions or alterations to structures shall be done in such a

manner that if such additions or alterations were to be removed in the future, the essential form and integrity of the structure would be unimpaired.

5. The Art and Architecture Committee, Report of First Meeting, August 16, 1983.
6. *Environment and Art in Catholic Worship,* 1:9, 10, 19–24; 2:27–32, 33, 37, 38.
7. Ibid., 1:11; 3:39–42, 49–51, 53; 4:58; 5:63–81; 6:104.
8. Design goals established for the Worship Space, Adjacent Spaces, and Final Touches by the Art and Architecture Committee were:

WORSHIP SPACE

1. Level the floor of the entire church to create a more flexible and less obstructed seating space and a more accessible sanctuary area. This may include filling the aisles to the level of the wooden floor under the pews and eliminating the extraneous platforming around the side altar and the former high altar.
2. Build sanctuary platforming that makes good use of available space; provides clear sight lines from all parts of the nave; and provides unobstructed movement and flexibility for a variety of liturgical actions.
3. Adapt and rework existing pews to provide a new seating plan that enhances the sense of community.
4. Create a place for the reservation of the Blessed Sacrament, as well as private prayer, under the baldachino, using recycled elements from the church. This might include setting the tabernacle on a marble column on the lowered floor with the altar frontpiece as a backdrop; visually enclosing the space with reworked portions of the altar rail; placing votive candles and kneelers inside the devotional space.
5. Design and build a new altar that conforms to episcopal guidelines concerning dimensions and that also reflects elements of the church.
6. Recycle the existing pulpit into an ambo that is harmonious with the new altar in dimensions and style.
7. Create a baptismal area on the left-hand side of the nave off the main aisle adjacent to the baptism window; use the existing baptismal font as a focus for this space.

ADJACENT SPACES

8. Insulate the worship space for the traffic flow between the rectory/undercroft/entrance by building a glassed partition along the front edge of the balcony and by closing off the St. Vincent chapel.
9. Create a gathering space near the main entrance of the church by removing the pews under the balcony, by removing the confessionals, and by eliminating other obstructions. The gathering space might be carpeted to reduce sound transmission.
10. Provide an alternative entrance to the undercroft.

FINAL TOUCHES

11. Repaint the interior of the church in a way that will highlight, rather than hide, the rich architectural detailing of the structure and thus enhance the historic feeling of the space. Incorporate the baldachin in a more harmonious way into the total design through the color scheme.
12. Install a new lighting system that will use hanging fixtures more in keeping with the historic nature of the church and that will use wall sconces as the primary source of illumination. All fixtures should be controllable for intensity.
13. Remount the A/V screen so that it is recessed into the ceiling when not in use.

Conclusion

1. Joseph Fichter, *Social Relations in the Urban Parish* (Chicago: University of Chicago Press, 1954), 199, 213; Debra Campbell, "The Struggle to Serve: From the Lay Apostolate to the Ministry Explosion," in Dolan, *Transforming Parish Ministry,* 222–52.
2. Campbell, "Struggle to Serve," 267.
3. The independent Thomas More Project of Baltimore, which places inner-city children in Catholic schools, has also provided scholarships for pupils at Queen of Peace School.
4. Fichter, *Urban Parish,* 211–12, quoting Fr. H. A. Reinhold.

ESSAY ON SOURCES

Two anniversary "histories" of St. Vincent de Paul Parish have been published: *Grand Official Programme and Souvenir of the Golden Jubilee of St. Vincent de Paul Church* (n.p., 1891), and *A Centenary Manual: Church of St. Vincent de Paul, Baltimore, 1841–1941* (n.p., [1941]).

With the exception of the sacramental registers, few records remain in the parish archives from any but the years of the present pastor. Valuable but incomplete, however, for the first two decades of its publication is "St. Vincent's Notebook," begun by the eleventh pastor, Rev. John Sinnott Martin, in 1940 and continued by his successor through 1969. It contains much information on the day-to-day operations of the parish, as well as a "Historical Sketch" of the parish by Father Martin.

In the archives of the archdiocese of Baltimore, the most valuable records are the annual parish reports, called "Notitiae," begun in 1873. Except for the pastorate of Rev. Edmund Didier, correspondence between the pastors and archdiocesan officials is scant. There is in the archives, however, a register of pew rents at St. Vincent's begun in 1849 and a ledger entitled "St. Vincent de Paul's Cemetery." Deeds and the files of deceased priests also contain useful information.

The Sulpician Archives of Baltimore contain a number of important records, including the settlement of the estate of the first pastor and the diary of Rev. Louis Deluol, which provides much information on the founding period.

Significant data have been extracted from the *United States Catholic Magazine,* the Baltimore *Catholic Mirror* and *Catholic Review,* and Baltimore secular newspapers, especially the Baltimore *Sun,* as well as from the national Catholic directories published since the 1830s under various titles such as the *Catholic Almanac and Laity's Directory.* Also useful were the Baltimore city directories and federal and city census reports.

Among the secondary works that proved indispensable for both parts of the book are Thomas W. Spalding, *The Premier See: A History of the Archdiocese of Balti-*

more, 1789–1989 (Baltimore: Johns Hopkins University Press, 1989); Sherry H. Olson, *Baltimore: The Building of an American City* (Baltimore: Johns Hopkins University Press, 1980); and Robert J. Brugger, *Maryland: A Middle Temperament, 1634–1980* (Baltimore: Johns Hopkins University Press, 1988).

Other secondary works that proved of more than passing utility are Thomas Scharf's *The Chronicles of Baltimore* (Baltimore: Turnbull Bros., 1874), and *History of Baltimore City and County* (Philadelphia: Louis Everts, 1881; rpt., Baltimore, 1971); John Tracy Ellis, *The Life of James Cardinal Gibbons, Archbishop of Baltimore, 1834–1921*, 2 vols. (Milwaukee, Wis.: Bruce, 1952); M. Hildegarde Yeager, *The Life of James Roosevelt Bayley, First Bishop of Newark and Eighth Archbishop of Baltimore, 1814–1877* (Washington, D.C.: Catholic University of America Press, 1947); [Michael J. Riordan], *Cathedral Records from the Beginning of Catholicity in Baltimore to the Present Time* (Baltimore: Catholic Mirror, 1906); and Owen B. Corrigan, *The Catholic Schools of the Archdiocese of Baltimore: A Study in Diocesan History* (Baltimore: St. Mary's Industrial School Press, 1924).

The church of St. Vincent de Paul itself served as the primary "document" for part 2. The "Notitiae," the Catholic weeklies, and the "Historical Sketch" mentioned above contain information about the church building, as does Tongue, Brooks, and Zimmerman, "Engineering Report: Property of St. Vincent de Paul R.C. Church and St. Leo's Orphan Asylum, Baltimore, Maryland" (Baltimore, 1940); Fr. John Sinnott Martin's *St. Vincent de Paul Church: Art and Architecture* (Baltimore: Frank T. Cimino Co., 1943); and the correspondence, reports, and minutes of the current Art and Architecture Committee of St. Vincent de Paul Parish.

Among the primary source materials for Baltimore's architectural history are Asher Benjamin, *The American Builder's Companion* (1827) and *The Builder's Guide* (1839); John Hall, *A Series of Select and Original Modern Designs for Dwelling Houses for the Use of Carpenters and Builders* (Baltimore: John Murphy, 1840); and "Recollections of George A. Frederick" (manuscript in the Maryland Historical Society).

Comparative architectural data was provided by the *Maryland Inventory of Historic Properties* of the Maryland Historical Trust, Crownsville, Md., and the architectural guides and inventories in Richard Hubbard Howland and Eleanor Patterson Spencer, *The Architecture of Baltimore* (Baltimore: Johns Hopkins Press, 1953). Among the works on architectural history that provided a framework for architectural analysis are Alan Axelrod, ed., *The Colonial Revival in America* (New York: Norton, 1985); Alan Gowans, *Images of American Living: Four Centuries of Architecture and Furniture as Cultural Expression* (New York: Harper and Row, 1964); Talbot Hamlin, *Greek Revival Architecture in America* (1944; rpt., New York: Dover Press, 1969), and *Benjamin Henry Latrobe* (New York: Oxford University Press, 1955). Also consulted were Henry Russell Hitchcock, *Architecture: Nineteenth and Twentieth Centuries* (New York: Penguin Books, 1977); Phoebe B. Stanton, *The Gothic Revival and American Church Architecture: An Episode in Taste, 1840–1856* (Baltimore: Johns Hopkins Press, 1968); and Dell Upton, *Holy Things and Profane: Anglican Parish Churches in Colonial Virginia* (New York: Architectural History Foundation, 1986).

CONTRIBUTORS

THOMAS W. SPALDING, CFX, Ph.D., is professor of history at Spalding University, Louisville, Kentucky. Brother Spalding is a graduate of Fordham University and the Catholic University of America. He is the author of *Martin John Spalding: American Churchman* (1973) and *The Premier See: A History of the Archdiocese of Baltimore, 1789–1989* (1989), both of which have received awards, and numerous articles in historical journals.

KATHRYN M. KURANDA, M.Arch Hist., vice-president of architectural services of R. Christopher Goodwin & Associates, Inc., Frederick, Maryland, directs the architectural history and history programs. A graduate of Dickinson College and the University of Virginia, Ms. Kuranda has also directed numerous cultural resource investigations throughout the Mid-Atlantic and Southeastern regions ranging from architectural surveys and building assessments to historic preservation planning studies.

MARTHA R. WILLIAMS, M.A., M.Ed., historic site specialist for R. Christopher Goodwin & Associates, Inc., is a graduate of Lebanon Valley College, the University of Pennsylvania, and George Mason University. Ms. Williams is also actively involved with a number of professional preservation organizations, including the Archeological Society of Virginia, for which she served as vice-president, and the Society for Historical Archeology, for which she is chair of the Committee on Public Education.

AUGUSTINE J. FAHEY, B.A., graphics coordinator for R. Christopher Goodwin & Associates, Inc., is a graduate of the University of Pennsylvania. Mr. Fahey specializes in computer graphics applications for cultural resource investigations.

INDEX